SOMERSET COUNTY

PRIDE BEYOND THE MOUNTAINS

MINER'S MEMORIAL PARK IN DOWNTOWN WINDBER. Monuments to miners and the town's veterans are surrounded by several historic markers and a bandstand in the park.

THE MAKING OF AMERICA

Somerset County
Pride Beyond the Mountains

Jaclyn LaPlaca

ARCADIA

Published by Arcadia Publishing,
an imprint of Tempus Publishing, Inc.
Charleston SC, Chicago, Portsmouth NH, San Francisco

Printed in Great Britain.

Library of Congress Catalog Card Number: 2003111120

For all general information contact Arcadia Publishing at:
Telephone 843-853-2070
Fax 843-853-0044
E-Mail sales@arcadiapublishing.com
For customer service and orders:
Toll-Free 1-888-313-2665

Visit us on the Internet at http://www.arcadiapublishing.com

CONTENTS

ACKNOWLEDGMENTS

Somerset County and its people have a unique character and story that the rest of the country have just begun to understand, as recent high-profile events have brought this rural area into national focus. I have faith that Somerset County residents, including myself, will continue to be proud of our area, including our past and more recent history.

This book would not have been possible without the assistance and support of the local community. Miners throughout the area have fought to keep the knowledge of their profession alive, especially Ed Kozdron. They have also shared with me valued information about my grandfather, Leonard "Nunny" LaPlaca, who spent 25 years in Windber's coalmines. Special thanks are due to Mary and Dwight Hostetler for their collection of postcards, books, and historical artifacts and their willingness to share those with me. Windber Public Library and Indiana University of Pennsylvania's Library and Special Collections Archive were of vital importance. The Windber Coal Heritage Center and its director Chris Barkley provided both information and pictures. The *Altoona Mirror*, Windber's Arcadia Theater, the Coal Heritage Foundation, and Somerset's Historical Society and numerous helpful residents have all provided significant contributions to this work. Finally, I would like to thank Millie Beik for the inspiration she has given me; Jo Wozny, my aunt, for sharing important reading materials; and especially my parents for their support.

This book is dedicated to the memory of my brother, Matthew Leonard LaPlaca, who grew to love Windber.

INTRODUCTION

Approached from the east by land, Somerset County comes into view suddenly, as you emerge from a long, straight tunnel cut through Allegheny Mountain on the old Pennsylvania Turnpike. The effect is of a particularly charming mountain scene in a diorama, a rolling landscape of pleasant farms and soft glades, painted in warm tones. The place is a visual surprise, given the economic dictates of its geology. Somerset is on the eastern edge of the Appalachian coal basin, and coal has been mined in the area for a century and a half.

Many of the small communities in the county, places such as Gray, Wilbur, Jenner's Crossroads, and Hooversville, originated as mining towns, some of them wholly owned—from the tidy little homes to the local bank—by the mining company that was the town's sole employer. One small mining town, Hyasota, laid out by the Hyasota Coal Company in 1912, consists of 20 company homes lined up on four streets, which are all still in use today—with only one street marker: "Hyasota Hill Rd." As recently as the mid-1960s, nearly half the people in the county had at least one family member working in the mines or in the steel mills fed by the coal mines, in nearby Johnstown and Pittsburgh. Mining in the area focused primarily on coal and iron ore, but fire clay was mined near Meyersdale and Windber for use in brick making, and limestone was quarried for use in constructing roads and in fertilizing soil. Even those who didn't work in the mines or the mills often mined coal for themselves, digging "dog mines" by the barn or even in the cellar for their winter fuel supply.

During the summer of 2002, the attention of the nation and the world was riveted by the rescue that brought nine Pennsylvania coal miners out of a mine in the town of Quecreek in Somerset County. With a population of 78,218, according to the 2000 census, the county's land area of 1,085 square miles makes it the seventh largest county in the state. In a period of economic recession full of anxieties generated by the 9/11 attack, the gripping drama of the rescue provided an inspiring, positive moment for the nation.

The most common characterization of the incident was "miraculous." The memory of many mining deaths in the area, the dedication and commitment of the rescuers, and the solidarity of the trapped men triggered an outpouring of community sentiment. The emotion of the moment was further intensified in the national media by the fact that the September 11 crash site of United Flight 93, with its message of courage and solidarity in the face of death, was only 13 miles away, also in Somerset County, in the town of Shanksville. That's a lot of attention for a community of small towns in rural Pennsylvania, but the historic struggle of the people of this county, their work ethic and values, was preparation for these events.

But the area's coal heritage is not obviously displayed. When the steel economy collapsed, so did the major market for much of Pennsylvania's bituminous coal. By the time coal operators reoriented themselves to a new primary market—generating electricity—the fundamental of the coal industry had changed dramatically. New technologies and mining techniques made coal mining a far less labor-intensive undertaking, and Pennsylvania coal production has steadily risen, even though in the 1990s the number of miners declined by nearly half. For example, among Somerset County's population of 80,000, only 282 people worked in underground mines in 1999. In modern times, most of western Pennsylvania's mines are small operations, and none are unionized.

The most plentiful job opportunities in Somerset County are in tourism and manufacturing, and the biggest private employer is Seven Springs resort. Throughout western Pennsylvania, Wal-Mart—with 94 discount stores and Supercenters, 20 Sam's Clubs, and 4 distribution centers in the state as a whole—has surpassed steel mills and coalmines as the area's largest employer.

This short historical overview of Somerset County is crucial to link its past with these modern-day events. The county itself was of considerable historical importance in an era when coal was king of the energy world. Coal furnished 90 percent of the nation's energy in 1900, when the United States replaced Great Britain for the first time as the world's leading coal producer. Pennsylvania, second in population only to New York, was itself an industrial giant, leading all states in its output of coal, iron, and steel. In its heyday, from 1900 to 1930, Somerset County lay well within the mainstream of American industrial life.

Secondly, Somerset County's history has to a large extent paralleled that of industrial America itself. As such, the story of its origins, rise, and decline is not unlike the stories of other industrial towns in important respects. In the past, one-industry mining towns have been notorious for coming into being and passing out of existence in the blink of an eye, or as the supply of the particular natural resource was successively discovered, utilized, and depleted. In the 1950s and 1960s most of Somerset County's mines closed down permanently, thereby posing a serious challenge to the county's continued existence and uprooting thousands of former miners and their families. Today, as American industry is threatened in many ways, it is too easy to relegate industrial workers and industrial towns to the "dustbin of history."

Thirdly, the population that came to reside within Somerset County was and is remarkable for its great ethnic diversity. For example, because of the town of Windber's plentiful immigrant groups and industrial importance, the Dillingham Immigration Commission chose the town as one of two Pennsylvania bituminous towns to use as a case study for its "Immigrants in Industries" series, published in 1911. At least 25 different nationalities were represented in a population that totaled about 10,000. Immigrants from southern and eastern Europe, who comprised the bulk of the local working class, were part of the wave of "new" immigrants who came to America in great numbers from 1890 until legislation of the 1920s severely restricted the number of newcomers from these areas. Windber's, and Somerset County's, rise and prominence as an industrial center coincided with the zenith of immigration from southern and eastern Europe on which it depended for its labor force.

Finally, the autocratic structure of the company towns that comprised Somerset County demands examination. As late as 1937, when the labor movement/New Deal coalition in the state of Pennsylvania secured passage of an important series of company-town–related laws designed to bring democracy where none had existed before, the Commonwealth of Pennsylvania counted 1,200 such towns within its borders. Several were in Somerset County. What happened in these autocratic company towns—that is, how and why class-based unionism came about—is an important chapter of American history. The roots and traditions of Somerset County's working class people are undeniably part of the story of diverse working people struggling to democratize the America they knew. Their history suggests something of the possibilities and limitations, strengths and weaknesses, of worker protest in the early twentieth century in the United States.

Chapter One

EARLY HISTORY OF THE LAUREL HIGHLANDS

The region in which Somerset County emerged was once wilderness populated by Native Americans and later farmlands for early white settlers. Most historians place the first Native Americans in Pennsylvania about the tenth century. Their life reflected their Stone Age background—tools, weapons, and household equipment were made from stone, wood, and bark. Transportation was on foot or by canoe and houses were made of bark and clothing from the skin of animals.

The Alligewi occupied the territory west of the Allegheny Mountains and east of the Mississippi River. The name Allegheny was derived from Alligewi-hanna, or "Stream of the Alligewi." The Delawares, who called themselves Leni-Lenape, occupied the basin of the Delaware River. White settlement forced them to move westward to the Wyoming Valley, to the Allegheny, and finally to eastern Ohio. A number of other tribes occupied western Pennsylvania: the Wyandots, Chippewas, Missisaugas, and Ottawas all established temporary villages. Eventually most of these tribes came under the influence of the Six Nations.

The Iroquoian Confederacy was originally made up of five tribes: the Onondages, Oneidas, Cayugas, Senecas, and Mohawks. The English knew them as the "Five Nations." The Tuscorora joined them after their migration from Georgia and the Carolinas. This Iroquois Nation was then known as "Six Nations." They were headquartered in the Mohawk Valley in New York. The Pennsylvania Indians—Delawares, Shawnees, Picts, Wyandots, and Mingoes—were ruled by the Iroquois. By 1700, the Iroquois Confederacy was in control of practically all of the Pennsylvania Indian tribes.

While it is known that the Shawnees were residents of western Pennsylvania during the years of the French and Indian War, we also know that the Delaware and Shawnee tribes occupied Somerset County as late as 1794. Today, Shawnee State Park is situated in Bedford County just off the town of Schellsburg on Route 30. This park attracts thousands each year for its wonderful fishing, swimming, camping, and picnicking facilities. A 400-acre lake occupies the valley floor. The land at the headwaters of Little Paint Creek was owned and controlled by the Native Americans. It was called Allegania. According to the Pennsylvania Historical Commission there are three sites of a well-defined phase of Indian culture in Somerset County: the Montague Site on the Youghiogheny River near the town of Somerfield, the Hanna Site on the east bank of Casselman River just south of Route 53 across the river from Harnedsville, and the Clouse Site near Youghiogheny.

Swedes who settled along the Delaware River in 1638 probably were the first Europeans to make their homes in any part of what is now called Pennsylvania. A settlement was established on Tinicum Island in 1643 under Governor Johan Printz. (Tinicum is now a state park in which the foundations of the Swedish government building still remain.) However, trouble broke out between the Swedes and the Dutch. In 1655, Governor Johan Risingh surrendered New Sweden to Governor Peter Stuyvesant of the New Netherlands. Nine years later, the English seized the Dutch possession in the name of the Duke of York. They held it until 1673 when the Dutch recaptured the territory. A treaty of peace the following year restored the region to English rule under Sir Edmund Andors as governor.

On March 4, 1681, King Charles II gave William Penn a charter for land west of the Delaware River. Penn, a Quaker, founded his colony as a "holy experiment" that respected religious freedom and liberal government. William Penn also showed some respect for indigenous people and purchased land, rather than seizing it. The 1701 Charter of Privilege was the colony's constitution, giving its elected assembly more power than any equivalent British body. Pennsylvania became the richest and most populous British colony in North America and played a major role in the independence movement. Due to the policy of civil and religious freedom and the abundant opportunity for individual advancement, Pennsylvania's growth in colonial times was rapid.

Pennsylvania was the last of the 13 original colonies to be organized into an English province. This was 75 years after the settlement of Jamestown, Virginia, and 62 years after the Pilgrims landed on Plymouth Rock. Maryland was already 50 years old. New York had been in English possession for 18 years. New Jersey had been established for more than a dozen years. In Penn's time, the word "Ohio" designated the area drained by the Ohio River and included Pittsburgh and most of the counties that today form western Pennsylvania. Ohio became a state in 1803—more than 120 years after the founding of Pennsylvania.

The French began the occupation of western Pennsylvania in 1733. Great land purchases were made in 1736 and 1737, the latter being the famous "Walking Purchase" that caused much resentment among the Indians. Then in 1744, contention began between Louis XV of France and George II of England about the territory west of the Alleghenies. France claimed it on the explorations made by La Salle in the Lower Mississippi Valley as early as 1679. George denied the claim, so in 1753 the French came to Pittsburgh and erected Fort Duquesne.

Since friendly relations were being strained with the Indians, a conference of the Six Nations was held in Albany, New York, in July of 1754. Here a deed was given to Thomas and Richard Penn, heirs of William Penn, for the consideration of £400. When the Indians returned home and mediated, they realized that all their lands west of the Alleghenies had been sold. Dissatisfaction and discontent increased and they sought an alliance with the French. These hostilities led to a great war between France and England, the Seven Years' War, 1756–1763. The defeat of France resulted in her release of all claims eat of the Mississippi to England.

A number of important Indian tribes, under the leadership of Pontiac, chief of the Ottawas, began an independent war along the whole frontier, especially west of the Susquehanna. Except for a few fortified places like Fort Pitt, the Indians were temporarily in full possession of the land. Colonel Henry Bouquet with 500 regulars was ordered to rescue the garrison at Fort Pitt, and in 1763 he defeated the Indians at Bushy Run, about 20 miles from Fort Pitt. White supremacy was thus re-established in western Pennsylvania.

The last of the land purchases, known as the "New Purchase," was made in 1768 at Fort Stanwix, New York. The deed, dated November 5, 1768, sold all Indian interest in all the land south of the Kittanning Trail in western Pennsylvania, including what is now Somerset County. The consideration was $10,000.

This area of the state along with most of western Pennsylvania was still considered the frontier. The earliest road followed Indian trails that were footpaths through the woods wide enough for men and horses but not wagons. Travel was extremely hazardous and very difficult. Western Pennsylvania remained largely unsettled. One reason was that before the Native Americans were subdued, it was too dangerous to risk bringing women and children into the region—it was too far from the eastern cities.

Early traders crossed the Allegheny Mountains to trade with the Indians. The forests were inhabited by a great variety of wildlife: bears, beavers, foxes, deer, groundhogs, rabbits, wildcats, minks, otters, weasels, muskrats, skunks, wolves, snakes, turtles, hawks, pigeons, grouse, quail, turkey, plover, and fish. Before the American Revolution there was mention of traders, pack-horse men, and hunters who established more or less permanent headquarters within today's Somerset County.

It is said that Edmund's Swamp, several miles south of Windber, was named after Edmund Cartlidge, one of the first traders to venture westward across the Allegheny Mountains. The early region called Allegania saw traders such as Peter Chartier, James LeTort, Jonas Davenport, and Peter Allen, who were also licensed by the provincial authorities. Another story claims that John Ray, Edmund Cartlidge, and James Dunning gathered beaver pelts from Shade and Paint Creeks 20 years before Christopher Grist, who has been generally credited as the first white settler in Somerset County.

George Crogan, referred to as the King of Traders, was first licensed in 1744 and was said to follow the Lower Path into the Alleghenies where he exchanged beads and blankets for buckskins that were cleaned and baled along the swift running waters of Shade and Paint Creeks. The Proclamation of 1763 still prevented white settlers from taking lands west of the highest ridges of the Allegheny Mountains. Boundary disputes between Pennsylvania and Virginia caused them to wait until the deeds would be valid.

Coal was discovered as early as 1742 in what is now West Virginia; British soldiers stationed at Fort Pitt (Pittsburgh) used coal to heat their barracks in 1759. Poor transportation, however, prevented shipment until canals and railroads were constructed. An old Indian trail is described in a history of St. Bartholomew's Church, Wilmore:

> . . . running from the Kittanning Path near the present town of Ashville,
> and Indian trail which wound up the ridge past the present town of Loretto,

thence southward, to the eastward of Munster and down that ridge and through Portage Township, crossing the Little Conemaugh in two places on the Great Bend, part of which was cut off by the Pennsylvania Railroad improvement of 1898, thence ascending the hill to avoid the swamp and laurel on the flat near the river diagonally across the depression in the hill on which stands the church of St. Bartholomew, down the "Forks," which point was designated as "Canoe Place" where the red man took to water in his light bark canoe of "Conemaugh Old Town," which was situated on the flat between Franklin Street and "The Point" in the present thriving city of Johnstown; and when going eastward the canoes were drawn from the water near the Forks, and the trip overland begun.

From the first settlers in the eastern part of Pennsylvania (1638), it took over 150 years to begin the development of the western part. The first house ever built by a European settler in Pennsylvania was near Chester by Caleb Pusey as late as 1643. By the end of the Colonial Era (1790), the three original counties of Philadelphia, Chester, and Bucks had grown into 21 counties with Bedford the only one in the current Somerset County area.

The Treaty of Fort Stanwix in November 1768 relinquished the area that was to become Somerset County from Indian ownership. Somerset County was the last county to take its name from an English shire. In Latin documents, Somerset appears as Astiva Regio, "region of summer." White settlers started to come into Somerset County after Penn's Treaty of 1754–1758 with the Indians. In the vicinity of White Horse, through the water gap in the Allegheny Mountain, Colonel Burd made a road in 1755 intended to help Major-General Edward Braddock's ill-fated expedition.

There were plenty of wild animals to eat at this time, especially venison and pork. Venison cost nothing but the price of the powder and shot used in slaying the deer, and as the animals were tame and plentiful and the pioneers expert marksmen with the flint-lock musket, or more modern percussion cap rifle, it did not take many shots to keep the larder well supplied with meat at all times of the year. There was no legal protection for deer or any other kind of game as there is now. Years ago the deer would travel back and forth between the Allegheny ridge and Negro Mountain, and some of the best deer trails passed right through the present site of Meyersdale and vicinity. During this time period, hogs cost very little, 20–25¢ for a four-week-old pig. And salt, which was almost indispensable, could not be had in the early days in this section of country. Some used certain wood ashes to preserve their meat, and in a few instances neighbors would take two horses each with pack saddles and go through the woods along trails so far east before they could buy a few bushels of salt, that it took a week or ten days before they returned. The pioneers in the Somerset County area often went as far as Winchester, Virginia for salt. A few bushels of salt supplied a family for several years. Coffee was also a scarce article, and many people used parched rye as a substitute.

Despite such sparse beginnings, many of those who helped settle Somerset County went on to do great things. The first Bible to be printed west of the Alleghenies came from the press of a Somerset printer. Charles Frederich Goeb, a German immigrant, came to Somerset about 1809. The first Bible, a German language edition of Martin Luther's translation, was published in 1813. The New Testament followed in 1814. A few copies of this Bible are still in existence, but in 1961 the American Antiquarian Society was able to discover only 31 copies.

Printing the Bible was an enormous undertaking. Goeb must have started setting the type by 1810 or earlier because the entire volume—both Testaments, the Apocrypha, and a table of feast days—must have required setting some five million pieces of type, including spaces. All the type had to be set by hand and then taken off again since no printer had the type or the space to keep all the pages up at once. Goeb may have even had to carve the large wooden type of titles and title pages himself, as well as the woodcut that closes the Old Testament, because there is no evidence of the usual alignment characteristics of cast metal type.

The Goeb Bible is more than a foot high and bound in leather over heavy oak boards nearly a quarter of a inch thick. Goeb's printing house stood on the present site of the Kantner building. He published a weekly newspaper called *Der Westliche Telegraph* from 1812 to 1819, along with almanacs and other works. All his publications are very rare finds now. In 1819 he went to Schellsburg, where he continued to publish. Born March 23, 1782, he died around 1829 and is buried in Schellsburg cemetery. His wife Catherine died July 13, 1870, at age 81.

Early History of the Laurel Highlands

In 1851 George Chorpenning and Absalom Woodward, both of Somerset, were awarded the first contract to carry mail between Sacramento, California, and Salt Lake City, Utah. Chorpenning's brother-in-law, Irvin Pile, was a driver, and he and Leroy Benford of Meyersdale drove the Conestoga wagon west for inauguration of the service. The first overland mail to cross the continent started eastward from Sacramento on May 1, 1851, under Chorpenning's personal supervision. Crossing the Sierras was especially difficult because of the snow.

On November 1, Woodward headed east with the mail train, taking all the available money to purchase stock, wagons, and supplies. His train was attacked near the Great Salt Lake and he was killed. In January 1859, the route changed to pass through central Nevada, which shortened the route by more than 100 miles. It was during this time that the idea of the Pony Express was first attempted.

Chorpenning had the idea to carry President James Buchanan's message across the continent. He decided to place a fresh horse at each relay station along the route and made arrangements with the President for an early delivery of the message text. As a result, Sacramento residents were able to read the second annual message of President Buchanan just 17 days after it had been delivered to congress in December 1858.

The idea of relay stations was followed up by a rich firm of freighters known as Russell, Jajors and Waddell. The Pony Express service was provided between St. Joseph, Missouri and Sacramento beginning April 3, 1860. Relay stations were set up 10 to 15 miles apart. As the rider approached each station, a fresh horse was saddled and ready to go. It took just two minutes for the rider to grab the mailbags and change horses. The Pony Express ended operation October 24, 1861, succeeded by transcontinental telegraph. In the early 1760s, Chorpenning had a claim against the federal government introduced in Congress for non-payment of the reimbursement for losses because of extra services performed or hostile Indian attacks while delivering mail. In December 1870, Postmaster General Creswell awarded Chorpenning $443,010, but it was never paid. Chorpenning's home in Somerset was on the site of the Stein building. It was one of the most beautiful homes in town, but it was destroyed in the great fire of 1872.

Other people were famous even before they chose to reside in Somerset County. For several years in the late 1800s, a house near The Diamond in Somerset served as a "summer White House" for President William McKinley, the nation's 24th president. The house was owned by his brother, Abner McKinley, a lawyer and businessman, and was located at the corner of Main and Court on East Main Street. Many times the President spent weekends at the house. The 17-room brick colonial mansion was the scene of many social gatherings, whether the guests were dignitaries from Washington, D.C., or an informal group of Somerset residents.

The mansion was originally built as a residence for General Alexander Coffroth. McKinley purchased the property in 1892. Abner McKinley was a native of Ohio, but he was married to the former Annie Endsley from Somerset. An article in the October 14, 1932 *Somerset Daily Herald* said Abner McKinley extensively renovated the house, including the installation of one of the first bathrooms in Somerset. In 1960, it was torn down to create a parking lot.

The President's last visit to Somerset was the most exciting. According to an account in the December 1959 *Somerset American*, the Pan-American Exposition in Buffalo, New York, was to be opened in August 1901. President McKinley had been asked to officially open the Exposition by remote control by touching a telegraph key in Somerset, which would illuminate the electric displays at the Exposition. The Western Union Telegraph Company office and equipment were at the rear of a haberdashery operated by Milton Black in the old Berrits building. A small crowd gathered to witness the proceedings, and at the designated time, the President entered a tent and hit the telegraph key. From Somerset the President went to Buffalo to attend the Exposition. While there on September 6, 1901, President McKinley was shot by Leon Czolgosz, an anarchist, and died September 14 from his wounds.

Some of the first people attracted to the tamed Somerset County were artists compelled by the beauty of the Laurel Highlands region. Most of the initial artists settled in what is today called Paint Township, outside of Windber, and spent their days working on sketches and oil paintings of the region's lush forests and pastoral landscapes. Many of the artists built cottages, forming an art colony. When the author Charles Dickens visited the area in 1842, he described it as "a valley full of light and softness." In an address marking the centennial celebration of the county in 1895, the Honorable William H. Koontz recalled that early pioneers, impressed by the abundance of natural meadows situated near the headwaters of many of its streams, had frequently and affectionately called Somerset County the "Glades."

One of the most famous artists to work in Paint Township would be George Hetzel, and his followers, who worked in the area soon after the Civil War. Hetzel was a quiet man who loved the woods, wildflowers, animals, and the changing seasons of the year. He spent days walking, sketching, and painting the countryside. Landscape painting, which Hetzel was most well known for, began in the New World as a form of documentation. Artists accompanied many of the early expeditions and brought back with them images of the immense countryside. But the arts in the nineteenth century were more international in nature than always acknowledged, with most aspiring native painters going abroad for schooling since institutions in America were lacking. Hetzel was among the artists who studied in Europe—he trained at the Dusseldorf Academy to observe naturalistic detail and render things in a precise manner. Therefore, the influence of both historical and contemporary movements in European art can be observed in the work produced in the United States once these students of art returned home. The Barbizon School, concurrent to the last generation of Hudson River School painters, was a French movement named, as with the Scalp Level School, for the area in which they chose to paint. What is remarkable about this artistic period is that for the first time in the history of art, landscape was the preferred subject of an entire group of artists and not just the specialty of a few.

While on a fishing trip for mountain trout in 1866 with John Hampton (lawyer/solicitor for the Pennsylvania Railroad) and the Pittsburgh artist Charles Linford, George Hetzel discovered an area not far from Johnstown, Pennsylvania, near the intersection of Paint and Little Paint Creeks called Scalp Level. Hetzel was so struck by the beauty of the area that he influenced every member of the Pittsburgh School of Design faculty to accompany him the following summer to paint landscapes from nature. Among the artists who would join him in the summer outings were Calerence Johns, Jasper Lawman, Charles Linford, Alfred S. Wall, William C. Wall, and Joseph Woodwell. A second generation of Pittsburgh artists who would travel to Scalp Level with Hetzel in the late 1870s and 1880s were A.F. King, Martin B. Leisser, Horatio S. Stevenson, George Layng, Olive Turney, E.A. Poole, A. Bryan Wall, Lila B. Hetzel, Laura Rinehart, Agnes Way, and Annie Henderson.

SOMERSET COUNTY

The following article appeared in the *Pittsburgh Evening Chronicle* on May 18, 1869:

> We have already alluded to the fact that Mr. Hetzel, the well known artist, is about to remove from this city to Philadelphia, where he proposes making his future home. We cannot but express out regret that Mr. Hetzel should deem this step necessary, but his abilities have not been appreciated here, and he desires to locate where he will meet with that encouragement he so fully merits. He informs us that it is his intention to dispose of the few pictures still remaining on his hands before departing for Philadelphia. We have no doubt that to his many admirers no further intimation will be required. His studio, always open to the public and his friends, will be opened tomorrow with special reference to those who may desire to purchase his pictures. Persons desirous of securing any of the pictures painted from Hetzel's last sketches will call upon him any day after tomorrow. We can assure them, from what we know of the terms, that such an opportunity will not present itself again.

Hetzel then exhibited paintings, most of which depicted rural landscapes of Somerset County woodlands, at the Pennsylvania Academy of the Fine Arts Annual Exhibition of 1869 in Philadelphia. Quite a number of established American artists would have been in the city for the event and he would have made many new friends.

Eventually, Hetzel spent the last months of his life on a farm in Somerset County. His son Jim purchased the farm from the heirs of Noah Roberts together with a large white framed farmhouse with some 230 acres on Lower Level Road a short distance from the city of Somerset. The Hetzel family moved in April 1898 for the last time. George was not well in the spring of 1899 and complained of failing health. On a visit to his brother John A. Hetzel's home at 813 Ohio Street in Allegheny City, George died of heart failure at 11:30 p.m., July 4, 1899, at the age of 73. His son James died of heart failure in Johnstown on January 20, 1901. George's wife Marie Louisa died at their Somerset home on October 6, 1923. On June 4, 1967, George's daughter Lila B. Hetzel died in a nursing home in Berlin and on July 4, 1977, his granddaughter Dorothy Hetzel Kantner committed suicide.

Under the provisions of his granddaughter's will, the Western Pennsylvania Conservancy in Pittsburgh received most of the Hetzel paintings and furniture, the Hetzel Studio farmhouse, which remains today, as well as 150 acres of land. To honor Miss Kantner's request that a memorial be established for her grandfather and mother, the Conservancy in November 1977 invited four institutions from Southwestern Pennsylvania to go to the Carnegie Museum of Art and select works from the Hetzel collection then arranged in a basement room of the museum. In specified order the Carnegie Museum of Art chose first, then the Westmoreland Museum of Art in Greensburg, followed by the Western Pennsylvania Historical Society in Pittsburgh and the Philip Dressler Center for the Arts in Somerset. The Conservancy kept two Hetzel paintings for its office in Pittsburgh.

Although Hetzel and others like him sought to capture and preserve the landscape of Somerset County, soon afterward the population of Somerset County would begin to grow and the landscape quickly began to develop.

Chapter Two

PIONEERING DAYS IN THE MOUNTAINS

The earliest land surveys of Somerset County were made in 1767. The first settlers, Germans of Reformed and Lutheran faiths, came to what is now the Berlin area in 1769. Mennonites migrated to the county in 1780.

Harmon Husband, a Quaker, was the first permanent settler of the village Somerset. He fled from North Carolina where he had protested British taxes and where a bounty had been placed on his head. It was Husband who petitioned the legislature in 1790 to form a new county—since then, the boundaries of the county have changed twice. Later, Husband was elected as representative of Somerset during the Whiskey Rebellion that began when the government placed an excise tax on all whiskey. Western Pennsylvanians felt unfairly discriminated against and demonstrated against the tax and the government. At first they carried out riots and demonstrations, and even tarred and feathered excise collectors, until Husband, a devout Quaker, was able to sway other delegates that peace was the only means for change. The government was at first conciliatory; however, later President Washington was concerned about the region west of the Alleghenies seceding from the union. He sent 13,000 militiamen to crush the rebellion—soon, federal troops arrived in Berlin and captured Husband, as well as 16 others. It is believed that Husband never had a chance to defend himself. He was falsely imprisoned and eventually released, but died shortly after on June 19, 1795. In 1800 the southwestern corner of Bedford County was annexed, and in 1804 a large northern section was lost to the creation of Cambria County.

The first deed recorded in Somerset County was for Lot 56 in Berlin, sold to Adam Miller for 15 shillings and an annual ground rent of one Spanish milled dollar. The deed states that "Jacob Keffer conveyed in 1784 to Jacob Glassner in trust for the Lutheran and Calvinistic churches, one-half of the 40-acre tract and that they laid out the town of Berlin on this tract."

The first road cut through any part of Somerset County was opened in the southwest part of Addison Township. It was surveyed by George Washington and came to be the forerunner of the great National Road or turnpike. Benson is the earliest settlement in the area at the bend of the Stonycreek River. The community grew up around the Bethel United Methodist Church, formed in 1874. The Baltimore and Ohio Railroad built a station to serve the area in 1881, and the area was then called Bethel Station. Another name change occurred in 1881, when the post office was opened under the name of Hollsopple in honor of Charles Hollsopple, an early pioneer. In some accounts, he is referred to as the town's founder, but other records do not credit him with a role in founding the community.

Berlin, named after Berlin, Germany, is located 10 miles southwest of Somerset and was first populated by a small group of German Dunkards and Baptists who came to the area in 1762. The French and Indian War forced them to move in 1763. The first written record of a permanent settler in the Berlin area is that of a farmer, Philip Wagerlein. The Wagerlein farm had a stockade used to shelter the neighboring families during Indian attacks.

Black Township was created out of Milford Township in 1886. It was named after Judge Jeremiah S. Black. James Wilson built a cabin in 1774 or 1775 in what was to become the township. He also built the first sawmill in the township. Jacob Critchfield built a house, which was also used as a schoolhouse and church as early as 1800.

Brothersvalley Township was one of the original six townships when the county was formed by the court of Bedford County during its first session on April 16, 1771. When formed, the township was larger than any other existing counties. Thomas Price started the first commercial mine in the area in 1875. The Wechtenhiser family possessed a draft for a tract of land where Central City is now. The draft was originally prepared in 1775. Theodore Garnish bought 1,150 acres in 1894 and started a logging business that failed, but a settlement called Walker's Sawmill remained there until Cessna Brothers of Bedford County bought the sawmill. In 1906, Babcock Lumber Company moved in and remained there until 1911.

John Penn was the first owner of the land where Davidsville is now located. Christian Miller sold 94 acres to David Stutzman for $600, including Ash Swamp on which Davidsville is now located. Plank Road Co. was chartered in the early 1850s to construct a plank road from Johnstown to Stoystown.

Pioneering Days in the Mountains

The small town of Confluence takes its name from its location at the confluence of the Casselman River, Laurel Hill Creek, and the Youghiogheny River. It is believed that George Washington was the first white man in the area when he was sent to survey the junction of the Casselman and Youghiogheny Rivers on May 21, 1754. According to the legend, Washington's Indian guide pointed out how the three rivers joined together to form the shape of a turkey's foot. The name of Turkeyfoot remains today as the name of the valley and the townships. In all, counting the outward and homeward journeys, "the father of his country" was within the limits of Somerset County not less than 11 times. His last journey through the county would be in 1784 after the close of the Revolutionary War, and his journal entry says:

> Sept. 10, 1784. Left Fort Cumberland. Dined at Mr. Given's, at the forks of the roads leading to Winchester and the Old Town, distant from the latter about twenty miles, and lodged at Tomlinson's, and in about one and a half miles came to what is called the Little Crossing of Youghiogheny. Breakfasted at one Mount's, on the Mountain 11 miles from Tomlinson's, the road being exceedingly bad, especially through what is called the shades of Death. Baited at the Great Crossing of the Yohogheny, on Braddock's Road (Somerfield), which is a large water distant from Mount's miles, and a better road than between that and Tomlinson's.

The Little Crossings referred to above is not in Somerset County, but in the state of Maryland, about two-and-a-half miles south of Mason and Dixon's line. The stream is Castleman's River in Somerset County, which in these times was known as the Little Youghiogheny River.

Elk Lick Township, the fifth township in order of formation, was formed by the Bedford County Court out of the southern part of Brothersvalley Township around 1785. The name came from one of those natural saline springs called a lick, a great area for elk and deer. An early tradition is that a hunter named Henry Hiller hid near the spring one night to shoot an elk. He saw a group of them approach and fired. His shot supposedly went through the backbone of one, into the leg of a second, and into the heart of a third elk.

William Tissue, whose name is also spelled Tyshu, Tyshoe, Tye and Tice, built a small gristmill on the tub-mill pattern on Tub Mill Run about the close of the Revolutionary War. The stream is believed to have been given its name from the mill that Ebenezer Griffith built around 1790, which was later rebuilt by Samuel Fike. In 1799 the Yost Zook farm had 80 acres of cleared land, the largest in the township.

Some of the largest businesses the county had before coal mining were Standard Extract Works built in West Salisbury in 1888, a business that extracted certain properties from chestnut wood to be used in tanning, and a large steam sawmill in Boynton, near the old sugar camp of the Douglas Boyd farm, which was built in 1880.

The town of Fairhope, in the smallest and most recently formed township in the county, was laid out a short period after the Civil War. According to reports, the residents considered it would be a "fair hope" that a rail line would be built through the village. The Baltimore and Ohio branch line was built through the village in the later part of the century. One of its biggest resources was a great amount of fire clay, used to line steel-making furnaces. Production of the fire-resistant bricks was centered in the village of Williams, in the southeastern part of the township.

The town of Garrett was laid out in 1869, but it did not build up until it became the south terminus of the Berlin branch of the railroad and the shipping point for several steam sawmills. Greenville Township was formed by the county in 1812 and Martin Weimer was the first settler in the township. He settled on and farmed a tract on a small branch of Pine Run in 1785. The township had a number of stream-driven sawmills, the first of their kind in the county. In the only village in the township, Pocohontas, Charles Miller built the first log house in 1844 and Peter Keefer operated the first blacksmith shop.

Jonas Hoover laid out lots along the banks of the Stony Creek River in 1836 and created Hooversville. People were already living in that area to mine iron ore and John Clark established the first gristmill before the town was laid out. George Lohr built the first store in 1850. In 1881, the railroad was built and a large vein of coal was found beneath the town.

Bakersville, near the central part of Jefferson Township, was founded by Henry Baker in 1847. He had a farm, a gristmill, a large distillery, and a tavern. Baker Whiskey, or moonshine, acquired a widespread reputation. Jenner Township was formed out of a part of Quemahoning Township in 1811 when Moes Fream came into the township and built a sawmill in 1813—there were already three gristmills in the area.

Jennerstown has always been known as a travelers' stopping point. It is situated at the crossing of Route 219 and Route 30, the Lincoln Highway, which was the old Forbes Road. James Wells settled on the farm that is now the site of Jennerstown—recently found family records of James Wells show three of his children died within a few weeks of each other in 1783 of smallpox. Joseph Haines advertised land for sale in this area in 1818 and the village was set to be called Laurel Hill, but when the new town was being laid out Dr. Edward Jenner developed the smallpox vaccine and the town was named for him.

In Larimer Township, named for General William Larimer who was a president of the Pittsburgh and Connellsville Railroad Company, the town of Deal was built around a gristmill in 1850. Two years later, the gristmill was destroyed by fire. It was rebuilt by Edwin Deal, for whom the town was named.

Somerset County's Lincoln Township was formed in 1890 and was named after President Abraham Lincoln. In the township, Michael Sipe, who was born in Meyersdale, founded Sipesville in 1820. He opened a store and the town grew up around the store, which was located on the first turnpike. The store and ten houses constituted Sipesville until the early 1900s. Also in the same township, the town of Quecreek was originally called Harrison when it originated in 1888.

Meyersdale was a summer base for Native Americans, who had several camps in the immediate area. John Olinger is considered to be the earliest settler in Meyersdale, having made his claim in 1779. Within a few years, Jacob Meyers Sr. moved from Lebanon County on land close to Flaughtery's Creek. Over the years, he built a sawmill, gristmill, fulling mill, and a distillery. During his time the village was known as Meyers Mills. In 1872, with the joining of two groups of plots, the town of Dale City was formed. In 1874, a movement began to join the two and incorporate. One group wanted to name the new borough Dale City and another group wanted the name Meyers Mills. The issue was put to a vote, but the resulting ballot ended in a tie. Judge William M. Hall of Bedford County, who was the presiding judge for Somerset County, proposed that the names be merged into Meyersdale—and so it was! Meyersdale has always been the leader in the matter of public improvements in

Somerset County. It was the first county town to have electric lights and water and to pave its streets. Later it would have the first four-year high school in the county.

Middlecreek Township, named after the stream of the same name, was created from Milford Township in 1853. Philip King built the first grist and saw mills not long after John Kooser built a gristmill in 1806.

In 1845, Henry Thomas Weld bought about 12,000 acres of timberland and built a sawmill that derived its power from Wills Creek. The village of Southampton Mills, in Northampton Township, grew up around it. Within the township, David Hay and Hiram Findley laid out the village of Glencoe around 1870, about the time the railroad was completed. Hay kept the first store in the township, but Augustus Dom kept the first store after the village was laid out and Hay built a hotel in 1874.

Ogle Township was formed in 1886 from almost a half of Paint Township. Why this was done isn't known, but it is believed that there was a dispute over taxes to support the schools. When it was first formed, Ogle Township was described as nothing but dense forest. The first, and for a time the only, industry was lumbering. George D. Wolf, D.B. Ernst, and others built the first sawmill around 1848. Known as the old Ashtola plant, it and many thousands of acres of other timberlands passed into the hands of the E.V. Babcock Lumber Co. around 1901. Three large sawmills were added, making it one of the largest lumber plants in the county.

Jacob Eash is said to have founded Paint Borough–Scalp Level, but no date can be found, nor could it be determined if he laid his town out in Somerset or nearby Cambria County or both. The story goes that Eash invited neighbors to help him cut trees and roll logs. He told them to "scalp the land level," which was what the area was then called. This theory was reaffirmed in a story from the *Johnstown Tribune-Democrat* on August 29, 1906:

> Eash (Mr. Jacob Eash), in order to clear the ground around his home, invited some of the people living in the surrounding country to a log rolling (a common practice to clear a patch or field of trees, logs, brush, etc.), and while some of the men were cutting up trees, others rolling them on piles, and still others grubbing and clearing out the underbrush, Eash made his appearance with a jug. Whisky was the prevailing drink in those days. It was

very cheap, and as it was also very good, everybody drank. When Mr. Eash came to the men clearing out the underbrush he made the remark, "Scalp them level," meaning, of course, close to the ground. Thus, this story says, the town was named.

Other stories have also been suggested—one story says that a band of hunters were killed in the area and scalped by Indians, another says that an ancient mountaineer made Saturday night visits to the town and after much drinking would threaten to "scalp 'em all off the level," and yet another legend suggests there was a long standing feud between two early families whose members constantly threatened to scalp each other. When the first passenger train arrived in the village on August 3, 1897, people decided the town would prosper and lots were laid out.

Quemahoning Township was the third township of the county in order of organization. The name comes from Indian words meaning a pine grove and water coming from a lick.

In 1857, Philip Wolfersberger bought land and laid out a town that was first called Mineral Point. But because there was another Mineral Point in Pennsylvania, the town's name was later changed to Rockwood to reflect its natural surroundings.

Prior to 1878, the town of Salisbury was a farming community. The completion of the railroad and mining in the Elk Lick Coal Basin brought people in from other areas.

Adolph and Helen Dupre bought the land that would soon be called Seven Springs in 1932 for $13 and opened a private ski club, which later became Seven Springs Mountain Resort, today the largest year-round resort in Pennsylvania. The story goes that Adolph was coon hunting in the area where he would eventually buy land when a moonshiner shot at him. Later he remembered the beauty of the land that reminded him of his native Bavaria, which he had left only four years earlier. By the end of the decade, people were coming to the area to make use of what was then one of the few ski slopes in the United States. An automobile was first used to tow skiers up a slope. A rope tow was added by 1935 and the first chair lift was installed in 1957. Dupre created a snowmaking system in 1960.

Buckstown is partially in Shade Township and partially in Stonycreek Township. John Lambert built the first house there in 1805. He opened a tavern in 1817. The only modestly successful iron producer in the county was Shade Furnace, the county's first iron works, built between 1807 and 1812 near a thin vein of iron ore. John Milnor managed the works, which included the furnace, a forge, a gristmill, and a sawmill. Rockingham was built on the site of the old Rockingham Iron Furnace, which was erected in 1844. Although the Rockingham furnace was abandoned by 1849, the Shade Furnace continued to produce iron until the late 1850s, and the Somerset Furnace, built in the same area, operated sporadically through the early 1870s.

Shankesvillle was founded by Christian Shank in 1789, who built a home and a gristmill on the banks of the Stoney Creek. He later built a woolen mill. Emanuel Shafer opened a store in 1820 and Daniel Brant kept the first hotel. The town was laid out in lots in 1829 and the post office was established in 1847. A fire on August 24, 1889 started in a store and destroyed most of the town, including the county bridge over Stony Creek.

The region of Somerset was first called Stony Creek Glades, but beginning in 1773, it was called Cox's Creek Glades because there was another Stoney Creek Glades. The name of Cox's Creek Glades came from Isaac Cox, a hunter and trapper who was a boyhood friend of Harmon Husband. In 1771, when Husband had fled North Carolina under the alias of Tuscape (or Toescape) Death, he decided to try to find Cox's camp. He instead found a cabin owned by William Sparks. On Sparks's land was the first soil in the settlement broken for cultivation. Sparks knew Cox and took Husband to Cox's cabin. Sparks thought that the name Tuscape Death was too formal, so Cox suggested Husband, who was a Quaker, be called the Old Quaker, which is what many called him.

Husband purchased Sparks's claim when Sparks decided to choose a better site before more settlers moved in. When Cox learned that a new county would be formed, he became upset that the people would drive beavers away and he moved west. John Vansel purchased Cox's claim, then sold it to Husband, too. Sparks later moved back to Juniata County because of a death in his wife's family. He sold his second claim to Husband.

Woolerick Bruner (who is listed in some accounts as Ulrich Bruner) and Peter Ankeny laid out a town known as Milford town in 1784 or 1785. But people spoke of it as the town that Bruner had laid out, or Bruener's Town, or in some spellings

Brunerstown. Adam Schneider and Ankeny replatted the town in 1795, after Somerset County was created; they named the town Somerset after the name of the county. In some records it is spelled as Summerset.

Governor Thomas Mifflin appointed William Findley, John Badolet, James Chambers, and Thomas Campbell as commissioners to choose a county seat. On September 12, 1795, they chose Somerset. Because Berlin was more of a town than Somerset, the people of Berlin were upset, but there was no appeal process. A room was rented for a courthouse until a building could be built. The first case before the court occurred when a member of the first grand jury, Adam Keffer, was found to be grossly intoxicated and unable to take part in the grand jury proceedings. His fellow grand jury members indicted him. He pleaded not guilty and was tried and convicted—paying a fine of $5.

The first deed recorded in Somerset County was on June 20, 1795, for a lot in Berlin. It was made out to Adam Miller by Jacob Keefer and Jacob Glassner, trustees of the Lutheran and Calvinistic congregations. The first will registered was that of Harmon Husband recorded on August 20, 1795. The first courthouse was built in 1798 and was used for 50 years. A second courthouse was completed in 1856. The current structure was completed in 1907.

Glade Road was the first road through Somerset, and the first railway tracks were built in the 1870s and would eventually be turned into the turnpike road leading from Bedford to Pittsburgh, now known as Route 31. Agriculture was the earliest industry in Somerset, followed by the manufacture of cloth. Iron ore, coal, timber, and limestone were plentiful.

Somerset suffered from three major fires. The first was in 1833. The second, and most disastrous, was in 1872. It began in a stable owned by Francis Weimer from a spark blown over from Somerset Foundry. The fire leveled most of the business district and many homes in just over an hour. The third fire occurred in 1876; it started in a stable owned by Somerset Foundry and spread to the foundry and other buildings. A direct result of the devastating fires was the organization of the first fire department.

Street lighting, with oil lamps, was inaugurated in 1875. The work for the first waterworks was completed on September 4, 1894. The sewage system was not installed until May of 1901.

Lavansville, part of Somerset Township, takes its name from its founder, David Lavan, a French blacksmith who came to the area in 1804. He wasn't the first person to live there. John Tantlinger built a hotel there in 1803. In 1847, Lavan converted his home to an inn and tavern because of the large amount of traffic on the turnpike.

The town of Friedens originally began as a small plot surveyed for a church. The land was patented in 1808 for the Lutherans and Presbyterians under the official name of Harmony. The citizens of the village decided to rename it as Friendsburg, but when it was found that another town had that name, it was changed to Friedens, which is a derivation of a German word meaning peace. Friedens was one of the first towns to have a one-room schoolhouse, which operated for many years and is now a community building for the area, according to Dwight Hostetler, long-time resident and postcard collector.

The sixth and last township of Somerset County is Stonycreek Township, formed in 1792 out of a part of Quemahoning Township. The township takes its name from the Stony Creek, which came from an Indian word meaning a swift mountain stream. The first, and at that time only, voting place in the county was at the home of James Black in Stonycreek Township. Abraham Lambert built the first house in Lambertsville in about 1855.

The village of Downey is located on Route 160, five miles northeast of Berlin. It was laid out in 1884 on land owned by Jacob G. Kimmel during construction of the Old South Penn Railroad and Allegheny Tunnel. Kimmel purchased the land from Jacob Lehman, who owned it as far back as 1786.

Stoystown, one of the oldest villages in the county, was founded by Daniel Stoy in approximately 1790. The land was first warranted to William Hunter in 1789, to Henry Bitel in 1799, and to Stoy in 1800—it was originally spelled as Stoyestown. It is not recorded when Stoy had the town platted, but it is believed to have been shortly after the laying out of the Pennsylvania Road, also called the Great Road, which was done in 1790 and passed through the town. In 1798, Stoystown was the most considerable settlement between Bedford and Greensburg.

Joseph Black kept the first store, according to local tradition. General Alexander Ogle kept a store in the township in 1796, having lived there before he moved to Somerset. Joseph Pisel kept a tavern starting in 1799. It is not known when Stoystown became a post office, but it is believed to have been at a very early stage.

Pioneering Days in the Mountains

In Summit Township Joseph J. Yoder, whose name is spelled Joder in some accounts, laid out Summit Mills in 1830. He was a famous ax-maker known as "Axie Yoder," an Amishman who mastered the art of tempering steel. Only 17 lots were on the original plat of Summit Mills. A hunter by the name of Flaherty or Flaugherty gave his name to the stream there. There are reports that it was named for him because he operated a still on the banks of the stream. In the early years there were three Amish-Mennonite settlements in Somerset County—the first was in the north near Johnstown, the second near Berlin, and the third near Springs-Grantsville. There are several growing Amish-Mennonite communities in Somerset County today—it is believed that these communities are among the fastest growing Amish populations in the United States.

In the same township, there are four or five different accounts of how Negro Mountain got its name. One of the more popular ones was that Jacob Castleman and his servant were hunting when a band of Indians began chasing them. The two men separated, the African American going up the mountain and Castleman toward the river. The African American was never heard from again. In another account, Captain Andrew Friend and a hunting party, which included his servant, were attacked by Indians. The African American was mortally wounded and urged the others to leave him so they could flee more quickly. Friend refused to abandon him. Another man, who had himself been saved by Friend, stayed with them. The two men stayed with the servant until his death, buried him on the mountain, and fled from the Indians.

The youngest community in Stonycreek Township is Indian Lake. This community has rustic homes surrounding a man-made lake. In 1960, the McIntyres, Baltzers, Neilans, and Bob Long built Indian Lake as a resort. It was incorporated as a borough on April 1, 1966. In 1972, it was sold to a group of Ohio developers. One year later, the new owners began to suffer a financial loss and in 1974 an auction was held to liquidate the holdings. Much of the resort was divided up in parcels. The lodge closed for about ten years, then the Lakewood Corporation purchased it in 1985. National Bank of Western Pennsylvania, lienholder of the lodge and related property, then purchased it at a sheriff's sale in 1989. The lodge, hotel, and golf course were purchased in 1992 by an investment group that includes Dr. Gerald W. Piffer, Pittsburgh; Edward J. Smith, Greensburg, and Jim and Paul Hengelsberg, Pittsburgh.

In Turkeyfoot Township near the end of the Revolutionary War, Oliver Drake built a gristmill on the waters that he named Drake's Run. The area was later called Draketown. His son Jonathon later built a fulling and carding mill. They were the first industries in the township and were later joined by a tannery owned by a Hendrickson and a Welsh in 1854.

Samuel Harned laid out Harnedsville about 1847. The village nurseries, which lay just outside of the town, were first started by Harrison H. Kemp in 1857.

Andrew Ream, an early settler, had a farm in the area that later became Ursina. The Honorable William J. Baer laid out Ursina in 1868, as surveyed by R.J. Botzer. Ursina is a derivative of the word "bear" in Latin. In the town, Ephra S. Kregar built a hotel, known as the Sycamore House, in 1868.

In the town of Windber, John Messerbaugh owned land along the Paint Creek and built a sawmill. David Shaffer, in 1865, purchased Messerbaugh's holdings along Paint Creek and cleared the land. Shaffer then built the first modern house in the town, which today serves as Windber's Museum, but the area did not attract many early settlers. James S. Cummingham, the advance agent in field operations for the Berwind-White Coal Mining Co., bought Shaffer's land in 1893. The syllables of Charles F. Berwind's name were transposed to give the community the name Windber. Cunningham, who bought more than 100 miles of territory for the mining company, is sometimes called the father of Windber. This, and many of the other communities mentioned above, would change greatly when coal would begin to be mined on a large scale.

Chapter Three

FROM FARMING TO

UNDERGROUND FARMING

Neither coal mining companies nor an immigrant population from southern and eastern Europe were present in Pennsylvania's Somerset County at the time of the 1890 census. But within the next decade there would be a transformation from a predominantly rural region into an important industrial center.

Somerset County was a picturesque setting for a new industrial area. Bounded by the Allegheny Mountains on its eastern edge and by the Laurel Mountains on the western edge, it had often been noted for its beautiful hills and scenery. Industrial development was on a small scale in this rustic setting for the early years of settlement. It is significant that state historian Sylvester K. Stevens barely mentioned Somerset County in his scholarly account documenting the rise of Pennsylvania industry. Stressing the uneven nature of nineteenth-century economic development, he argued that rural sections of the state, as late as 1870 or beyond, often resembled the Colonial era more than the emerging industrial one.

In any event, the first railroad to enter the county limits did not do so until 1873, and in 1890 most residents continued to make their livings as farmers, much as they and the nation had done throughout the century. The rolling hills, dense forests, and extensive farmlands of this county would become the site of a future metropolitan coal center.

The percentage of people born in the United States in Somerset County was much higher in 1890 than it was in the nation as a whole. Nearly 97 percent of its inhabitants had been native born; the corresponding national figure was slightly more than 85 percent. While the county's population had increased from 28,226 in 1870 to 37,313 in 1890, the number of foreign born had actually decreased during that period. Thus, by 1890, the county's foreign-born constituted only a little more than 3 percent of its total population, whereas in the nation they constituted nearly 15 percent.

SOMERSET COUNTY

If the relative balance between the native-born and foreign-born population in Somerset County differed significantly from that of the nation, the ethnic distribution of its foreign-born more closely mirrored it. In both cases, northern Europeans, headed by Germans, constituted the vast majority. On the national level, Germans alone accounted for more than half of the total 9,249,547 foreign born. In Somerset County, where they had been settling throughout the nineteenth century, they made up 64.3 percent of the total. Nationally, the Irish were second in importance, followed by a third group of English, Scots, and Welsh. In Somerset County the position of these two groups was simply reversed, but immigrants from the British Isles, Scandinavia, and northern Europe nevertheless comprised 94.24 percent of its foreign born.

In neither the national nor the local instance did those who were considered part of the new immigration from southern and eastern Europe constitute more than a mere fraction of the total foreign-born population. In the nation as a whole, no southern or eastern European nationality group numbered more than 200,000 in 1890, and the sum total of all such groups in Somerset County was only 68, or 5.59 percent of the total foreign born. Italians, who comprised 4.7 percent of the county's immigrants, formed the only sizable cluster in the scattering of these nationalities.

Thus, Somerset County's population was predominantly white and born in the United States. It was also, not surprisingly, Protestant. Even as late as 1906, when the influx of new immigrants into the area was sizable, a historian counted only six Roman Catholic congregations but a multitude of older, well-established Protestant ones representing many different denominations. Lutheran bodies alone numbered 55, and there were 38 Reformed congregations.

In politics, the county traditionally favored the Republican party, which had easily carried its presidential and gubernatorial candidates to victory in a vast majority of elections since 1860. For example, in the critical realignment contest in 1896, William McKinley outpolled William Jennings Bryan, 15,861 votes to 2,295. Political contests in the late nineteenth and early twentieth centuries were more likely to occur between rival local factions of the Republican party than between Republicans and Democrats, and at the turn of the century the Prohibition party was the most powerful of a number of minority parties. Temperance and Sabbatarianism were issues that many Protestants took seriously. Anti-Saloon

From Farming to Underground Farming

League and Women's Christian Temperance Union organizations were growing in numbers, size, and influence, reflecting a nationwide movement in the direction of prohibition.

It was in this setting, on July 4, 1895, that residents gathered in Somerset, Pennsylvania, to proudly celebrate the county's centennial amid predictions that the next 100 years of its history would greatly outshine the prosperity of the previous century. The basis for such optimism was the value of the vast deposits of bituminous coal that geologists had reported underlay much of Somerset County. Although the county had, in terms of development, historically lagged behind other areas endowed with similar riches, change was imminent. The editor of the *Somerset County Democrat* proclaimed, "Her [Somerset County's] vast fields of coal are only commencing to be developed; in the next ten years the development will be in full blast and that means prosperity." He then lauded the belated arrival of railroads into the mountainous area: "Her desirable territory will be crossed and recrossed by bands of steel on which the products of her soil, the wealth of her mountains, and the results of the industry of her people can be carried to a market, and this means greater prosperity." The editor concluded on this bright note:

> In fact Somerset County in the next decade is destined to advance to the proud position of one of the leading counties in the state, a position which belongs to her by right of her natural resources and by reason of her hardy, progressive, intelligent and capable class of citizens.

These optimistic predictions of imminent industrial development of the county turned out to be substantially correct. Somerset County came into its own just as the state of Pennsylvania and the nation were concluding a period of historical development that has often been dubbed "the golden age of industry." In 1900, Pennsylvania ranked second only to New York in terms of its industry and population. By any standard—such as the percentage of wage earners in manufacturing or the value of manufactured products in the state—Pennsylvania attained its greatest relative importance in industrial production vis-à-vis the nation during the period 1870–1900. While still important for decades afterward, the share of its contribution to national industrial productivity declined after 1900, as did that of most other older, established states in the eastern United States.

The great industrial growth of Pennsylvania and the United States in the late nineteenth century was in large part based on coal. By 1900 the two different types—anthracite (hard coal) and bituminous (soft coal)—were supplying approximately 90 percent of the nation's energy, with soft coal furnishing more than 70 percent of that amount and hard coal about 30 percent. Post–Civil War railroad development, combined with technological developments in the iron and steel industries, such as the open-hearth furnace, had produced a great demand for soft coal. Approximately half of Pennsylvania's bituminous production from 1880 to 1900 went into the making of Pennsylvania coke, which was subsequently used in the new blast furnaces of the Pennsylvania steel industry, which in turn came into historical importance in its own right.

Throughout most of the twentieth century, Somerset County has been among the top six or seven bituminous-producing counties in Pennsylvania, which led all other states in such production until 1927, when West Virginia surpassed it. According to a report published by the Pennsylvania Geological Survey in 1928, Somerset County ranked fifth in original bituminous deposits in the state. Moreover, the amount of coal actually mined bore a close relationship to these rankings. Only the counties of Fayette, Greene, Washington, Westmoreland, and Allegheny, all of which are located in southwestern Pennsylvania, historically produced more.

Coal mining did not become an industry of any importance in Somerset County until the 1880s, but after 1897, when Berwind-White opened the first of its 13 mines, its growth was spectacular. By 1903, local newspapers were citing geological statistics, commenting on the previous five years of growth of Somerset's coal industry, and attributing the recent rise in county production solely to the new Berwind-White mines.

Windber-area mines continued to be the mainstay of the county's coal industry in subsequent years. Peak production was reached during the years 1910 to 1913, when nearly 4 million tons were produced annually. The zenith of all Somerset County production in the state reached its high mark in 1918. Nonetheless, throughout the 1920s and beyond, Berwind-White and an affiliate, the Reitz Coal Company, produced approximately half of all the coal produced in the state's important 24th bituminous inspection district, which encompassed Windber and the adjacent Johnstown region.

By the time the Berwind-White Coal Mining Company came to Somerset County, it exemplified the new type of impersonal, large-scale corporations that were coming into being in the United States in the period following the Civil War. Four of five Berwind brothers, the children of a Prussian-born cabinetmaker who had settled and prospered in Philadelphia in the 1840s, did eventually take active part in the coal business through the Berwind-White Coal Mining Company. The company had grown from the Berwind brothers' earlier, small-scale partnerships in the 1860s and 1870s until it reached modern form in January 1886, when it was reorganized and incorporated as the Berwind-White Coal Mining Company.

Throughout the 1860s and 1870s, the Berwinds initiated and expanded their business interests. They leased mines, bought up mineral and surface rights, invested in related enterprises, and entered into contracts that guaranteed markets for their coal. Their first mine, Eureka No. 1, was opened in the early 1870s in Houtzdale, Pennsylvania, where the Berwinds also established their first company store, known as the Eureka Supply Company. Through direct ownership, leases, and interlocking cooperative arrangements, the company rapidly achieved considerable success in the bituminous coal industry. Like other large corporations, the company's success in the highly competitive industry of bituminous coal had been ensured by its growing vertical integration, which included control not only over the coal resources themselves, but also over transportation, docks, finance, marketing, and other enterprises related to mining.

Berwind-White's development was greatly aided by its important and controversial long-term association with the Pennsylvania Railroad. In 1875, Edward J. Berwind had gone to New York to obtain contracts from steamship companies, which agreed to buy coal for the transatlantic trade from Berwind mines and the Pennsylvania Railroad. Until then, the Pennsylvania Railroad reportedly had no share of this important soft-coal market. Berwind was highly successful in this endeavor, in a manner that was repeated over and over again in the future with other companies and public utilities. With or without an intermediary, he sold coal from his own mines to other enterprises in which he had become an important investor or director. Such questionable conflict-of-interest practices led to a number of scandals and governmental investigations. One of the most important occurred during the strike of 1922, when New York City investigated the company's financial and labor practices because Windber coal fueled the city's subway system, on whose board Berwind sat.

The vast holdings and wealth that Edward J. Berwind acquired in his lifetime led one contemporary competitor to dub him "the 'biggest' name in bituminous coal mining." Upon his death in 1936 at the age of 88, *The New York Times* reported that Berwind was "reputed to be the largest individual owner of coal properties in the United States" and the last survivor of a circle of J. Pierpont Morgan's followers and associates. During his lifetime, he was president of six coal companies, including Berwind-White, and director of four others. Yet, the obituary noted, Berwind was also known for his business activities outside the coal industry. He had served as a director of approximately 50 of the nation's other leading corporations, including railroad, banking, insurance, steamship, and communication companies.

Nonetheless, the Berwind-White Coal Mining Company played a key role in the Berwinds' accumulation of wealth and power, and evidence suggests that Windber-area miners were the most productive and profitable of all its historical operations. In the 1870s and 1880s the Clearfield region of Pennsylvania had been the chief focus of its activities. Seven years after Windber's founding, the company established new towns and mines in West Virginia. Yet Windber was chiefly responsible for Berwind-White's claim for coal empire status early in the twentieth century, and throughout the period 1897–1940 Windber occupied the central place in the corporation's extensive operations. It was the showpiece of the company's 50th anniversary advertisement in 1936 and was important enough for a woman who married into the Berwind family to discuss her introduction to—and growing consciousness of—the town in her memoirs.

Berwind-White could not have developed its new coal holdings without an adequate transportation system. Throughout the early 1890s, Somerset County papers had been speculating about potential railroad competition and development. In the end, the Pennsylvania Railroad Company built or controlled the lines necessary for development.

By the 1890s the Berwind-White Coal Mining Company was widely reputed to be a Pennsylvania Railroad concern, and the widespread perception of their interlocking interests in the region was such that at the turn of the century newspaper reports sometimes used the names Berwind-White and Pennsylvania Railroad interchangeably. The railroad's president, Alexander Cassatt, occasionally came to Windber to inspect railroad lines to the mines. More important, in 1906, Interstate Commerce Commission investigations into charges of car and rate discrimination by the Pennsylvania Railroad on behalf of Berwind-White substantiated such charges, uncovered other favors and cooperative arrangements, and revealed that railroad magnates and lesser officials had received gifts of stock in the coal company.

Railroad and coal development in Cambria and Somerset County did not begin until the Johnstown flood of 1889 had made new routes into the area possible. In 1891 the South Fork Railroad Company completed construction of one line, which facilitated access to the new coalfields. Built directly through the break in the breast of the dam, this railroad, linked to the Pennsylvania system, connected Berwind's mines in South Fork and Dunlo in Cambria County with its new operations in Somerset County.

In March 1897 a state charter was issued to the Scalp Level Railroad Company, which the Pennsylvania Railroad and the Berwind-White Coal Mining Company controlled, to build a line connecting South Fork and Windber. Since surveys had already been made, contracts were quickly let and construction rushed in hopes that mines might be opened by July 1897.

A test run of the first passenger train, with dignitaries aboard, took place early in August 1897; the pioneer shipment of coal from Berwind-White's first mine in the area, Mine 30, occurred in September 1897. The South Fork Railroad Company and the Scalp Level Railroad Company merged in 1902. Built to develop Windber-area coal lands, they were absorbed directly into the Pennsylvania system in 1903.

Rumors of railroad and coal development in the Central Pennsylvania region attracted the attention of a third interest, which usually accompanied the other two in the opening of new territories. Timber was a commodity of great commercial value, and lumber industrialists sought to exploit the virgin hemlocks and other forests in the area. While a number of firms were involved in this industry, the largest by far was the Babcock Lumber Company of Pittsburgh. In October 1897 its president, Edward V. Babcock, acquired an initial tract of 6,800 acres of forested land in the Ashtola district of Somerset County. Berwind-White, however, retained ownership and rights to the underlying minerals.

SOMERSET COUNTY

By 1900 the Babcock Lumber Company was employing 400 men, and by June 1902 its payroll had increased to 1,244. In subsequent years, it purchased many additional acres of forests in the region and bought out most competitors. Babcock closed the last of its local operations in 1913, after the timber had been depleted, but during its active operations in the early years of the century its various lumber camps were located on the outskirts of the new town of Windber. Although it established its own housing and stores, newspaper reports suggest that Windber's hotels, clubs, and speakeasies attracted many lumberjacks, as well as miners, on Saturday nights.

As must often have been the case with timber and coal interests in a given area, the Babcock and Berwind companies were complementary and not in competition with one another. Their respective owners and officers entertained each other socially, especially in the rustic setting of Babcock's newly constructed luxurious lodge, and if newspaper reports are accurate, they typically supported the same political candidates. Certainly they shared in policing the region in the frontier era of Windber's history. Although the first burgess of Windber was a superintendent of Babcock Lumber Company, Berwind-White, not Babcock, had originated regional development, and coal, not timber, was the reason Windber had come into existence.

There is an abundance of coal and timber all throughout Somerset County that made industrial progress possible. Early coal enterprises suffered two problems that hindered the development of coal reserves: a lack of inexpensive transportation and the inability of local businesses to attract large amounts of capital, especially from outside investors. Despite the early mining efforts of the Union and Wellersburg Coal companies, it was not until the 1870s that the coal reserves of Somerset County were exploited on a large scale. The expansion of railways in the area hastened the growth. The completion of the Pittsburgh and Connellsville Railroad in 1871 and the Salisbury and Baltimore Railroad in 1876 were two of the keys that unlocked the doors for the southern part of the county.

By 1874 there were 11 coal companies operating in the county, including the Keystone Coal and Manufacturing Co. near Meyersdale. A total of 11 companies employed a few dozen men and produced 6,500 tons of coal annually for an average of about 600 tons each. The Cumberland and Elk Lick Coal Co. found investors and was about to construct 100 coke ovens in 1886 in southern Somerset County.

From Farming to Underground Farming

Around the turn of the century, Daniel B. Zimmerman helped establish one of the county's largest coal concerns, the Quenmahoning Coal Co. Operators established mines and communities such as Goodtown and Ralphton that were named after family members or company stockholders. By 1900, 28 coal companies were operating 35 mines in the county. The combined production boosted the county's rank to eighth among the state's bituminous coal–producing counties. Two large coal companies, the Berwind-White Coal Mining Company, as mentioned above, and the Somerset Coal Company, emerged and overshadowed competitors.

The Somerset Coal Company was incorporated in New York in 1901. It acquired 18 mining properties, including those of the Pine Hill Coal Co., the Cumberland and Elk Lick Coal Co., and the Listie Coal and Manufacturing Co. During its first year of operation, Somerset Coal produced 1.325 million tons of coal, more than one-fifth of all coal mined in the county. It was then bought by Consolidation Coal Co. of Baltimore. Berwind and Somerset Coal together produced nearly one-third of the county's coal.

The opening of mines brought with it company towns adjacent to the mine sites, such as Keystone southeast of Meyersdale in 1872 by the Keystone Coal and Manufacturing Co. The most elaborate company town was Windber, where employees had the option to buy homes instead of just renting. Residents could shop in any store in the area, but many just shopped at the company Eureka stores that stood in each of the towns. Companies frequently ran other enterprises, including the local electric, grocery, heat, and lumber companies. They also owned movie theaters, which often showed silent pictures in the earlier years. Berwind-White operated more than a dozen mines at one time and nearly all were in Somerset County.

The completion of the Buffalo Valley Railroad in 1874 marked the starting of the coal industry on a large scale in Brothersvalley Township. A number of large mines opened along the railroad, starting above Garrett. They were owned by Enterprise Coal Mining Co. and Hocking Coal Co. located at Fogletown. Somerset Coal Co. had the Allegheny Mine at Althouse and two other mines at Goodtown and Raineytown.

John Ream and John Stoner had large mines at Berlin. Brothersvalley Coal Co. opened mines at Salco and Macdonaldton. Many of the mines changed owners over the years. Somerset Coal Co. became Consolidated Coal Co. It later merged with

Pittsburgh Coal Co. and was called Pittsburgh Consolidated Coal Co. The company was then sold to Continental Oil Co. Hillman Coal Co. had a deep mine at Jerome.

While iron ore was among the first commercially mined minerals in Somerset County, the iron industry never flourished. Many of the materials necessary for iron production, including limestone for flux and timber for charcoal, were present in the area, but local iron ore deposits were irregular and of little commercial value. The limited supply of iron made it necessary for local forges to import pig iron from Bedford or Cumberland, Maryland.

The only modestly successful iron producer in the county was Shade Furnace, the county's first ironworks, built in 1807. Located in the northern part of the county near a thin vein of iron ore, Shade Furnace was in reach of the Johnstown marketplace, about 16 miles away. By 1820, the furnace site included a forge as well as a gristmill and a sawmill. It employed 70 to 100 men, 6 boys, and 15 women who backed and washed for the men. In 1849 the company made 30 tons of bars. The operation continued at various intervals until it closed in 1858.

Rockingham Furnace was located along Dark Shade Creek, about 2 miles upstream from Shade Furnace, near the village of Rockingham along Route 160 between Windber and Central City. The ore used at the furnace was obtained by open pit mining in the surrounding area.

Around 1809 Peter Kimmell and Matthias Scott built a forge for the manufacture of bar iron on Laurel Hill Creek in Jefferson Township. Also during the same period, Robert Philson erected a catalan forge in Turkeyfoot Township. The ore was mined in the vicinity or hauled from Laurel Hill Creek. It made blooms and bar iron directly from the ore. It was a tedious and expensive process as well as a most primitive method. It is believed to be the only forge of its kind in Somerset County. Its operations ceased in 1823.

In 1811 Joseph Vickroy and Conray Piper built Mary Ann Forge along the Stony Creek about 5 miles below Shade Furnace. It was named after Piper's wife, who was also Vickroy's sister. One of the county's coal companies also operated an iron furnace. In 1855, the Union Coal and Iron Company constructed the Wellersburgh Furnace. During its first years of operation, the furnace produced 1,200 tons of iron. But it operated sporadically and by 1866, the company abandoned the operation.

From Farming to Underground Farming

Next to coal mining, the manufacture of firebrick was one of the most prevalent industries in the early history of the county. The Savage Fire Brick Company was erected at Keystone Junction, about 10 miles east of Meyersdale. It was known for having the most extensive supply of fire clay in the United States, with the clay being from 7 to 25 feet in thickness. In addition, one of the finest silica quartz quarries in the state was located on the company's land. The Keystone plant was destroyed by fire on May 15, 1898. It was immediately rebuilt and equipped with all the modern appliances known to the business.

A clay mine opened about 1910 in Shade Township on the Philip Reitz property along Dark Shade Creek. The clay was shipped to other parts of the country for various products. Around 1955, white clay, believed to be of excellent quality, was obtained by strip mining on the Wagner and Brant property, about 2 miles east of Central City. The clay was sent to factories out of the area.

Clay was also mined at Hollsopple and used by Hiram Swank's Sons in Johnstown. Swank had offices in Japan and India. Its main product was clay nozzles for the steel industry. Other brick plants were developed in Windber and Boswell. Welsh, Cloniger and Maxwell owned a brickyard in Fairhope Township. It played a large part in making bricks for the Falls Cut Tunnel in 1897, also for Sandpatch Tunnel in 1913. Many bricks were used for paving, sidewalks, and buildings throughout the tri-state area. The employees were paid 13¢ an hour. The Maxwell Brickyard also crushed stone for silica; however, the dust was harmful for the employees. Fire destroyed the brickyard in 1917.

John Buckley, Jacob Fisher, John Hider, Matthias July, Michael Hoover, and Rudolph Moyer had sawmills in Brothersvalley Township in 1795. The first attempt towards developing the lumber on a large commercial scale was done in Ogle and Northampton townships. In 1848, George D. Wolf and William J. Baer erected the Ashtola Mills in Ogle (Paint) Township for sawing lumber. Even though it was an extensive plant, reports say it was hampered by lack of transportation to move the lumber to the market. During the same time period, Henry Thomas put in Southampton Mills in Southampton Township, where the lumber was hauled by wagon to Cumberland.

The development of the railroads helped make the industry flourish. In 1880 the firm of Dill, Watson and Co. began operations as the largest producer of lumber in the county. The timer was in Greenville Township, but the mills were in Boynton, Elk Lick Township. In 1882, reports say the mills cut more than 6 million feet of lumber. After exhausting the supply of trees, the plant was abandoned.

Another company was on the horizon in a much larger scale. E.V. Babcock and Co. started in Paint and Ogle Townships. In 1897 the company acquired 7,000 acres of the Ashtola property on which an estimated 150 million feet of timber could be harvested. The mill was up to producing 4 million feet a month. When the timber supply was exhausted, Babcock moved its mills to other areas.

Charcoal became a byproduct of the lumber industry. One of the pioneers was David Hess, who began operations near Somerset in 1874. His son-in-law, James McKelvey of Somerset, succeeded him in around 1880 and produced about 8,000 carloads of charcoal. It was used to smelt iron ore. As early as 1899, there were 43 manufacturing establishments of various kinds in the area that fell within the scope of factory laws. They employed 711 men and 83 women.

Chapter Four

FROM EUROPE TO SOMERSET COUNTY

An examination into the geology of Somerset County will show that nearly all of the area lying between Allegheny Mountain and Laurel Hill is one vast coalfield, every vein of coal from the great Pittsburgh seam downward being represented in it. The first official U.S. census was taken in 1790 and showed Pennsylvania's population at 434,373. The number of people in western Pennsylvania totaled about 75,000—about 17 percent of the state's total. Bedford County—then made up of Cambria, Blair, Somerset, Bedford, and Fulton—was only credited with 13,124 or about 3 out of every 100 commonwealth residents. Somerset County's peak coincided with the peak in soft coal production in 1940 with 84,957 people. Since its first official census (1800), it showed a continuous growth for the next 120 years.

Immigrant workers were of crucial importance to the development of Somerset County—and to the extraction of the coal. The controversial and influential Dillingham Immigration Commission chose to study Windber in 1909 and reported that "operations in the mines of Community A (Windber) were begun with immigrant labor, and the general expansion of the mining industry and the development of the locality have been due principally to immigration from Europe." It concluded: "The mining company has been successful principally through the fact that it could secure immigrant labor, their [*sic*] being no supply of native labor available."

From the standpoint of Berwind-White, from 1897 until the 1920s, the company faced a perennial struggle to secure and retain a labor force of sufficient size to meet the needs of its new mines in the Windber area. In this era of industrial expansion, scarcity of labor was a problem that coal operators frequently cited in coal journals. E.J. Berwind himself stressed recruitment problems in testimony before the U.S. Industrial Relations Commission on January 21, 1915: "I know one thing—that there has never been a day in this 10 years, until this war broke out, that we could get the men to man our works."

Berwind went further. He insisted to the commission that this labor shortage was chronic, and therefore a reason to reject congressional proposals that would legally restrict immigration. At the time, the Berwind-White Coal Mining Company was a large financial contributor to the National Liberal Immigration League, an important lobbying organization that sought to convince the public that immigration should remain open and unrestricted. When a commissioner suggested that labor might be too abundant and that large employers sometimes took advantage of this overabundance to suppress wages, Berwind admitted: "The scarcity of labor raises wages more than anything else." Yet, he persisted, he needed more, not fewer, workers for his mines.

Berwind's continual search for miners resulted in a polyglot company work force drawn from diverse sources and numbering approximately 4,000 at any given time throughout these early years. The Dillingham commission reported that, as representatives of 25 or more nationalities found jobs in area mines during the decade from 1900 to 1910, movement into Windber was constant and movement out frequent. But what do we know about who these people were and what had prompted them to come to Somerset County?

Opening up new mines required expertise and skill, so in 1897, when Berwind-White began to develop Windber-area mines, it turned first to its own supervisory and engineering staff in such towns as Houtzdale. By transferring a number of its own officials as well as experienced engineers and miners, it laid out the new mines and prepared operations so that less-skilled miners and machines could then take over the rigorous task of extracting coal and loading it for shipment to market.

Many of the top company officials who served in the Windber area in the town's early years had worked for the company or associated enterprises for a decade or more. Among these were W.A. Christ, Harry D. Edelblute, and John Lochrie. Having been general manager for Berwind-White in Houtzdale for years, Christ became the first general manager in the Windber region in 1897. Edelblute, the first head of the company-store system in the new town, had risen to a supervisory position in the company's Eureka store in Horatio, Pennsylvania, while the assistant superintendent of mines at Windber, Scottish immigrant John Lochrie, had begun his family's long-term working relationship with the Berwinds in Houtzdale in 1878 shortly after his arrival in the United Sates. On the other hand, the initial ties that certain ethnic leaders, such as Frank Lowry, had to Berwind-White are less clear. Yet Lowry, an important labor contractor who supplied and supervised work gangs composed of fellow Italians for the company's many Windber-area projects, had built a career as a labor contractor for railroads even before 1890.

Local management was easily transplanted, but Berwind-White still needed skilled operatives to carry out its initial operations. It therefore asked a few individuals who possessed special skills to leave its operations in Houtzdale and move to Windber. John Adam Novak, a recent Slovak immigrant, was one of those who moved to the new town to help open mine headings there. Yet the numbers involved were not sufficient for the tasks at hand. Because the local rural population was sparse and there were no immigrants in the immediate area, except a few Italians employed in railroad construction, the company turned to outside employment agencies to obtain about 1,500 workers from other locations. The Dillingham Commission reported that 80 percent of this initial work force of 1,500 was English in origin and had previous experience in mining. The remaining 20 percent was a mixture of many different ethnic nationalities.

As mine development progressed in 1899 and 1900, the company continued to increase the size of its labor force, and as less-skilled labor was needed for its ongoing operations, southern and eastern Europeans began to come into the community in great numbers. The Dillingham Commission asserted, but did not prove, that the English miners hired earlier had begun to leave the area en masse before 1900, presumably as a result of this influx. The commission's hostility to new immigrants was such that it habitually assumed and then concluded—without evidence—that new immigrants would push out or displace Americans and northern Europeans, thereby lowering wages and working conditions. In fact, however, as the company's president later said, Berwind-White's new operations required many workers and then more workers, and the company was able to absorb all the skilled and unskilled labor it could recruit and retain in these early years. Where that labor force came from was of secondary importance, when important at all, to the primary need for workers.

In 1909 the Dillingham Commission estimated that the Windber-area population of Somerset County, and outlying mining settlements, totaled approximately 10,000 and that Windber residents alone numbered 7,500. One year later, federal census-takers counted a slightly larger population. According to the official census, Windber then numbered 8,013 inhabitants and the two other towns 2,423. Outlying camps brought the mining area's total to nearly 12,000 people.

The region's growth in the preceding decade is evident when these figures are compared with those in the 1900 census. Then Scalp Level had only 450 people, compared with 1,424 in 1910. When the census was taken in early 1900, neither Windber nor Paint Borough had yet been granted formal borough status. As a result, the populations of the two emerging boroughs were included with and not distinguished from other residents of Paint Township. The entire township, however, totaled only 6,835 in 1900.

After 1910, the area continued to grow. Windber's urban population peaked in 1920, but Scalp Level and Paint Borough's did not do so until 1940. When the populations of the three towns are combined, it is evident that, overall, the regional pattern showed growth until 1920, stagnation or a tiny decline by 1930, small growth again by 1940, followed by a relatively sharp decline and the beginning of a trend reflecting increased exodus from the region due to the onset of permanent mine-closings there.

If the Dillingham report and the 1910 census were in relative agreement about the area's population size at the end of the century's first decade, they present somewhat different pictures of the community's ethnic composition, and especially of the balance between Windber's foreign-born and native-born populations. The Dillingham Commission referred repeatedly to "the preponderatingly foreign character of the population" and had in fact selected Windber as one of two bituminous coal towns in Pennsylvania to study precisely because of its influx of new immigrants. According to commission calculations, three-fourths of the 10,000 residents, or 7,500 people, were foreign-born, but that included all children whose fathers were of foreign origin. This method of calculation—classifying native-born children according to their father's birthplace rather than their own—automatically diminished the size of the native-born population and exaggerated the numbers of foreign-born. If, through ignorance or error, English-speaking census enumerators often underrepresented southern and eastern Europeans, the commission did exactly the opposite. Its focus on immigrants and its sympathy for immigration restriction may have contributed to its use of a methodology that systematically distorted and underrepresented American-born and English-speaking people. In any event, its investigators estimated that only 2,500 Americans resided in the entire area.

When another standard of judgment is used, a different conception of Windber's ethnic composition emerges. For example, when all those born in the United States are considered native-born and U.S. census figures are used, Americans constituted a majority of 55 percent of the area's total population in 1910, instead of the minority of 25 percent cited by the Dillingham Commission. By these calculations, 57 percent of Windber Borough residents had been born in the United States, and usually in Pennsylvania.

Despite these reservations, the Dillingham Commission was absolutely right to select Windber to study because of its preponderance of immigrants, most of whom came from southern and eastern Europe. After all, 45 percent of the area's population, including 43 percent in Windber proper, were born in foreign countries. At the same time, in 1910 only 17 percent of the inhabitants of Somerset County or 19 percent of the residents of the state of Pennsylvania could claim a foreign heritage.

The zenith of foreign-born representation in the overall population of Windber and surrounding areas was reached in 1910. By 1920 the outright foreign-born comprised only 29 percent of Windber's population. Immigration restriction in the 1920s contributed to a further decline of this portion of the population. By 1930, the foreign-born constituted 22 percent of the total population; by 1940, 18 percent; and by 1950, 15 percent.

Four nationalities—Slovaks, Magyars, Poles, and Italians—unquestionably constituted the bulk of Windber's immigrant influx. These four leading ethnic groups comprised 84 percent of the area's entire foreign-born population and 38 percent of its general population in 1910. According to the manuscript schedules of the census taken that year, the Slovaks were overall the most numerous of the four, but only slightly ahead of the Magyars; Poles were in third place, followed by Italians.

The numerical dominance of these four foreign nationalities varied somewhat according to specific place of residence. Each of the three towns or outlying mining settlements had a slightly different ethnic makeup. Italians were highly concentrated in Windber proper and considerably outnumbered the Poles there. However, there were so few Italians in the two other towns and outlying mining areas that they did not rank in the top four ethnic clusters in any of them, and other, generally less numerous, nationalities surpassed them in these localities. Also, Magyars, not Slovaks, led the roster of nationalities living in Scalp Level, Paint Borough, and Mine 37, while the reverse was true in Windber proper.

The four leading nationalities were the basis on which the various immigrant communities were founded. They pioneered in establishing their own churches and fraternal societies. Their size itself gave them a certain degree of power and influence, especially among other, less numerous ethnic groups from southern and eastern Europe. No attempt to integrate disparate nationalities into a working-class movement, such as the United Mine Workers union, could afford to ignore any of the big four nationalities.

It is more difficult to be precise about the numbers of the less numerous nationalities living in the area. There were many inherent problems in identifying and classifying people according to nationality, which was not always self-evident to either enumerators or immigrants themselves. If the Dillingham estimates erred by underestimating the American-born and English-speaking population, the census erred in the opposite direction by underrepresenting people from southern and eastern Europe. Nevertheless, it is possible to draw some basic conclusions about the size and composition of the less numerous resident ethnic groups.

First, many different nationality groups had a presence of some sort in the Windber area. Outside of the big four, 25 different nationalities were easily represented in the general population. Among these were people from northern and western Europe, central and eastern Europe, southern and Mediterranean Europe, and northern Africa. Ethnic diversity was a distinguished feature of the local mining communities.

Second, additional evidence suggests that the Dillingham figures about the numbers of southern and eastern European nationalities in the area are closer to the truth than was the census. If this is so, then new immigrant groups, not the old ones, constituted a majority of the less numerous foreign-born populations. Three groups in particular—Romanians, Jews, and Carpatho-Russians—were almost certainly larger than the modest numbers counted in 1910. Each of these examples is worth examining.

From Europe to Somerset County

Evidence that the Romanians once had a local population of some size and importance derives from religious sources and newspapers. An article in the Catholic Encyclopedia, published in 1909, cited both Windber and Scalp Level as chief areas of settlement for Romanian Greek Catholic immigrants in the United States. Also, Scalp Level's Romanian Greek Catholic Church, founded in 1908, was only the second such church to be established in the entire country, and it served as the center for all Romanian Greek Catholic missionary activities in Pennsylvania. The Dillingham report claimed that this church had a membership of 75 families, or 400 people, and a regular Sunday attendance of 150. While the census itself showed only one resident of this nationality in Windber proper, it found a concentration of Romanians in Scalp Level and Mine 37; the church was located close to this cluster in what was described in local newspapers at the time as "Romanian hill."

Jewish people in Windber certainly numbered more than the 22 listed as Yiddish in the census of 1910. Individuals known to be Jewish were enumerated as Germans, Magyars, Poles, or Russians, reflecting their place of origin or degree of previous assimilation. While no known Jewish people were involved with mining, a number were active in Windber's early, rapidly changing businesses. Historians of Johnstown's Jewish community claimed that frontier areas like Somerset County attracted itinerant Jewish peddlers and businessmen early in the twentieth century because the opportunities there seemed great. But not all who came remained. For example, one of Johnstown's most prominent businessmen, Moses Glosser, had stopped off and operated a store briefly in Windber before moving on to the larger city, where he opened a highly successful department store in 1907.

Windber's Jewish community was not large enough to support a synagogue or temple of its own, so it relied on the Johnstown population for an active social and religious life. The Reform rabbi from the larger city traveled to Windber frequently in the town's early years to perform traditional ceremonies. In turn, according to local newspapers, Jews from Windber supported and attended social and religious festivities en masse in Johnstown. However, Windber Jews were organized enough on their own to have established a short-lived B'nai B'rith chapter, which conducted a fund-raising drive for the relief of persecuted Russian Jews in 1905. In subsequent years, they formed fraternal insurance societies and social clubs or joined

Johnstown chapters and groups. But the internal divisions that split Johnstown Judaism into Reform and Orthodox factions in 1902 also affected Windber. Windber's Orthodox wing, whose membership came primarily from Russia or Poland, was numerous enough to have had its own kosher butcher and rabbi, Isaac Slesinger. Although a synagogue was never erected, quarters in various town buildings were rented for weekly services. During the decade from 1910 to 1920, this community was of sufficient size and importance to attract Jewish people from more isolated or adjacent towns to come to Windber to celebrate important religious holidays there.

Carpatho-Russians—the third example—were vastly underrepresented in both the census and Dillingham report because they were almost always enumerated as other nationalities, especially as ethnic Russians or other groups who had originated in the old czarist empire. One important reason for this confusion is that the masses of Carpatho-Russian immigrants had no sense of a distinct national identity until after 1914. The term "Rusyn" had been used in early centuries to denote all Eastern Slavs, otherwise undifferentiated, and was derived from the word Rus, the geographical region where they had all once lived. Gradually, through the years, Russians, Belorussians, and Ukrainians became differentiated nationalities, so that by the twentieth century only Eastern Slavs in the Carpathian Mountains were still known as Rusyns. The name Carpatho-Russian today suggests this "Rusyn" people's geographical origins in the Carpathians, their Slavic culture and linguistic origins, and their religious connections to Eastern Christianity. In the past, Carpatho-Russians were frequently called Ruthenians, but they had been known as Rusnakes, Uhro-Rusyns, Carpatho-Rusyns, or Carpatho-Ukrainians.

Parish histories and local newspaper accounts reported that Ruthenians were instrumental in 1900 in founding one of Windber's first two Catholic churches, the one that adhered to the Byzantine, or Greek Catholic, rite. This new Windber church, the first Greek Catholic church to be established in Somerset County, attracted an original ethnically mixed membership of 1,500, many of whom were Ruthenians. Because of its Ruthenian, Slovak, and Hungarian Greek Catholic populations, in 1924 the Vatican placed it under the jurisdiction of the Byzantine Ruthenian Rite Catholic Church in the Pittsburgh diocese, not its Ukrainian counterpart in Philadelphia, when ethnic and religious conflicts on the national level led to the creation of two separate Byzantine Rite dioceses in the United States. Despite a bitter national and local schism that split Greek Catholics into two churches in 1936, it is significant that the two local churches retained the use of the Ruthenian language in their Sunday services for years afterward.

That Windber-area and Somerset County immigrants came from Austria-Hungary, Italy, or the Russian empire in 1900 might tell us something about them, but such information is clearly insufficient or even misleading for many purposes. Immigration is not a random occurrence, and not all countries, provinces, towns, or villages sent immigrants in equal numbers to the United States. Sometimes the pioneers influenced relatives, friends, and neighbors from the same place to leave in what is usually described as a chain migration. In other villages and towns, few people, or perhaps none, left their birthplaces. Nor did all nationalities emigrate equally or even in numbers proportional to the general population.

Knowing the specific provinces or regions from which Somerset County-area immigrants left in great numbers can provide us with important information about the areas they left behind and their motivations for leaving. Moreover, at the turn of the century, immigrants frequently defined themselves in terms of their province or region of origin, rather than in terms of a nation-state. Contemporary nationalism had barely affected the peasant masses of a number of southern and eastern European societies, even though, by then, middle-class intellectuals and religious leaders in middle Europe were espousing nationalistic causes. Carpatho-Russians have already been cited, but there are other examples. Thus, Italians settling in American towns and cities usually identified themselves not as Italians but as people from northern Italy or southern Italy, from Abruzzi or Sicily, while Slovak newcomers to the United States typically referred to themselves as Sarisania or Zemplincania, or some other term that reflected their county of origin. Although there were some exceptions, the masses of new immigrants from many of these societies developed a national consciousness and interest in nationalistic causes in Europe only after they were living in America.

Because immigration was a selective process and migrating people often thought in regional terms, it is useful to break down ethnic populations into smaller geographical units of origin, whenever possible. Doing so requires going beyond censuses and most governmental reports, to church and fraternal society records, which often contained the name of the province or town of a person's origins. Unfortunately, the plethora of foreign nationalities, churches, and fraternal groups in Windber makes a comprehensive breakdown of the area's population into smaller units virtually impossible, however desirable. But it is possible to convey an analysis of certain sectors of that population in this and subsequent chapters.

The vast majority of all southern and eastern European immigrants who came to Windber in the early twentieth century were Roman or Greek Catholics in terms of religious affiliation, although discernible numbers of Jews and Protestants, especially Slovak Lutherans and Hungarian Reformed Church members, had also migrated. Nonetheless, by 1900 this immigrant majority, adherents of Catholicism, had established two large Catholic parishes in the new town. St. John Cantius Church was originally designed to serve all Roman Catholics regardless of nationality, while St. Stephen's Byzantine Catholic Church (later renamed St. Mary's Greek Catholic Church) served a similar purpose for all Greek Catholics. In time, four additional Roman Catholic churches and one Byzantine Orthodox church eventually emerged or seceded from these two original bodies. Consequently, the membership of these two churches provides us with a useful overview of the origins of many of the town's new immigrants early in the century. The records of the 363 Greek Catholic and 430 Roman Catholic marriages that took place in these churches from 1899 to 1912 are the most useful gauge for assessing church membership and origins.

These marriage records indicate that each church drew constituencies from particular regions of Europe. Greek Catholics came exclusively from counties in northern, especially northeastern, Hungary and the province of Galicia, otherwise known as Austrian Poland. Two-thirds of all 363 brides and 363 grooms married at St. Mary's during this era had emigrated from three provinces, Zemplen and Saros in Hungary and Galicia in Austria. Except for a small number of the betrothed whose origins were unknown, and a few who had either been born in the United States or whose records had incorrectly cited current residences rather than place of origin, all other Greek Catholics had come from Hungarian counties adjacent to these three provinces. Thus, Windber's Greek Catholic community originally came from a limited and concentrated region that encompassed the northern and southern slopes of the Carpathian Mountains and traversed the territory along the Hungarian-Galician border. At the present time, this area is located in the Lemkian region of southern Poland and the Presov region of Slovakia.

The ethnic diversity that characterized Windber and Somerset County, then, was not new to St. Mary's parishioners, who had originally come from ethnically mixed provinces in a multiethnic empire. All three of the major nationalities that made up the church's membership—Carpatho-Russians, Slovaks, and Magyars—had coexisted in this region. According to the Hungarian census of 1910, Zemplen's population at the time consisted of 56.5 percent Magyars, 27.1 percent Slovaks, and 11.4 percent Ruthentians; Saros had a majority of Slovaks (58.3), more Ruthenians than Zemplen (22 percent), relatively few Magyars (10.4 percent), and a smattering of Germans (5.4 percent). As far as Galicia was concerned, the Austrian census of 1900 indicated that Poles made up 46 percent of the province's population, Ruthenians 42 percent, and Jews 11 percent.

In contrast to Byzantine Rite Catholics, Roman Catholics in Windber came from a much more dispersed geographical area, and one that went far beyond northern Hungary and Galicia, into other parts of Europe and across the Atlantic to the United States. A considerable percentage, 16 or 17 percent of the 430 brides and 430 grooms married in St. John's, listed towns in Pennsylvania or other states as their place of origin. This figure is misleading, though, because in half of these cases respondents or visiting priests had erred by citing Windber or other current residences, not birthplaces, as the place of origin. Nevertheless, more Roman than Greek Catholics had either resided in the United States for a long time or been born here.

Ireland, which had historically supplied so many Roman Catholic adherents in large cities, never furnished more than a handful of church members in the Windber parish, but Italy provided a far greater number than the marriage data indicated. Linguistic and ethnic differences in the parish had led priests, as early as 1903, to keep separate records, not included in these totals, for Italians, who split off from the church in 1906. Meanwhile, Slovaks and others from northern Hungary also formed a separate parish derived from St. John's in 1905. In the earliest years of St. John Cantius, then, the percentage of church members from Italy and Hungary was higher than in subsequent years and higher than these marriage totals suggest. Despite all these qualifications, these marriage records do convey a good sense of the original geographical and ethnic diversity represented within the church and in Windber.

Although the parish population was diverse, the core constituency of St. John's membership from its inception had been the Roman Catholic immigrants from the sections of historic Poland partitioned and annexed by Austria and Russia in the eighteenth and nineteenth centuries. Austrian Poland or Galicia alone supplied 35 percent of all brides and grooms married in the church during this period. Another 10 percent came from provinces in Russian Poland, in particular Lomza, Plock, Warsaw, and Lublin, while 6 percent had migrated from Russia's Lithuanian provinces of Vilna, Kovno, and Suval, where numerous Poles also lived. Except for a small number of Lithuanians, then, these people were Polish in nationality.

Northern Hungary supplied the next largest number of brides and grooms married at St. John's in these early years. Zemplen and Daros, which had furnished so many Greek Catholics, led a list of nine counties in northern Hungary that were represented in the Roman Catholic marriage data. Hungarian and Slovak Roman Catholics originating in these counties therefore constituted an impressive 24 percent of all those married. Smaller percentages of the brides and grooms came from Prussia, Belorussia, or Austria-Hungary's Slavonia and Carniola provinces, which suggests that the church also had members of the German, Belorussian, and Slovenian nationalities.

Several striking observations result from this breakdown of the membership of the two churches into respective provinces of origin. First, St. John's broader geographical and ethnic inclusion should not obscure the fact that, regardless of political boundaries and ethnic differences, virtually all Greek Catholics and about 60 percent of the Roman Catholics in the Windber area came from the same contiguous region in central Europe—the Carpathian Mountains of Galicia and northern Hungary. As Emily Balch, an economist, activist, and pioneer of immigration studies, pointed out long ago in her classic study of Slavic immigration, Slavic and other nationalities converged in this area. Once immigration had begun, it was a contagious phenomenon, not limited to any one nationality or any one nation-state but one that gradually spread eastward throughout the Carpathian region.

Second, the great diversity of peoples, cultures, and languages coexisting in this area meant that their juxtaposition in a new place like Windber was not a new phenomenon. Old World conflicts were sometimes transplanted, but, as in Europe, the peasants who formed the bulk of the immigrant influx were least likely to be hostile to peasants of other nationalities or religions. The emerging nationalism that affected upper-class elements in these societies, and the Hungarian government's oppressive discriminations against non-Magyars, had not injured relations at the village level. Balch herself stressed the nonexistence in Europe of ill-feeling between the masses of Slovaks and Magyars and concluded: "The peasants of both races are profoundly unconscious of any reason for hating one another, regard one another as friends, and intermarry freely." In many cases, it was the experience of having become a foreigner in the United States that brought a new consciousness of ethnic identity and nationalism. Whether ethnic awareness ultimately led to interethnic cooperation or to conflict in Windber would depend on many variables, and not on the mere juxtaposition of populations that spoke in different tongues.

Third, that Somerset County's new immigrants generally mirrored the larger wave of new immigration, in terms of provinces of origin and multiple ethnic composition, can be seen in the specific case of Hungary. Between 1880 and 1914 the most important regional and mass migration from Hungary as a whole occurred in eight northeastern counties located on the right bank of the Tisza, the same area that had furnished so much of Windber's foreign-born population. Slovaks, Ruthenians, and Germans left this ethnically mixed geographical region of Hungary in unusually large numbers early in the century. But so did the resident Magyars. The general heterogeneous nature of migration from concentrated areas suggests strongly that its root causes lay in particular geographical, social, and economic conditions rather than in national or political oppression.

Despite territorial boundaries, similar social and economic conditions prevailed in the areas of central and eastern Europe that sent so many immigrants to Windber at the turn of the century. The entire region was in the midst of an uneven social and economic transformation. Austria-Hungary and Russia, which had ended serfdom in their empires only in 1848 and the 1860s, generally lagged behind western Europe in terms of the capitalistic development of agriculture and industry.

Somerset County's immigrants reflected the general wave of new immigrants. Many are known to have come from rural districts where they farmed their own land or that of other people. Although displaced artisans and small merchants often preceded the rural peasant exodus, 70 to 80 percent of all immigrants to the United States from central and eastern Europe after 1890 came from rural areas where the lack of industrial development of the land offered them few alternatives to migration. Small and medium-size landholders came first, with the landless coming in greater numbers after 1900. The proportions of small landowners and the landless varied considerably, reflecting national and regional differences. Thus, approximately 50 percent of all Magyars, Carpatho-Russians, and Poles who arrived in the United States from 1900 to 1914 were landless, perhaps young sons of small landholders, while only 10 percent of the Magyars, 19 percent of the Slovaks, 24 percent of the Carpatho-Russians, and 29 percent of the Poles were small independent farmers.

Moreover, on the national level, 80 percent or more of certain groups, such as Slovaks, came to the country as unskilled laborers, most of whom entered industrial occupations afterward. The Dillingham Commission reported that Slovaks alone comprised 13.1 percent of the nation's steel workers and 12.8 percent of all bituminous coal miners. The rural background of the new immigrants and their lack of previous mining experience were also cited. Only 8.2 percent of all the southern and eastern European immigrants employed in coalmines in the United States had been employed in that occupation in their native lands. By contrast, 87.6 percent of the Welsh miners and 82.6 percent of the English miners who worked in American mines had worked in European mines before their emigration.

The initial influx of new immigrants into Somerset County mirrored national trends in that it was predominantly male. Mining was "men's work," and 13 years after the town's founding, males still comprised a far greater portion, or 59 percent, of the local population than did the females, who made up only 41 percent of it. Census officials noted that a greater percentage of males than females had emigrated to the United States during the decade from 1900 to 1910, and that the ratio of males to females among the foreign-born was higher (131.1 males to 100 females) than it had been in previous decades. Certainly the immigrant influx of particular ethnic groups was predominantly male. Paul Magocsi has pointed out that single or recently married young men made up a full 75 percent of the Carpatho-Russian immigrant population before 1914. Moreover, men who came without their families in search of work predominated during the peak years of immigration from places such as Hungary.

From Europe to Somerset County

It is not surprising that many immigrant males who expected to work in difficult, strenuous, industrial jobs emigrated when they were in the prime of life. Nearly 60 percent of those who left Hungary during the peak emigration years of 1905–1907 were under 30 years of age and most of these were in their most productive working years. About seven percent were under the age of 14; only three percent were 45 years of age or more. Miners interviewed often said that mining required strong (presumably youthful) backs. The Dillingham Commission indicated that Berwind-White had found just such men during Windber's early years. Of 2,833 foreign-born company employees in Windber, the largest segment, or 52 percent, were between the ages of 20 and 29; those in their 20s and 30s made up 90 percent of this work force.

National census figures suggest that female immigrants were similarly youthful or even younger. The bulk of females who entered the country fell in what was considered the primary marriageable age range, 14 to 21; only small percentages of new immigrant women were over 30. These figures varied with each nationality, but 73.7 percent of arriving Magyar females and 84.6 percent of Slovak females arriving fell within the age range of 14 to 21.

A majority of the men who came to Somerset County to find work were married. Of the 2,821 foreign-born miners for whom Dillingham investigators had information, 55.5 percent were married while 44.1 percent were not. The comparable rate for a much smaller number of native-born miners varied only slightly from this figure. Moreover, the 1910 census survey of the large boarding population living in the Windber area indicates that approximately one-third of all boarders were married men whose wives lived elsewhere.

The immigrants who came to the area during its early years were predominantly recent arrivals in America. At least 75 percent of all foreign-born residents in the Windber area in 1910 had come to the United States sometime between 1900 and 1910. More than 42 percent of them had come within the previous five years, and it seems reasonable to conclude that many of these either migrated directly to Windber or moved there within a short time of their arrival. The groups with the highest proportions of their local populations to arrive in America after 1900 included the four most numerous nationalities from southern and eastern Europe. By contrast, the vast majority of northern Europeans had originally arrived 20 or more years earlier.

SOMERSET COUNTY

The time Somerset County's various ethnic groups arrived in America closely parallels national immigration trends. Locally and nationally, the bulk of northern European immigrants historically preceded the bulk of southern and eastern nationalities by at least a decade. Slovaks were relative pioneers of the new immigration wave. They had begun to migrate to the anthracite mining region of Pennsylvania in the 1870s and 1880s, when coal companies recruited new immigrants under contract labor conditions in the aftermath of Molly Maguire labor troubles there. (The "Molly Maguires" were miners in the anthracite coal region of Pennsylvania who organized into a union during the 1860s and 1870s. These miners were chiefly, although not exclusively, Irish and the union was called the Workingmen's Benevolent Association. In general, the members of this union were also members of the Ancient Order of Hibernians, a semi-secret fraternal society, which had its origin in Ireland as a completely secret and anonymous association. This organization of Irish miners was dubbed the "Molly Maguires" after a group of Irish peasants who dressed up as women to antagonize their landlords. The group was infamously known as murderers and assassins and the press and police in America applied the name to the Irish miners. The label was used by both the press and the owner-operators of the mining companies to their distinct advantage. They called anyone who was pro-union a "Molly," inferring that they were criminals at best. This helped to subdue, even if only slightly, uprisings in the work place.) A relatively large proportion, 30 percent of the local Slovak population, had arrived in America before 1900.

Circumstantial evidence derived from oral histories, contemporary newspapers, parish records, fraternal society correspondence, naturalization documents, the census, and the Dillingham report indicates that many Windber-area immigrants initially expected to be in America only temporarily. Historians of immigration generally concur that, until World War I, most immigrants from Hungary and other places in central and eastern Europe left there with the intention of finding temporary work, accumulating savings, and eventually returning to their homelands. Estimates of actual return rates have ranged anywhere from 25 percent to 60 percent, depending on particular nationalities, regions, and historians. It is significant that northeastern Hungary—the primary locus of origin for many of Windber's immigrants—had one of the highest return rates in Europe. John Bodnar cited estimates that the Magyar return rate was 64 percent and that the Slovak rate was 59 percent.

Decisions to remain permanently in the new country were usually made after immigrants had lived here for some time and were often prompted by some compelling national or familial circumstance. Nor was it unusual for laboring men to travel back and forth across the ocean several times before a final decision was reached. In its national findings, the Dillingham Commission itself concluded that 40 percent of the new immigrants eventually returned to Europe and that two-thirds of these stayed there permanently.

Throughout the early twentieth century, steamship agents advertised widely in local newspapers that routinely carried items about immigrant workers who were returning to Europe. In one such announcement, in December 1902, the *Windber Era* reported that agent Andrew Zemany had sent 11 people to Slavonia via Bremen on the *Kaiser Wilhelm*. Other articles stated that work in the Windber area was migratory and seasonal in nature for a number of the foreign-born who owned land in Europe. On March 31, 1903, for example, the *Windber Journal* reported that 16 people were leaving to resume farming in Europe and that more were expected to follow them in the next few days. Other workers seem to have left Windber in the winter but were expected to return in the spring.

According to the papers, economic recession also influenced return rates. For example, late in 1903 the *Windber Era* noted a great exodus of foreigners from the coke regions of western Pennsylvania during an economic lull, but also commented on the departure of many local Italians and Poles. On occasion, contemporary journalists acknowledged that some immigrants who had accumulated savings were returning home permanently. In one such instance, in July 1903, the *Windber Journal* reported that 16 foreigners, including several women, were about to leave for Europe. Apparently they did not expect to return to the United States, because the steamship agent who had arranged their passage told the reporter that all "were well supplied with American coin, and they can now live luxuriously in their fatherland."

One standard way of measuring the expected temporary or more permanent nature of an immigrant group's residence in America is to see where the wives of miners lived. Caution is needed here in drawing conclusions. In general, it is true that ethnic-group males who emigrated with wives and children intended to stay permanently from the onset. On the other hand, married men who came alone may have simply lacked the resources necessary to bring their families over immediately.

The Dillingham report, the only source for information on the location of wives, found that of the 1,507 whose whereabouts were known, 54.1 percent were living elsewhere in the United States and 45.9 percent were still abroad. Among the recently arrived ethnic groups, Italians, Magyars, and Russians had more than 50 percent of their wives in Europe. More northern Italian wives, 58.2 percent, than southern Italian wives, 50.9 percent, were abroad, as were 54.5 percent of the Magyar spouses. Of the four most numerous nationalities in Windber, two groups, Slovaks and Poles, had a majority, approximately 60 percent, of their wives in America. Because Slovaks had been a pioneer ethnic group in immigration to the United States, the higher resident rate of Slovak wives is perhaps understandable, but this rationale does not explain the Polish finding.

Also, although northern European immigrants had a greater percentage of their wives located in America, a significant portion also had wives abroad. A surprising 20 percent of the German miners and 19 percent of the English miners had wives who still lived overseas. That a sizable segment of these immigrant groups had not yet reunited their families, even though their ethnic groups generally had been in America longer, casts doubt on artificial distinctions sometimes made between the nature of the old versus new immigration and strongly suggests that the immigrants' class position and length of residence, and the life cycle and stage of immigration itself, explain many differences better than national origin does.

References to wives and children residing abroad appeared frequently in local newspapers in routine reports on fatalities resulting from mining accidents. Typical was the short obituary that followed a longer description of the accident that resulted in the death of Vidor Roseleski in August 1904: "Roseleski was thirty years old and had a wife and two children in the old country." In addition, fraternal societies kept detailed information for insurance purposes. A perusal of national Slovak fraternal records showed that it was still common in the 1920s and 1930s for wives or other relatives living abroad to write letters of inquiry about benefits owed the beneficiaries of a deceased husband, son, or brother who had once worked in Windber.

A George Hetzel Painting of Paint Township from the Early 1800s. Hetzel, a famous artist, was one of the first to discover the natural beauty of Somerset County. Through landscape paintings, Hetzel and his school of artists brought acclaim to the area. (Courtesy of Windber Coal Heritage Center.)

Art colony in Early Somerset County. Somerset County was made famous early on by the prestigious artists who came to paint landscapes of the beautiful scenery. (Courtesy of Windber Coal Heritage Center.)

Highland Falls in Rockwood. The natural beauty of Somerset County, especially through parks and resorts, has always been a continual draw for the area. (Courtesy of Dwight Hostetler.)

Whites Creek in Unamis. The town of Unamis got its Store and Inn by 1913. (Courtesy of Dwight Hostetler.)

Early Meyersdale. At first Meyersdale was a summer base for Indians who had camps in the area. (Courtesy of Dwight Hostetler.)

EARLY LISTONBURG. Ten miles east of Listonburg is the highest point in Pennsylvania—Mt. Davis at 3,213 feet. (Courtesy of Dwight Hostetler.)

AN EARLY SCHOOLHOUSE. *For many years small schoolhouses were used to teach all age groups, until the first high school in the country was established in Somerset Borough in 1887. (Courtesy of Windber Coal Heritage Center.)*

"STEPPING STONES" IN SOMERSET. *Somerset Borough was incorporated in 1804 and soon after,* The German Farmer, *the first newspaper in the county, was published. (Courtesy of Dwight Hostetler.)*

EARLY ROCKWOOD PASSING. *This was the first bridge across the Casselman River and was built in 1816; later it would be known as Schaff's Bridge. (Courtesy of Dwight Hostetler.)*

FISHING IN EARLY ELK LICK. *The name of this township came from the natural springs in the area, called licks, which attracted a great deal of elk and deer. (Courtesy of Dwight Hostetler.)*

OLD COVERED BRIDGE. This bridge stood for many years on Whipkey Dam. (Courtesy of Dwight Hostetler.)

MAPLE SUGAR CAMP. This camp in Berlin, and others in the Meyersdale area, remind us that spring is around the corner when they tap the sugar maple trees to make maple syrup. Each year this occasion is celebrated with the Pennsylvania Maple Festival in Meyersdale. (Courtesy of Dwight Hostetler.)

"BLACK DIAMONDS" LEAVE SOMERSET COUNTY. At peak production, 25,000 tons of coals were shipped daily from the area. (Courtesy of Dwight Hostetler.)

BERWIND-WHITE IN SOMERSET COUNTY. The company's first mine to fully operate was Mine 30 in the Windber area. (Courtesy of Windber Coal Heritage Center.)

HUNGARIAN FUNERAL IN WINDBER. Many traditions came with the immigrants to Somerset County. (Courtesy of Windber Coal Heritage Center.)

MEAT DEPARTMENT AT EUREKA STORE. The company store took care of the miners in good times. (Courtesy of Windber Coal Heritage Center.)

A Picnic Gathering. As more women came to Somerset County, social events became common. (Courtesy of Windber Coal Heritage Center.)

Police Forces Emerge. Rather than relying on the coal companies for order, police forces slowly became established in Somerset County. (Courtesy of Windber Coal Heritage Center.)

SOCIAL OUTING. Coalmining executives and lumber executives in Somerset County were known for having a good social relationship. (Courtesy of Windber Coal Heritage Center.)

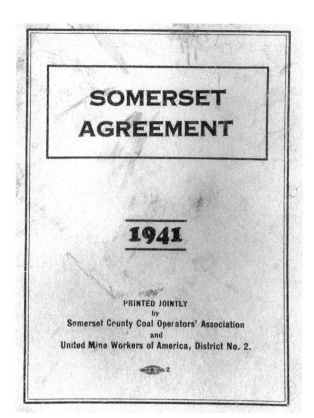

1941 SOMERSET AGREEMENT. UMWA District 2 issued this strike call to non-union miners. (Courtesy of Windber Coal Heritage Center.)

MINE 30 IN WINDBER. Today Somerset County is trying to preserve several of its mines. (Courtesy of Dwight Hostetler.)

SUSIE SHUSTER. Susie Shuster, a union supporter who signed an affidavit against the Berwind Coal and Iron Police, poses with her children—Katherine, Anne, Joe, and John—during the strike of 1922. (Courtesy of Windber Coal Heritage Center.)

PAINT CREEK. This picture shows a washhouse and repairshop for motors near Mine 35 in the late 1920s. (Courtesy of Sara LaManna [Alesandrini] Osis and John Osis.)

COAL SHAFT. Most coal shafts in Somerset County were less than five feet tall during the peak production years. (Courtesy of Dwight Hostetler.)

PEN MAR MINE. Men pose in front of mine number 3 in MacDonaldton around 1909. (Courtesy of Dwight Hostetler.)

MINE 32 IN WINDBER. *Michele and Margharerita Alesandrini in the late 1930s sit on telephone poles stored by Berwind Electric Company with their dog, Stubby. Stubby was later hit by a Eureka Store truck driver and thrown in Windber's creek. Later Ray Alesandrini, Michele's son, fished the dog out of the creek and gave him a proper burial. (Courtesy of Sara LaManna [Alesandrini] Osis and John Osis)*

MINERS ON STRIKE. *For publicity and relief-raising efforts, this photo of several thousand Somerset County miners, dressed for the occasion, was taken in an open field soon after their decision to continue the strike for union. (Courtesy of Indiana University of Pennsylvania.)*

CHILDREN'S DAY PARADE. *The town of Berlin held "Old Home Week" August 9 through August 15, 1908.*

CHILDREN OF SOMERSET COUNTY. Families began to have financial problems when the mines in Somerset County cut back production. (Courtesy of Windber Coal Heritage Center.)

ABRUZZI IN WINDBER. "Fraternal" societies began to appear all throughout the towns—as with churches, there was one for each ethnicity. The club shown here is the Abruzzi, for Italians, in Windber. (Courtesy of Windber Coal Heritage Center.)

FAMILY REUNION. Throughout the 1930s, more family members immigrated to Somerset County and gatherings became common. (Courtesy of Windber Coal Heritage Center.)

FROZEN WATER TANK. This water tank in Well's Creek in 1909 demonstrates why Somerset County is known for harsh winter weather. (Courtesy of Dwight Hostetler.)

SNOWSTORM OF 1936. Before snowploughs were used to cope with the harsh Somerset County winters, men and cranes cleared snow. This picture shows the road between Somerset and Confluence. (Courtesy of Dwight Hostetler.)

SCHOOL CELEBRATION. Local schools grew and developed despite the faltering mines. (Courtesy of Windber Coal Heritage Center.)

REITZ, 1905. Lumber was the first large industry in Somerset County. This picture shows men loading logs at Reitz in 1905. (Courtesy of Dwight Hostetler.)

LUTHERAN CHURCH IN BAKERSVILLE. There were several churches in each town as Somerset County grew—usually one church for each large ethnic group. (Courtesy of Dwight Hostetler.)

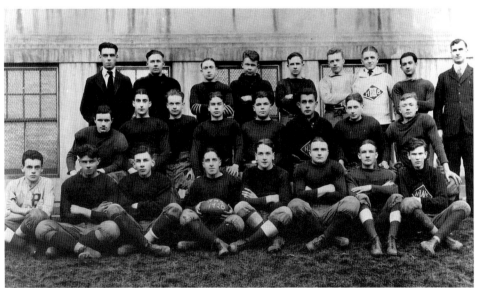

FOOTBALL TEAM. Athletic sports became extremely important to Somerset County, providing a strong bond for all the nationalities. This picture shows Windber's 1920 football team. (Courtesy of Windber Coal Heritage Center.)

GIRLS' BASKETBALL TEAM. *Girls soon got involved in organized sports as well. Shown here is a Windber High School girl's basketball team. (Courtesy of Windber Coal Heritage Center.)*

BASEBALL TEAM. *For both students and miners baseball became an important sport—shown here is Hooversville's baseball team.*

SOMERSET TROOPS. Carousing here are the men of the Pennsylvania National Guard in 1909. (Courtesy of Dwight Hostetler.)

NAVY MEN. Somerset County is well known for its military service. Here we see two men in Navy uniforms with their families in Windber. (Courtesy of Windber Coal Heritage Center.)

MEYERSDALE. The swinging bridge in Meyersdale was an early attraction. (Courtesy of Dwight Hostetler.)

A PEEP AT SOMERSET, PA.

SOMERSET. This picture is an overlook of the county seat. (Courtesy of Dwight Hostetler.)

OUTDOOR WINDBER CONCERT. *Put on by Laddie Timko and his orchestra, this outdoor concert was a big hit in the area. The Timko family owned a series of pharmacies in Somerset County. (Courtesy of Windber Coal Heritage Center.)*

THE GRAND VIEW SHIP HOTEL ON THE OLD LINCOLN HIGHWAY. *Dinners and dances were held at the hotel, which boasted a view of three states and seven counties. The hotel, about to undergo restoration, burned to the ground around 2000. (Courtesy of Sara LaManna (Alesandrini) Osis and John Osis.)*

MEYERSDALE. A streetcar passes through Meyersdale over a bridge. (Courtesy of Dwight Hostetler.)

GRAHAM AVENUE. Towns continued to celebrate their heritage; this picture was taken on Graham Avenue during July 4th celebrations. (Courtesy of Windber Coal Heritage Center.)

CONFLUENCE RAIL STATION. Shown here is the rail station in Confluence, which used to be a large shipping point on the Pittsburgh division of the Baltimore and Ohio Railroad in the early part of the nineteenth century. (Courtesy of Dwight Hostetler.)

Somerset Courthouse. This picture is an interior shot of the Somerset Courthouse. The same courthouse remains today and was remodeled in 2003. (Courtesy of Dwight Hostetler.)

WINDBER TODAY. Many of Somerset County's main streets are being restored—shown here is Windber's Arcardia Theatre, which was once a movie house for the town.

MINE 32. Armand Catenaro as a young artist sits with an easel, with Mike Petro (left) and other friends. Catenaro went on to become an artist making backdrops for numerous films and CBS productions until his death in 2003. (Courtesy of Sara LaManna [Alesandrini] Osis and John Osis)

ONE OF THE EARLIEST ETHNIC STORES IN SOMERSET COUNTY. Leone's Market was founded in 1922 in Windber. On the left is the founder, Tony Leone, and on the right his successor, Erino "Harry" Leone. Harry married the current owner, Rhoda M. Leone, who continues the store's rich tradition of fine Italian foods. (Courtesy of Rhoda M. Leone.)

SEVEN SPRINGS. This picture shows the old ski slope at the popular Somerset County resort, Seven Springs. Today the resort is the county's largest employer. (Courtesy of Seven Springs Mountain Resort.)

WIND ENERGY. *The area of Somerset and Friedens is one of the only areas on the East Coast to have significant wind-produced energy. This project is currently expanding.*

FLIGHT 93 TEMPORARY MEMORIAL. *Gifts are held here in Shanksville for only a few days so they do not get damaged by the weather. They are then moved to a storage area. A permanent exhibit, which will include people's gifts left at the memorial, is being planned.*

QUECREEK MINING COMMUNITY, 1940. *More than 60 years later, the same community gathered for the rescue of nine miners who were trapped underground for 77 hours. (Courtesy of Pat Betts.)*

From Europe to Somerset County

Another traditional barometer of the transience of various ethnic groups is the amount of money sent abroad. One major goal of most immigrants was to earn high wages and save as much money as possible. Money was essential for supporting the family unit and for purchasing land in the home country, if returning was contemplated, or for a house in the United States, if a decision to stay permanently had been made. The amount of money sent to Europe also paid the passage for other relatives to emigrate. Government officials in Austria-Hungary sometimes first became aware of mass immigration from a particular region because of the amount of dollars and money orders sent there from America, and the Dillingham Commission cited statistics to show that large amounts of money were involved. More than $500 million had been sent abroad via the postal service alone from 1900 to 1909. Windber's immigrants took part in this characteristic immigrant activity. Again, the only source for concrete information on the local level comes from the Dillingham study.

No written sources convey a sense of the poignancy of the original intention of many immigrants to return as well as oral histories do. One elderly couple interviewed spoke movingly of the lot of the man's Magyar parents, immigrants who had come to the United States early in the twentieth century. From the time of their arrival in Windber before 1910 until their deaths decades later, the parents had dreamed of accumulating a nest egg to use to return to their native village, where they hoped to buy a modest house and open a small store. They even sent their eldest American-born son to religiously oriented summer schools with the conscious intention that he learn to read and write Hungarian better than they themselves could. He had to be educated to run the store in Europe and keep its books. Once or twice in their lifetimes the unfortunate couple did manage to save enough money to make the return, but some event or other intervened to deplete their funds or otherwise cause them to change their plans. In one case, a world war prevented their return. In a second instance, they were bilked of their entire savings by an unscrupulous salesman involved in a fraudulent land scheme. Never fully at home in their new environment, the man labored in the mines for the rest of his working life. Lacking the means necessary even for a visit, the foreign-born couple was never able to realize their dreams or see their native village again. In the late 1960s, the eldest son and his wife were able to visit the cherished birthplace.

SOMERSET COUNTY

Berwind-White and the other Somerset County mine operators needed men to mine coal in its new operations in Windber. Slovaks, Magyars, Poles, Italians, and other nationalities supplied the work force. They made the journey from Europe to Windber, either directly or indirectly, because an international system existed that brought working people from the Carpathians and elsewhere together with industrial employers in the Alleghenies. The diverse populations of Europe had by that time become an integral component of an emerging worldwide labor market, and the formative stages of American industrial capitalism required plentiful labor.

Contrary to popular myth, until about World War I most new immigrants who came to the United States expected to return to their native countries, where they hoped to buy land or other property from the wages they had earned during a work stint in the New World. The primary reason for the general exodus from selected areas at the turn of the century was economic, although other reasons, such as czarist persecution of Jews, were influential in particular instances. The regions that immigrants were leaving behind were undergoing uneven social and economic transformations of their own, and migration for work—neither a new nor necessarily permanent phenomenon—became one strategy for confronting the imperatives of the new economic system. Once they had settled in Windber, they continued their struggle for a better life in an autocratic setting that presented them with many new problems and challenges.

Chapter Five

MEN AND WOMEN AND
THE GROWTH OF MINING TOWNS

Somerset County's dependence on immigrant labor from the outset forced the coal corporation to develop recruitment practices that were consciously designed to appeal to the foreign-born. These practices, however, were only the first step in a broader corporate policy that linked the companies to their multiethnic work force. The success of the companies in obtaining a diverse population to mine their coal enabled them to engage in deliberate, if commonplace, employer strategies and techniques that aimed at dividing and dominating its workers. The company-town setting that Berwind-White had created ensured that its efforts to maintain authoritarian control, maximize profits, and avert unionization would not be confined to the workplace but would extend to the entire community. Nevertheless, the workplace rapidly became a key arena of contention between capital and labor.

The new immigrants who came to work in Somerset County mines found themselves inhabitants of towns that were predominantly working class. The vast majority, 78 percent, of the area's working population, according to the 1910 census, held unskilled, manual laboring jobs. Another 8 percent were employed in the various trades, while 4 percent worked in white-collar clerical, bookkeeping, or sales positions. Only a minority, 10 percent, were engaged in business, the professions, or management, which were traditional middle-class occupations.

The new immigrants were also entering a highly stratified society. The towns' prevailing class structure embodied a particular hierarchical arrangement of ethnic groups that left the Americans and certain northern European nationalities at the top of the social order and clearly distinguishable from the new immigrant groups in terms of occupation, political clout, economic power, residence, and status. As a result, the major dividing line within the communities was simultaneously a class and ethnic one.

SOMERSET COUNTY

Certain ethnic groups tended to specialize in particular occupations in Somerset County. For example, census records indicate that 25 percent of all Syrian residents, including unemployed women and children, were merchants and approximately 45 percent of all Jewish people were merchants, peddlers, or salesmen. At the same time, the very small numbers of the lowest groups in the social hierarchy, Asians and blacks, were confined to certain manual laboring jobs. All three Chinese residents were laundrymen, and of the 13 blacks in the area, nine were employed: six as laborers, primarily as carriers, one as a teamster, one as a hotel porter, and one as a combination housekeeper and servant.

As a group, southern and eastern Europeans were not the bottom rung, but close to it, of the ethnic and racial hierarchy that pertained to jobs and the communities. Aside from the small minority of their fellow compatriots who were engaged in other jobs in town, new immigrants were clustered in the many unskilled and semi-skilled laboring and mining jobs.

Over the years, the coal companies employed various mechanisms to recruit miners for its Windber-area operations. After the initial use of employment agencies, transfers of company personnel from other places, and publicity about the opening of new mines, the companies turned to overt advertising in American newspapers. In 1899, for example, in the midst of Berwind-White's first serious battle against unionization, it sought to lure men away from neighboring mines by placing a want ad for 500 miners in a Johnstown paper. In later years, the coal companies advertised widely in foreign-language newspapers in languages and in terms thought to appeal to ethnic populations.

But steamship agents, immigrant bankers, and ethnic labor contractors were even more important as suppliers of labor early in the century. Particular ethnic leaders had railroad, steamship, and financial connections that enabled them to serve as intermediaries for new arrivals in America and as de facto or authorized agents of the company. In addition, the coal corporations periodically sent representatives who were noted for their linguistic talents to New York and other ports to meet incoming ships to try to persuade men to come to Somerset County. These individuals were also sent to other mining towns for the same purpose. Once foreign-born miners had settled in the Somerset County area, they themselves became active, if sometimes unintentional, agents of recruitment through letters and dollars sent to friends and relatives abroad.

The laborers who took part in the activity of bituminous mining performed a variety of skilled, semi-skilled, and unskilled jobs. Traditionally, mine work was organized on the basis of the numerous occupations entailed in the operations of the mines. Mining jobs can be classified in a number of ways, but a first important division, one incorporated in state mining reports, was between the occupations that were carried on inside the mines and those that were performed on the surface or outside mines. The work underground included the basic tasks necessary to the extraction and transportation of the mineral to the surface, while the outside jobs involved subsidiary tasks, such as the weighing and shipping of coal to market, bookkeeping, carpentry, and blacksmithing. Underground employees were necessarily preponderant, and statistics show that work below the surface was vastly more dangerous. Although the workforce of Somerset County varied considerably from 1897 to 1918, the ratio between those employed inside and outside the mines remained more constant. On the average, 89 percent of the entire work force held underground jobs, while 11 percent had jobs outside the mines.

Southern and eastern Europeans dominated the unskilled mining and loading jobs of the Windber-area mines. Figures taken from the manuscript schedules of the federal census of 1910 indicate that 90 percent of those listed as inside miners, loaders, or coal cutters were new immigrants. The big four nationalities—Magyars, Slovaks, Poles, and Italians—alone constituted 85 percent of such workers. Magyars made up 28 percent, Slovaks 26 percent, Poles 20 percent, and Italians 11 percent of the Somerset County mines.

At the same time, southern and eastern Europeans held other unskilled jobs in the mines. They were the majority of tracklayers and trackmen and a sizable portion of the company's laborers. Only a handful of these ethnic workers held semi-skilled jobs, such as motormen and spraggers, or more highly skilled jobs, such as electricians or coal carpenters. Blacksmithing was one exceptional arena in which new immigrants were more highly represented. Nearly one-third of all company blacksmiths were of new immigrant origin.

Because mining was a new occupation for the many Europeans who had farmed as small landowners or agricultural day laborers in Europe, prospective miners often faced a necessary and difficult transition from a rural to an industrial mining work-life. Even the relative absence of a factory-like discipline still made mine work unbearable to many, and the new and unfamiliar working conditions did not appeal to everyone who was looking for work. One elderly miner described the lure of America for people who remained in Europe after family and friends had emigrated: "When they (the immigrants) come here, they would write letters and tell them how nice it was here and everything. The ones that were left back there . . . thought that the streets in America was paved with gold, opportunity. But," he emphasized, "they never told them what had to be done." This same miner had a family member who was enticed to emigrate but who rejected mine work as an occupation after a short stint in the mines:

> Myself, I had a cousin—my mother's brother's son. He always wanted to come here from Europe. He was left back on the family farm over there in Europe. . . . And he came over here. He wanted a job in the mines. His father was here so he took him in the mines. When he went, he loaded for about a week. He worked in the mines, and he said he's not going to mine no more. He said, "There's no windows or anything in there in the mine." He went in there in the dark, underground. Then he worked one week and quit.

Turnover was a continual problem for Somerset County companies. Irregularity of work, along with periods of boom and bust, were characteristic of the mining industry as a whole. Soon the eight-hour day became a major goal of the American labor movement, partially because of these problems with the mining industry. The United Mine Workers of America (UMWA) believed that they had achieved an important national victory in 1898 when the union won operator recognition of the shorter day in the central competitive field, a region that set the standard for settlements in other mining districts. In 1903, union officials in the UMWA's District 2, where the Somerset County miners were located, won the eight-hour day for unionized mines. However, Windber miners did not share in this victory, because Berwind-White mines were nonunion and did not honor many of the working conditions specified by union contracts.

Men and Women and the Growth of Mining Towns

The eight-hour day came to Somerset County mines in 1917, at a time when World War I had created a huge demand for coal, when labor was scarce or leaving for higher-paid jobs in factories and war industries, and when the UMWA was taking new initiatives on the regional and national levels. Although local mines were not unionized, Berwind-White could not ignore the growing strength of the labor movement or the ongoing need to be competitive vis-à-vis other operators in order to keep its labor force. In January 1917, for the first time in Windber's history, the company reduced the length of its workday—from ten hours to nine hours. Five months later, it cut the hours again from nine to eight. Modest wage increases accompanied each of the hourly reductions.

The golden era of Somerset County's productivity and steady work in mines encompassed the years 1897 to 1921, but it also witnessed the most numerous number of fatal mining accidents in the company's history. In other words, the life of a Somerset County miner was considerably cheaper in the first decades of the twentieth century than it was in later decades. What was true for local mines was generally true for mines all over the nation as well. Fatalities in American mines peaked during the five-year period from 1906 to 1910, when an average of 2,658 deaths a year occurred, and critics began to point out that American mines were more lethal than their counterparts in leading European countries.

The one major reorganization of work that did occur in Somerset County mines in this period seems to have been prompted by the new state laws regarding safety and mandatory worker compensation and by a new industry-wide interest in greater efficiency to meet the huge demand for coal brought on as a result of World War I. That reorganization entailed an increase in the number of foremen and assistant foremen, so that greater supervision could be exercised over the miners and company men. Increasing the quantity of supervisory personnel was one way companies could cut down on accidents, thereby reducing compensation costs, and increase cost-efficient production at the same time, thereby maintaining their competitiveness in an industry noted for a lack of concentration and fierce interstate competition. Moreover, the bituminous code of 1911 in Pennsylvania had added to the duties and responsibilities of the mine foremen, so that compliance often entailed increasing their numbers as a matter of practical necessity. According to the 1893 code, the foreman of every mine, or his assistant, was expected "to visit and examine every working place therein at least once every alternate day while the miners of such place are or should be at work." From 1911 on, foremen or assistants were expected by law to make visits to each working place on a daily basis.

Somerset County supports the general picture of gender imbalance found in most contemporary and historical descriptions of frontier mining and steel communities. Characteristic of such places was the abundance of men and the shortage of women. Thirteen years after the founding of mines in Somerset County, males still comprised a far greater portion, 59 percent, of the local population than did females. One female resident who recalled the era explained: "There was a woman shortage in this area. So when a young girl would come, my gosh, there would be a dozen men to visit one girl."

Young, single immigrant miners found it difficult to find wives in the early years of the area and led many of them to rely on marriage, family, and village networks for selection of their spouses. People interviewed told how men often traveled to previous residences, such as Houtzdale, Pennsylvania, or to large cities, such as Pittsburgh, New York, or Perth Amboy, to select wives from their respective ethnic groups. Women sometimes described simple or elaborate networks that eventually brought them to Windber.

Kathryn A. Haigh, now deceased, who was born in Meyersdale in Somerset County, remembers traveling with her coal-miner father, of English and Irish descent, from mining town to mining town, often getting offers of marriage. When she married, she recalled:

> Sam and I had six children; his parents until they died and my mother, who was blind, until she died all lived with us. And during the Depression, we lived on my home canned and dried vegetables and fruits. I had over one thousand jars packed away and even used milk bottles to jar jelly because there was a large crop of berries that year.

In Somerset County, the Depression brought an end to an era of great effort to increase agricultural production. The company store allowed $1 a day per person in the family to be charged to their bill, which Haigh said helped with necessities. She also mentioned that although women played a major role in the mining community, they were bad luck in a mine. Despite this, the Danels, who run a miner's museum in St. Michael, Pennsylvania, insist that there were several women miners in Somerset County. One female coalminer, who still lives in Somerset County, spoke at a school history day in Windber in 2003, describing her dual role as leader of her house and miner in the 1950s.

In general, from Women's Bureau figures, it appears that even fewer women in Somerset County were gainfully employed than in the overall bituminous industry. In 1910, only 15 percent of the town's entire working-age female population, consisting of all classes, held jobs as wage earners. It is also striking that the total percentage of employed females changed little or not at all in the next decades. In 1940 the U.S. Census listed 15 percent of Somerset County's working-age females as employed in regular jobs. An additional 1 percent, however, were employed in public emergency work programs created for the unemployed during the Great Depression, and another 3 percent were seeking work.

While fathers or other male relatives trained young boys or men to mine coal, mothers and other female relatives trained daughters in all sorts of domestic duties. Gender roles were reproduced. At an early age, females learned to bake, cook, sew, wash clothes, and care for the ill. Young girls often assumed major domestic responsibilities for the first time when their mothers had a newborn child, usually delivered by a neighbor who was also a midwife. Mothers needed the help of their daughters because families tended to be large. Despite some additional schooling and some household improvements, the younger generation of the 1920s had little time to dream of alternatives to domestic, clerical, or sales work, and even fewer opportunities to realize any such dreams in the area. As in the case of their male counterparts, childhood was still a brief interlude at best. Women interviewed told frequently of their great disappointment when they had to leave school to help out at home. In 1940, some 69 percent of all Windber residents, male and female, over the age of 25 had completed only eight grades of school or less. For both sexes, work began at an early age and remained a fundamental reality.

Chapter Six

CULTURAL CHALLENGES TO THE
EARLY COMMUNITIES

As the coal industry took hold on the Somerset County region and immigrant workers came to the area, some divisive elements began to occur in the communities of the county. The most benign of the challenges were the ethnic churches and fraternal organizations that appeared in the segregated ethnic enclaves throughout the area. These groups were encouraged by coal companies as part of broader labor management policies that were designed to keep foreign-born miners satisfied, unorganized, and separated from American miners.

In 1903, Will Hendrickson, the *Windber Journal* editor, accused the company of "nursing" the foreign element in order to divide miners and arbitrarily deny workers' basic rights. A U.S. Department of Labor investigator reached the same conclusion in 1919. To placate new immigrants, the company routinely allowed immigrant miners to take time off to attend fraternal events and occasionally even closed the mines for foreign national and religious holidays. In public testimony before the Industrial Relations Commission in 1915, E.J. Berwind chided his foreign-born miners for a propensity to take days off, but hinted strongly that company toleration of such absences was considered necessary to keep his miners content, which, in his worldview, meant nonunionized and less likely to migrate elsewhere.

Many of the coal companies in Somerset County seriously underestimated immigrants and immigrant communities, which were continuously producing ethnic leaders with working-class loyalties even as the company, work experiences, and life in company towns were producing class-consciousness among the general mining population. These alternative leaders fully appreciated the need to integrate miners of disparate nationalities into a class-based industrial union, such as the United Mine Workers. To do so successfully, they understood, required displacing the company's ethnic aristocrats and mobilizing the masses of miners to take charge of their own ethnic institutions—national parishes and fraternal societies.

The region was also influenced by national cultural trends, with the Ku Klux Klan emerging as a major actor in the central and western Pennsylvania story. Dormant since the post–Civil War period, by the 1920s the Klan reemerged with a vengeance. Although it primarily drew upon its southern roots, the KKK of the 1920s made major inroads into the northern industrial states of Illinois, Indiana, Ohio, and Pennsylvania. Affiliation in Pennsylvania's organization ranked among the largest in the nation with the western part of the state boasting a membership of over 125,000. Most of its activities included organizing large-scale demonstrations, cross burning, picnics, and other social affairs. Because they were perceived as competitors for jobs, Italian and eastern Europeans as well as African Americans were prime targets for Klan intimidation.

The organization used Johnstown, on the border of Somerset and Cambria Counties, as its regional headquarters for launching recruiting drives among Anglo Americans in the small commercial towns that dot central Pennsylvania's rolling foothills. By 1921 Johnstown's chapter numbered over 1,000 with an additional group started in nearby Ligonier. Rumors circulated in Indiana County that it would be next in line for an affiliate. But it wasn't until the second month of the 1922 strike that the Klan became a reality in Indiana County when a rally complete with the burning of a fiery cross was held at Bath Hill overlooking Indiana borough. The county's chapter later became the second largest in the state.

In 1922, thousands of Somerset County miners and their families joined hundreds of thousands of their fellow workers in the largest coal strike that has ever occurred in the history of the United States. The national coal strike and other strikes occurring that year marked the ending of the most significant strike wave (1916–1922) in American history. During World War I, a variety of skilled, semi-skilled, and unskilled workers had responded to existing industrial conditions with rising expectations and a drive to secure higher wages, "workers' control," and the right to organize and bargain collectively. After the war, ordinary workers in Somerset County and elsewhere began to apply President Woodrow Wilson's notion that the United States had fought the war in Europe to make the world "safe for democracy" to demand that they, too, deserved democracy, "at home," in the industries and localities where none existed. In this spirit, in 1919, delegates to the national United Mine Workers convention endorsed a "Miners' Program" that included nationalization of the coalmines, a 6-hour day, and a labor party. The strike of 1922 grew out of the postwar efforts of the coal operators to return to the wages and conditions that prevailed before 1914. The grievances of Somerset County's nonunion coal miners follow:

1. For collective bargaining and the right to affiliate with the union.
2. For a fair wage.
3. For accurate weight of the coal they mine. (Experience teaches us that this can be secured only when the miners have a checkweighman.)
4. Adequate pay for "dead work."
5. A system by which grievances could be settled in a peaceful and conciliatory spirit by the mine committee representing the miners and a representative of the operator.
6. But above all they struck to secure their rights as free Americans against the state of fear, suspicion and espionage prevailing in nonunion towns. Against a small group of operators controlling life, liberty and pursuit of happiness of large numbers of miners. To put an end to the absolute and feudal control of these coal operators.

Unlike those miners who already had secured the right to organize and bargain collectively, many of Somerset County's miners, including all the Windber miners, possessed none of these or other democratic rights in 1922. When they came out en masse for union in April 1922, they were striking for union—and all it represented to them—primarily because of local conditions, but also to support the union and their fellow miners in the larger world. For nearly 17 months, despite the horrors of armed repression, meager food allotments, evictions that forced them to live in hen houses or chicken coops or to migrate to other places, they endured and fought on valiantly for the right to organize. They continued their struggle for one full year after August 1922, when the national union's officers settled the national strike on highly controversial terms which John L. Lewis claimed were the best they could hope to get at the time. Somerset County miners and other miners from across the country who had been unorganized before the strike began were left out of the national contract. But, with some help from the national organization and a great deal of aid from District 2 of the United Mine Workers, they nevertheless renewed their commitment to continue their strike for union and made history by their actions.

Although many Somerset County miners were unable to secure union recognition and collective bargaining in 1922–1923, their contributions and efforts for union during this struggle were nationally significant at the time and of critical importance in shaping the labor movement of the 1930s, New Deal labor legislation, and democratic social reforms. Many of the miners, including Windber area miners, did successfully organize and achieve union recognition and collective bargaining rights in 1933, under the terms of the National Industrial Recovery Act.

During the ongoing strike, Somerset County's nonunion coal miners made six general demands that the UMWA's District 2 president, John Brophy, outlined in a brief presented in 1923 to the U.S. Coal Commission. The comprehensive nature of the miners' grievances indicated that unionization could never be a narrow issue related merely to wage rates. The right to organize was fundamental, linked to the wage issue and to other issues at the workplace and in the community. Basically, at stake was whether or not the autocratic nature of coal life in company towns would continue to prevail or be supplanted by democracy and American civil liberties.

After the settlement of the national strike, Windber and Somerset County miners pioneered new methods of gaining public support for their ongoing strike for union. By far, the most creative and innovative action taken by Windber-area miners was an initiative that took a delegation of them to New York City in September and October 1922. They went there to petition the mayor and to ask the city's top financial administrative body, the Board of Estimate, for assistance. New York City—and its people—had a direct financial, if no other, interest in what was happening in the private Interborough Rapid Transit Company (IRT), on whose board of directors E.J. Berwind sat. In what was an obvious conflict of interest, Berwind used his influence on the IRT to get the city to buy its coal directly from his privately-owned mines at the prices he determined. New York City subways ran on Windber coal!

Windber miners testified before the Board of Estimate on September 26 about their many grievances and the autocratic conditions under which they labored and lived. Because of the city's financial interest, however, they stressed that, before the strike, the city was paying Berwind-White $7.35 per ton of coal for the subways, while Berwind-White was paying its own miners only $1.28 for each ton of coal they mined. Then, in 1922, at the beginning of the strike, the Berwinds abruptly raised the city's price for coal to $8.35 per ton, as they simultaneously reduced their miners' wages to $1.01 for each ton. The miners specifically asked for the city's help in getting E.J. Berwind, who adamantly refused to meet his own miners, to confer with them. They also asked the city to appoint a committee to investigate their laboring conditions.

Before long, Berwind reneged on a publicly made promise that he would arrange a meeting with his miners but only in Windber. Then, the Windber miners returned to New York to picket the company's corporate offices. On October 26, 1922, Mayor John Hylan appointed a committee of prominent New York officials to investigate conditions in Windber and make recommendations. The committee members were: David Hirshfield, commissioner of accounts, chairman; Mrs. Louis R. Welzmiller, deputy commissioner of public markets; John Lehman, assistant corporation counsel; Amos T. Smith, mechanical engineer, of the office of the Secretary of the Board of Estimate and Apportionment; Thomas F. Moran, examiner of the Bureau of Investigations, Department of Finance.

This committee of New York officials did come to Windber, held hearings, collected documents, took photos, and gathered evidence. The following excerpts are from its official report, which was published in January 1923:

Conditions Found at the Coal Fields

On Sunday, October 29, 1922, your Committee, accompanied by representatives of the mineworkers, visited the Berwind-White Coal Mining Company's coalfields at Windber, Scalp Level and Seanor. The day was cold and blustery and ice was evident everywhere from the heavy frost of the night before.

At the Windber mine, the Committee found no strikers, and, according to information, those who had been evicted at this mine had moved to other fields nearby.

At Mine 40, located at Scalp Level, about thirty-two families, including one hundred and eighty children, were found living in tents on the bare ground, without stoves or other protection from the cold. These families, it was stated, were the remainder of a group of 200 families who had been evicted from their homes at this mine by the Berwind-White Coal and Iron Police, shortly after the commencement of the strike in April, 1922. Some of the evicted families had been taken care of in barracks erected by the union and in the homes of relatives, while others who, in some manner, had secured sufficient funds to move away, had obtained employment in union mines. The families without funds and without friends could not leave the district but were compelled to stay where they were and depend for their subsistence upon the meager sum advanced them by the union.

At Mine No. 38, located at Seanor, only ten families were found out of the original 150 families evicted from their homes at this mine. Some of these families were living in hen houses, cowsheds, cellars and under tents. Here also, the union supplied these people with enough food to keep them existing.

At all the mines which the Committee visited, it found most of the women and children barefooted and scantily clad. The feet and limbs of most of these unfortunates, particularly those of the children, were scarred and bleeding from walking on hard ice, through underbrush and over stone. The picture was most depressing.

The influences of all the years of meager living and struggle for mere existence among these barren hills, had left an imprint on these miners and their families, that amounted almost to despair. Their women folks become old and hollow-eyed before their time. The children were found undersized, and with supplicating eyes begging for help.

Most of the miners in Somerset County are Poles, Russians, Slovaks, Hungarians, with a few Welsh and very few Irish. Many of them have been there for many years. In some instances, two generations have been working

in these mines and the second generation is just as poor as was the first.

At the time of its release, and probably because of its critical conclusions and progressive recommendations as well as Berwind-White's larger political influence, the New York City report did not gain prominent widespread coverage in the nation's media. It did get some lesser coverage, though. While it did not end the strike or produce reforms, it remains invaluable today as a document that accurately presents the miners' case for the strike and the conditions that existed in the town and in Berwind-White mines there.

Despite great obstacles, Windber and Somerset County miners and their families continued their strike for union into a second year. Finally, in August 1923, nearly 17 months after they had gone out on strike, they were forced to concede defeat. To any and all but the most biased company people and open shop advocates, their actions alone had proved their uncompromising desire for, and commitment to, unionization—and all that represented to them. As the final document indicates, when they had to end this particular effort, they did so with the same courage and pride with which they had conducted the lengthy strike. In 1933, they eagerly seized upon a new opportunity, built upon such earlier struggles, and successfully unionized to continue their long-term efforts for democratic freedoms and social justice into a new era.

On Mitchell Day, a miners' holiday celebrating the commencing of the eight-hour workday, in 2003, Windber unveiled a marker commemorating the 16-month miners' struggle with Berwind-White Coal Mining Company in 1922–1923. The ceremony brought miners and residents from all throughout Somerset County and included a panel discussion, an educational event for local school children, an ethnic food celebration, and a film presentation. The marker, which some opposed due to the sensitivity of Berwind-White's stance during the strike, now stands at a prominent place in Miner's Park in downtown Windber. "This marker stands for all miners," said Ed Yankovich, UMWA District 2 president. "Somerset County's miners' struggle was a struggle that involved all of them: For wages, health care, medical care for their children and better working conditions. We find ourselves in the year 2003 still fighting for those issues."

Chapter Seven

PROFILES OF PERSEVERANCE

Alcohol was forbidden by law on January 16, 1920 and the Prohibition years would last until December 5, 1933. It was a law that some in Somerset County did not heed. This was an area where people made "the drink" to serve during the holidays—the people of the county believed that it was part of their tradition and a matter of pride. "Windber ain't the town it used terr be" became a favorite saying in the town. On January 1, 1903, the Windber Brewing Company was chartered in Somerset County with George W. Flowers being the solicitor for the application. The objective of the company was to manufacture and brew malt liquors. Somerset County's beer production in 1916 totaled 37,615 barrels. Of this amount, 19,996 barrels were produced in Windber. The signs "Serve Windber Bottled Beer To Your Friends, Its The Art of Hospitality" or "Just The Beverage To Set Before Your Guest" were no longer in style. Federal officers came into Windber to empty all the vats, but the "huge containers were full of water by the time the Feds got here," report most Windber residents. Local hotel men were arrested as the government sent in undercover men to watch the businesses that had previously sold alcohol. From time to time Chief McMullen would find some local moonshine with a homemade still and mash. Joseph Magazzu recalls that each family was permitted by law to make enough wine for their own use. It was used to serve when guests were in your home. Joe says, "When the wine ran out you didn't get much company."

One story that was printed in the local newspapers in July 1928 was an incident that took place at the old Hoffman farm, near Elton. Two farmers were shot, one fatally, by hijackers who were seeking the "Shine." The murderers mistook the Hoffman brothers for moonshiners. Lewis was shot to death and Herman was seriously wounded. The men had gone to the Hoffman farm for the purpose of robbing the moonshine plant located on the end of the farm which had been leased some time before.

SOMERSET COUNTY

By 1932 the Great Depression had hit the country with full force, sending 13 million men into the unemployment lines and women and children into food lines. Since coal production in Somerset County had peaked in the 1920s, by the time of the Great Depression coal production had plummeted to half of its 1927 level and the lumber industry was a distant memory. During the Depression era, "Pinchot Road" construction provided employment for many miners. Despite poor economic conditions, the county population remained healthy at almost 81,000 in 1930.

The miners of Somerset County were having a tougher time than most. On May 15, 1933, during the early days of the New Deal, several thousand men, women, and children marched under the auspices of the United Unemployed Councils of Somerset County to the courthouse in Somerset to present 19 demands to the Emergency County Relief Board. They came from Holsopple, Scalp Level, Windber, and many other towns. Of the 4,800 families representing 24,000 individuals who were on the county's relief rolls at the time, 3,101 were families of unemployed miners. The protestors' demands included the removal and reorganization of the committee in charge of relief, a range of payments depending on the age and marital status of those in need, cash payments instead of merchant orders in order to be fair to all businesses, free medical aid, assistance without a work requirement for those over 60 years of age, free milk for children with compensation to the diary producers, no poll tax for the unemployed, no evictions of those unable to pay rent, and no discrimination against those taking part in the hunger march. From 1931 to 1933 similar marches occurred in many places throughout the United States.

Another problem that grew throughout the Depression years was the growth of the Ku Klux Klan in Somerset County—often supported in the 1930s by organizations such as the Patriotic Order Sons of America, the fire company, and certain Protestant denominations that spoke and acted against the "un-American Catholics and foreigners." And there was some good news: Somerset County area miners would finally win union recognition and a union contract in 1933, following many years of struggle. As the region recovered from the Depression, the county population reached its highest level ever of 85,000 in 1940.

Then on December 7, 1941, World War II was declared. Over 5,000 men left Somerset County to fight for their country. On December 11, after the sneak attack on Pearl Harbor, the Windber Legion supervised Civilian Defense Units that were organized with three fully equipped Air Raid Stations. A rifle squadron was organized as a possible nucleus for a home defense unit. Air raid drills were conducted with "lights out" practiced. No one in Somerset County was permitted to walk the streets or drive a car until the all clear whistles blew. Air raid wardens went on duty making sure everyone participated according to the rules, and food and gas coupons were issued.

One of the worst symbols of the war, however, was at the local train stations. The young draftees lined up on the platforms while relatives and friends tearfully gathered together to watch them board the trains that would take them away. No longer was it a time when they would be going to camp; they were now going to war. The seriousness of the condition touched every family in Somerset County.

Young Benjamin Bossi and his twin brother, Frank, were stationed at Pearl Harbor in Hawaii at the time of the attack by the Japanese. Ben wrote home to his family on 22nd Street in Windber:

> Dear Mom, I guess there is no use to answer my letters because I may never receive them. Frank is alright they came close but that is all. Zeke is alright too, tell Aunt Katie. Try to get word to Joe Furda, Tom Senella, and Merle Bartholamew's mothers that they are alright. They did a lot of damage here, they bombed our barracks. Give my regards to everyone in Windber. Love, Ben.

The fearful ordeal for both those going away and those waiting for them to return lasted until May 7, 1945 when the unconditional surrender of Germany was announced. In all the towns of Somerset County fire whistles blew, church bells rang, car horns tooted, and people laughed and screamed for joy or just sat down and cried. At least 87 of the community's young men died during World War II. Towns mourned their dead and mothers hung Gold Star flags in their windows. Twenty-four-year-old Frank Bossi, mentioned in the letter to the Bossi family above, was shot down over Germany and died on July 7, 1944.

Following the Second World War, Somerset County returned to concentrating on its communities. Construction of the Pennsylvania Turnpike helped lift Somerset

County's economy and brought some new industries to the area. It was on March 18, 1948, that the first Somerset County Maple Festival, which was to play such an important part in the postwar development of Meyersdale and surrounding communities, began. Pennsylvania Governor Daniel B. Strickler, guest speaker, addressed a crowd of 1,500 gathered on Main Street in front of the New Colonial Hotel. His words of praise for our enterprising and industrious community were followed by the coronation of Miss Agnes Jean Hornbrook, who had earlier won the right to the title of Pennsylvania's Queen Maple I. U.S. Representative William F. Crow performed the honors. A dinner and tour of local maple camps concluded the day.

The story of how this important local tradition became a modern tourist draw is unique. One scene that has become forever inseparable from a history of small-town America is a local store, a pot-bellied stove, and a handful of men gathered 'round it. Proving no exception to the rule, any recounting of the history of our quiet rural community of Meyersdale must give special prominence to just such a "Currier and Ives" tableau. For it was actually around a potbellied stove of the Shipley Hardware Company Store, one blustery winter night some 50 years ago, that plans were formulated, which, in the years since, have succeeded in launching Meyersdale into a position of international renown as "Maple City, USA." On that night a group of farseeing men had a vision—a celebration, a festival in Meyersdale to promote the sweetest of all Pennsylvania's commodities, our own Somerset County maple syrup, a Maple Festival—and that vision, that dream, became a reality.

Somerset County, the "Roof Garden of Pennsylvania," has long been recognized as the Commonwealth's largest producer of maple products. Obtained from the sugar maple, one of the most beautiful and stately of American trees, maple syrup was first made by the Indians and continued by the white settlers who followed. The making of maple syrup is truly an American art.

The American Indians celebrated the "maple moon" or "sugar moon" as the return of spring. They hacked the maple trees with tomahawks and collected the sugar water in troughs or crude vessels. The Indians condensed sugar water or sap by dropping heated stones in wooden troughs containing the liquid. The maple industry faced many changes over the years. Hand augers and later power drills were used to drill holes in the maple trees. Into these holes were inserted wooden, and later metal, spiles to catch the sugar water as it dripped, drop by drop, into wooden, metal and later, plastic buckets, known in Somerset County as "keelers." Also, a newer method being used in some maple groves is plastic tubing, which transfers sap from the tree to central gathering tanks.

This process, called tapping, will not harm the trees. If a tree is 10 inches in diameter, it can support one tap; 15 inches, two taps; and 20 inches, three taps. An average maple tree will produce 15 gallons of sap from each taphole per season.

When the weather is such that there is a freeze at night and a thaw during the day, the sap collecting and gathering follows. Men with carrying pails collect from each tree and empty the buckets into covered tanks hauled on trucks or by tractor. Much sap is pumped from roadside tanks into a tank truck, to be hauled to central storage tanks at the "Sugar House." These have germicidal lamps over them to prevent bacterial growth until sap can be evaporated.

Unlike the Indians, who used heated stones to evaporate sugar water, and the settlers, who used large iron kettles fired with wood, we now use fuel oil to boil the water. As the sap flows along in a constant boil, the water escapes in the form of steam and the liquid becomes sweeter and changes to an amber color with the increasing sugar content. As it comes from the tree and enters the evaporator, sap has about two to two-and-a-half percent sugar content. After this boiling process, it leaves the evaporators with a sugar content of over 65 percent. Thus, 1 gallon of maple syrup weighing 11 pounds was condensed from 40 to 50 gallons of sugar water. Then transferred to flat pans for final finishing, the syrup is forced through special filters to remove any accumulated sediment and stored in 550-gallon sterile metal tanks, which have germicidal lamps under the lids. Later it is pumped back to finishing pans, reheated to 185 degrees Farenheit, refiltered through pressure filters, and packed into cans, bottles, ceramic, or plastic containers. This final packaging is carried on throughout the entire year and employs several people. After packaging, the syrup may travel halfway around the world by mail, or it may appear on your grocer's shelf in your hometown.

The background for this amazing story of transition from a local tradition to large-scale development and growth centers around that ever-popular American songstress, Miss Kate Smith. One day in the first part of 1947, Smith, on her daily noontime broadcast, mentioned that she would appreciate a taste of some good

Vermont maple syrup. Through the combined efforts of a few local citizens who accepted this as somewhat of a challenge, the idea of sending the radio star a sample of Somerset County's maple syrup was conceived and implemented. On her April 17, 1947 national broadcast, Miss Smith sang not only popular tunes but also the praises of our community's gift to her, pronouncing our local syrup to be the "sweetest she had ever tasted."

This publicity furnished the impetus for a hard-driving promotional campaign that began that May under the auspices of the Meyersdale Chamber of Commerce. However, as the long winter days began to loom ahead, enthusiasm waned, and it was not until that "summit of the potbellied stove," January 20, 1948, that this campaign received the final push it needed to start it on the road to success. With Chamber of Commerce President W. Hubert Lenhart at the helm, a planning committee was decided upon, and preparations for the very first Maple Festival to be held in Pennsylvania got under way.

The story of Meyersdale's Maple Festival is one of growth. From a handful of men gathered around a potbellied stove, it has come to include literally hundreds of workers. From a crowd of 1,500 spectators, it has become an attraction drawing tens of thousands of visitors annually. Today, to mention Meyersdale anywhere in Pennsylvania, anywhere in the tri-state area, and still very much farther than that, is to bring forth the reply, "Oh! the Maple Festival." The Maple Festival has truly succeeded in putting Meyersdale on the map.

While residents were basking in the glow of their maple sugar fame, the county was struck by another terrible disaster, one that would force some to become heroes.

On October 15, 1954, Hurricane Hazel caused extensive damage throughout the county. Five people died in the wake of the storm. The southern part of the county was particularly hard hit by floods. Between Meyersdale and Sand Patch Tunnel, Eber K. Cockley, B&O agent in Meyersdale, reported that the downpour measured almost 7 inches. The heavy rainfall affected all of the area streams, including Flaugherty Creek, Casselman River, Elk Lick Creek, and Blue Lick Creek. At Glade City southeast of Meyersdale, Lester A. Chilton and his wife Julia of Easton, Pennsylvania, who was pregnant with their first child, were on their way to Meyersdale after visiting friends. They were on the Glade City road when the floodwaters swept their car away. It was snagged by a rope strung between the homes of William Herwig and Edward Hostetler Sr. Mrs. Chilton got out of the car as Edward Hostetler, with a clothesline around his waist, waded out to get her. Both were swept away, the clothesline broken by the force of the water. Their bodies were found in the Meyersdale fairgrounds area. Lester Chilton lost his grip on the car and was swept downstream. Two hours later, the car broke loose and crashed against him as he clung to a pole. Somehow he was able to climb into the back seat of the car and he started to blink the dome light in the hope of being rescued. The Herwigs pulled him out after tossing him a rope. Hostetler was posthumously honored by the Carnegie Hero Foundation of Pittsburgh.

In the other three storm-related deaths, Roy Barkley, 44, of Listonburg drowned while trying to aid a stranded mother and two children. William A. Petry, 70, a Salisbury contractor, sustained a fatal heart attack while digging a ditch around his home. George A. Hillegas, 73, of Boynton, also suffered a fatal heart attack shortly after wading in rising water near his home. The flood caused damage to electric and telephone lines, but most were repaired within a few days. One of the most unusual effects of the flood was found along Route 219 between Meyersdale and Boynton, where the waters lifted a long section of railroad track and set the ties up on end, like a snow fence, for more than a mile.

In what could be called the calm before the storm, Somerset County began to be recognized for its athletic achievements. Once firmly established, traditional sports, such as baseball, football, wrestling and track, spread like wildfire and continue to the present day. Beginning in 1935, basketball and other sports programs expanded to the point where it was necessary to separate the larger schools from the smaller ones. During this time, schools were divided in Class A and B leagues.

The most notable athletic star of the area was Johnny Weissmuller. He rose to stardom as Tarzan in Edgar Rice Borough's jungle stories that flashed across the movie screens of America for three decades. His father, Peter Weissmuller, came to America after serving as a captain in the army of the Emperor Franz Josef in Vienna. Although it was believed in the past that Weissmuller was born in Windber in 1905, recent documents have revealed that he was born in Romania and immigrated to Windber with his mother when very young. Later Weissmuller would use his brother's birth certificate, who was born in Windber, in order to compete as a U.S. citizen in the Olympics. A marker still remains in downtown Windber stating that Weissmuller was born in the town. Weissmuller's parents lived a few blocks from Delaney Field and his father ran Windber's Brewery, just as he had run a brewery in Romania.

Johnny began swimming at age six and the rest is history. Once billed as "the fastest swimmer in the world," Weissmuller won gold medals in the 1924 and 1928 Olympic Games. He won hundreds of swimming meets and set 67 world and 52 American records in distances ranging from 100 to 880 yards. The Associated Press sports writers, in 1950, voted him the greatest swimmer of the past 50 years. He moved to Hollywood and starred in 16 Tarzan movies in the 1930s, 1940s, and 1950s. His first movie was *Tarzan the Apeman* in 1932. On April 20, 1950, Johnny Weissmuller, who was married six times, paid his first visit to Windber during his adult life. Nearly 4,000 people turned out at the Windber Stadium to hear Weismuller give his famous Tarzan yell. He said, "This is the biggest thrill I ever had in my life."

In 1967 Weismuller visited nearby Johnstown where he was inducted into the Cambria County War Memorial Hall of Fame. Bob Sefick, a writer for the Johnstown newspaper, was sent to meet the star. Sefick found him to be "just a regular guy." He had met the Queen of England and knew plenty of big time movie stars, but he admired the coal miners. In 1979 he was inducted into the Windber Hall of Fame. In January of 1984, Johnny Weissmuller died at his home in California at the age of 79 years. Sefick wrote, "Farewell, we hope you were in heaven before the devil knew you died, so long Johnny and thanks for the memories."

Another famous entertainer from Somerset County is Alan Freed, the disc jockey credited with naming rock & roll. Freed was born Albert James Freed on December 21, 1921 in Windber. In 1933 the Freed family moved to Salem, Ohio. In high school Freed formed a band known as the Sultans of Swing, in which he played trombone. In 1942 Freed landed his first broadcasting job, at WKST (New Castle, Pennsylvania). He took a sportscasting position at WKBN (Youngstown, Ohio) the following year. In 1945 he moved to WAKR (Akron, Ohio) and became a local favorite, playing hot jazz and pop recordings.

In 1949 Freed moved to WXEL-TV in Cleveland. Record store owner Leo Mintz convinced him to emcee a program of rhythm & blues records over WJW radio, and on July 11, 1951, calling himself "Moondog," Freed went on the air. At his "Moondog Coronation Ball" at the 10,000-capacity Cleveland Arena in March 1952, upwards of

20,000 fans (almost all black) crashed the gates, causing the dance to be cancelled. This is considered to be the first "rock" concert. It also marked the point at which Freed's audience began to include an increasing number of whites—who subsequently heard Freed refer to rhythm & blues as "rock & roll."

In September 1954 Freed was hired by WINS radio in New York. The following January he held a landmark dance there, promoting black performers as rock & roll artists. Within a month, the music industry was advertising rock & roll records in the trade papers. Freed also emceed a string of legendary stage shows at the Brooklyn and New York Paramount Theatres; was heard nationally via CBS radio; and starred in several rock & roll movies. In 1957 ABC-TV gave Freed his own nationally-televised rock & roll show, but an episode on which Frankie Lymon danced with a white girl enraged ABC's southern affiliates and the show was cancelled. In the spring of 1958, when violence occurred outside the Boston Arena after a Freed stage show, local authorities indicted him for inciting to riot. The charges were eventually dropped, but WINS failed to renew Freed's contract. Freed moved to WABC radio and also hosted a locally televised dance show.

When the broadcasting payola scandal erupted in November 1959, Freed claimed payments he had received from record companies were for "consultation," not as an inducement to play their records. He was fired from his radio and television programs. In 2003 Windber added a "star" to its downtown memorial to remember the founder of rock & roll.

An athletic standout who would rise to national fame is Los Angeles Raiders quarterback Jeff Hostetler, a native of Somerset County, who started his illustrious football career at Conemaugh Township Area High School. A three-sport standout for the Indians, Hostetler also played baseball and basketball and was named to All-County teams in 1978 and 1979. He was noted the WVSC Outstanding Senior in basketball—leading the Indians, coached by Joe Majer, to the PIAA state finals—ending his high school basketball career as the second highest scorer in Somerset County history with 1,853 points.

Hostetler, who followed in the footsteps of his older brothers, Ron and Doug, was a promising high school quarterback, but was shifted to the tailback slot his senior year, and was named to the Parade All-American list—as a linebacker. In 1978 Hostetler was named to The Associated Press All-State football team. The following year Hostetler played in the Pennsylvania Big 33 football game. Hostetler attended Penn State University for a short time and then transferred to West Virginia University because he wanted to be a starting quarterback. He totaled 4,411 career yards on offense at WVU and had ten 200-yard passing games. He earned national recognition during the 1982 and 1983 seasons when he led the Mountaineers to back-to-back 9–3 seasons.

WVU coach Don Nehlen said Hostetler's opening performance of 321 yards in a 41–27 victory at Oklahoma was his biggest and most memorable game at WVU. *Sports Illustrated* named Hostetler player of the week following the outstanding performance against Oklahoma. In 1983 Hostetler was named Amateur Athlete of the Year by the West Virginia Writers Association and he was a Heisman Trophy candidate his senior year, finishing seventh in the balloting.

The New York Giants selected Hostetler in the third round of the 1984 draft and he stood in the shadow of the Giants' starting quarterback, Phil Simms, for seven seasons. Simms, sidelined because of a foot injury, gave the Hollsopple native his first opportunity to start as a quarterback in the National Football League playoffs. In 1991, Hostetler delivered victories over the Chicago Bears and defending Super Bowl champion San Francisco 49ers. He reached the pinnacle of success in the NFL when he led the Giants to a 20–19 victory over the Buffalo Bills in Super Bowl XXV. Hostetler's Super Bowl performance was rock-solid. He completed 20 of 32 pass attempts for 222 yards and one touchdown.

After winning the crown jewel of professional football, Hostetler became a national celebrity. He was invited to the White House and appeared on *The Tonight Show*. He gave motivational speeches and attended numerous awards banquets. The people of Somerset County also celebrated and paid tribute to their hometown hero. The county commissioners proclaimed Super Bowl Sunday as "Jeff Hostetler Day" in Somerset County. In February of 1995, Hostetler threw a touchdown pass to the Pittsburgh Steelers' Eric Green as the AFC overwhelmed the NFC, 41–13 in the Pro Bowl played in Honolulu, Hawaii.

Although these years seemed golden for a few, more challenges would face Somerset County in the following years. The worst flood came on July 19, 1977 when Johnstown, Windber, and other areas of Cambria and northern Somerset County were ravaged by floodwaters in the early morning hours. The local weather forecast for July 19 read: Chance of thunder shower tonight; low near 70. Partly cloudy, hot and humid Wednesday; high near 90. Chance of rain 30 percent tonight and 20 percent Wednesday. Laurel Run Dam, just west of Johnstown, Cambria County, burst as a result of the pressure of eight hours of heavy rain in which nearly 12 inches of precipitation fell on the area. When the final tally was conducted, the floodwaters had killed 77 people and caused hundreds of millions of dollars in damages throughout the two counties. That included 640 homes destroyed; 2,580 homes with major damage; 405 small businesses destroyed; 100 miles of road closed; 20 bridges washed out or damaged; 3,300 motor vehicles destroyed; and 8.2 million pounds of food lost.

Damage to highways, bridges, and streets totaled $94 million; public utilities, $30.7 million; homes, $25.7 million; and community facilities, $62.7 million. Federal money spent in aid totaled more than $210.2 million. State money spent within the first year totaled $5.6 million with another $56 million expected. Damage was high in Windber, Scalp Level, Paint Township, Conemaugh Township, and other communities in the northern part of the county.

Five people died in Somerset County, including three in Scalp Level Borough and two in Windber. George Zidzik, 50, of Johnstown had gone to try to convince his mother Susan Zidzik, 84, and sister Helen Zidzik, 62, to leave their home at 604 Main Street, Scalp Level, when their house was swept away. Andrew Koharchik Jr. and his wife Ann were killed when they were trapped in the basement of the Slovak-Slovenian Club in Windber, which they were cleaning after closing time.

Windber's main street, Graham Avenue, was devastated from 14th to 20th Streets. A post office, supermarket, state store, and two car dealerships received extensive damage. The watermark in the post office was 6 feet high. The Stony Creek wiped out 10 houses and a mobile home in the small town of Seanor. The Little Paint Creek in Scalp Level carried more than 100 old mine cars from the hillside and destroyed just about the entire area on Main Street between the two railroad bridges. The waters carried away homes and destroyed Trinity United Methodist Church. From Scalp Level, Little Paint merged with Paint Creek and together they demolished the four-lane highway of Route 56, closing all travel toward Richland and Johnstown.

The waters continued into Stonycreek River, which is joined by Little Conemaugh River at the Point in Johnstown to form the Conemaugh River. The Conemaugh Dam held and collected 20 acres of debris. President Jimmy Carter declared Somerset, Bedford, Cambria, Clearfield, Indiana, Jefferson, and Westmoreland Counties disaster areas. On July 22, late afternoon thunderstorms with heavy rain and wind gusts up to 65 miles per hour complicated cleanup efforts.

Windber Mayor Thomas Panetti established a 9:00 p.m. curfew. Some 300–400 people from Windber and Paint Township were being fed and housed in mass care centers, including the high school cafeteria. The high school gymnasium was transformed into a disaster center, which provided help in housing, food, or other emergency assistance, home or business loans, farm assistance, unemployment benefits, property cleanup, food stamps, and many other serious needs. The center was open until August 9.

The Russian Club building was open for 15 days, serving meals, providing medical services, and distributing food, clothing, and cleaning supplies. Destruction of water lines caused a serious drinking water problem. Fire departments from Somerset County, the National Guard, county dairy farmers, Bellefonte firemen, and Forty Fort volunteers furnished and transported fresh water daily.

David Shaffer, one of the firemen from the Rummel area, was among those who first answered the whistle. He, like many others, did not return to his home for over 24 hours. As he approached the area near the Windber High School, his vehicle stalled out in the high water. Running through the dark water that was covering the street, he made it to the Fire Hall as lightning lit up the town. The crew was sent from the area fire companies to pump basements and to see to the safety of the people who were stranded in the murky water. The floodwaters rushed from Seese Run and Paint Creek covering the town. It had peaked by 1:30 a.m. on July 20, reaching a depth of 6 feet on Graham Avenue and 8 feet in other areas. When morning light came the residents saw the horrible scene. Wreckage was piled up both sides of the Paint Creek and 100 families had been evacuated from their homes.

Windber was the hardest hit in Somerset County with 464 homes damaged. The clean up began and once again the people of the area showed their community spirit. Volunteers came early to help and stayed late. Some searched for bodies and some dug mud until they could no longer lift their shovels. There were those who sat on pieces of broken furniture sobbing as they viewed the loss. The Trinity United Methodist Church in Scalp Level was one of the hardest hit victims with only a few walls remaining. Railroad cars were swept onto the nearby banks. Telephone service was out with only a few emergency lines available. Windber's water system was out of operation, roads were washed away making travel in or out of the town impassable, bridges were washed away at Seanor, Camp Hamilton, and Elton, and entrance and exit ramps were closed.

The little villages of Seanor and Hillsboro, at the riverbanks, staggered under the blow. Families were in the second floors of their homes for hours before rescue crews could reach them. Care centers were immediately established for over 400 people who had no place to sleep and no food. Windber High School and the Rummel Church of the Brethren served as disaster centers.

A previous flood, the St. Patrick's Day flood in 1936, had been almost as damaging when a downpour of more than 4.5 inches of cold rains covered hundreds of acres of land and caused thousands of dollars of damage in the county. The Casselman River tore through Rockwood, Garrett, and Confluence, while the Stonycreek flooded Hooversville and Hollsopple. Four feet of water gushed over the streets in Garrett, spilling into first-floor windows. For the first time in the history of the town, floodwaters reached the post office. The steel bridge connecting the north and south sections of the borough broke away from its foundations after being pounded by the Casselman River.

Half of the buildings in town were reported to be under water up to the first floor, and much of the lower south side of the town was completely covered. All roads leading out of Salisbury were covered with from 1 to 4 feet of water. It was impossible to get from Salisbury to Meyersdale. The Meyersdale fairgrounds were completely covered. In Confluence, the floodwaters were rising an average of 2 feet an hour. The bridge over the Casselman Creek was swept away. The west side of town was isolated from the rest of the town. Water stood 3 to 4 feet deep in store basements. Schools closed early so children from outlying areas could get home. By 2:00 p.m., the road between Ursina and Confluence was under 3 feet of water. The river completely covered Rockwood, with water rushing over the bridges over the Casselman Creek.

Water Level Road from Somerset to Rockwood was impassable by early afternoon, covered with 3 to 4 feet of water in places. Barns owned by Chester Miller and Dr. George Speicher were swept from their foundations and carried downstream to the concrete bridge at the borough limits. The debris became entangled in the arches of the bridge and had to be burned by Rockwood firefighters to prevent water from backing up into the town. By 7:30 p.m. the stone foundation of the old red covered bridge spanning the Casselman River in Rockwood could no longer withstand the floodwaters, and it washed downstream. By that evening, the water level had decreased from 6 feet to 2 inches in the town.

All houses on the south side of Main Street were flooded up to the first floor level, while basements on the north side were filled within 3 or 4 inches of the first floor. The basement of the Miller Building, where the *Rockwood Leader* had its office, was flooded to sidewalk level, and only the publisher's records were saved. Snyder's Bakery suffered extensive damage. When the waters receded, they left behind mud 2 feet deep in the entire first floor. Large chunks of highway were torn up all through town. In Somerset, several businesses closed with several feet of water seeping into their buildings. At the town bridge, the water level reached several feet above the bottom of the bridge. The central part of Somerset, which is set higher than the rest, was not severely affected.

In Bakersville, the lowlands were submerged, but the highways were not covered to any great extent. Five-and-a-half-foot-high floodwaters ran through the main street of Hollsopple, flooding local businesses and residences. In Hooversville, Mrs. Marshall Cessna was washed downstream more than a mile after a boat capsized during an attempted rescue. Her body was found early the next morning. Her husband had also been thrown overboard and knocked unconscious, but he was rescued. More than 25 houses and garages were washed from their foundations.

In Windber, Paint Creek attained a height of 12 to 14 feet, the highest to that date. Melting snow on top of the mountain above Mine 42 contributed to the flow. Every property along Railroad Street and Graham Avenue from 18th to 14th Streets was affected. The worst damage was to residents of 16th Street, Veil Avenue, and the creek region below Graham Avenue bridge. Along 18th Street water reached the height of the first floor and drainage facilities were inadequate. Sewers backed up to 18th Street, and Graham Avenue was covered with 2 feet of water. One area along 16th Street disintegrated and sank about 2 feet from its intersection at Graham Avenue. Some 22 families suffered the loss of household goods, along with 32 families in Paint and Scalp Level Boroughs.

Similar effects were felt during one of Somerset County's earliest recorded floods—that of June 7, 1887. The village of Hollsopple was all but destroyed by a flood. After extremely heavy rains on the watershed of the Stonycreek River, water rose to a height of 16 feet. All buildings in the flood zone were damaged or destroyed. Bethel United Brethren Church was swept away, floating a mile downstream before disintegrating. Many bridges were destroyed at the headwaters of the Stonycreek. The town soon recovered from the effect of the flood as new buildings were constructed and new businesses moved to town. But as we have seen, floods were still uncontrollable.

As the floods proved, if there's one thing Somerset County is known for besides its mining and maple sugar, it's harsh weather. A memorable winter example was in 1944 when a snowstorm began December 11 and a week later the county was buried under some 34 inches of show. The heaviest came on December 12 with 19 inches.

On Sunday, November 26, 1950, Somerset residents opened their homes to about 500 motorists stranded in one of the "worst unseasonal storms" up to that time. The *Daily American* reported that the snow started falling around midnight Thanksgiving. By Saturday afternoon, all secondary roads were blown shut, and by Sunday, 20 inches of snow lay on the ground throughout the county. By Sunday, most of the travelers were able to leave, but by Wednesday the snow had reached 28 to 30 inches; 90 percent of the secondary roads remained closed; and snow drifts 12 to 15 feet high were reported near Husband, northwest of Somerset.

Because of a weekend snowstorm on January 30–31, 1966, more than 250 travelers stayed in the Somerset National Guard Armory, the home of Company C, 2nd Battalion, 103rd Armory, and the 28th Infantry Division. In 1970, January temperatures dropped as low as 22 degrees below zero. A record snowfall February 12–13 deposited 21 inches of snow and caused more than 23 turnpike accidents. On February 19, 1972, the county was socked with 37 inches of snow. Winds peaked at 50 miles per hour, causing high drifts. More than 250 motorists were stranded at the Somerset National Guard Armory and the First Christian Church when they encountered high drifts on all the major highways.

Travelers again had to seek refuge in the armory and churches when a snowstorm that paralyzed the county for over a week began in the early morning hours of

SOMERSET COUNTY

Sunday, December 1, 1974, with heavy, wet snow, high winds, and thunder and lightning. Thousands of travelers returning home from the Thanksgiving holiday weekend were caught by the snowfall, when highways, including the Pennsylvania Turnpike, closed. The Civil Defense Office estimated more than 1,200 people were staying at churches, the Somerset National Guard Armory, and the Somerset Borough building. In local motels, people jammed into hallways and lounges when the rooms were full. Some travelers stayed with area residents. The snow began in the early morning hours, and the Somerset area received about 10 inches of snow the first day. That climbed to anywhere between 18 and 30 inches in the Somerset area by Monday night. Electrical and telephone service in the county was completely disrupted by the wet snow, which quickly accumulated on trees and wires, causing a large amount of damage when the weight proved to be too much. At one point all of Somerset County was without electrical service for a five-hour period from about 3:00 a.m. on Tuesday.

An additional burden hit Jenners, where residents were without water. Without electrical power, the water company couldn't pump water from the treatment tanks into the storage tanks to the customers. On December 3, Somerset Borough was without water for several hours and some people were without heat, with temperatures in the teens. By Thursday, December 5, crews from other parts of Pennsylvania and New Jersey worked beside local crews to help restore power. On Friday, power was still completely out for Penelec customers in Confluence, New Lexington, Addison, Ursina, Kingwood, and Springs, plus scattered locations all over the county. The Rural Electric Cooperative (REC) and GTE telephone company had customers still without service.

Saturday, December 7, the American Red Cross set up a feeding station at the Confluence Community Center, serving two meals a day, and there was no electricity within a 15-mile radius of Confluence. Civil Defense said the National Guard had been activated to assist line crews in getting electrical service back to about 3,000 people in the county. Lieutenant Governor Ernest Kline declared the southwest portion of the state a disaster area. Penelec estimated costs of $2 million for restoration of service, while REC estimated $1.25 million. The American Red Cross spent about $10,000, mostly for food but some for blankets at shelters.

Respite lasted but for a few years. In January, February, and March 1977, bitterly cold Arctic air hung over most of the United States. Several times the temperature failed to rise above zero. On January 17, weather observers recorded 17 degrees below zero in the county. At the height of the freeze in January, Governor Milton Shapp closed all schools to cut down on fuel usage. The county also experienced heavy snows; snowdrifts reached 25 feet in some places.

Schools may close, but very little can stop the U.S. Postal Service. However, on January 21, 1985, for the first time in the history of the Somerset Post Office, mail wasn't delivered to homes because of the cold weather. The decision to cancel home delivery was made by the Johnstown management office for the 250 post offices in the area, which includes Somerset County, Johnstown, Indiana, Altoona, and State College.

Recently, after several relatively mild winters, Somerset County residents were reminded of how brutal winter can be. The winter of 1992–1993 had several snowstorms. From December 2–6, 12 inches of snow fell on the Somerset area. Then during a storm from Thursday, December 10, to Saturday, December 12, 1992, the county received 28 inches of snow, with 10 inches from Friday to Saturday, according to John Mayak, a National Weather Service observer in Somerset. Ogletown reported receiving 30 inches by Friday morning, declaring a snow emergency. The storm brought the most snow since the Sunday after Thanksgiving in 1974.

That storm was just a prelude to the so-called "Storm of the Century," which hit the entire northeastern part of the United States over the weekend of March 13 and 14, 1993. The state issued a winter emergency declaration. The storm dumped up to 36 inches of snow in Somerset County, while wind gusts created drifts of 6 to 8 feet high. No storm-related deaths, power outages, or accidents were reported, but the storm closed many roads, including the Pennsylvania Turnpike.

Then in 1994, for the second year in a row, Somerset County was hit with a March blizzard. But that was just icing on the cake for the winter of 1993–1994. The year 1994 began with heavy snowstorms and bitterly cold temperatures. By March 4, 1994, the area had experienced its 15th winter storm. A blizzard warning was in effect January 3–4 with wind gusts up to 35 miles per hour and wind chill factors of 20 to 30 degrees below zero. The storm left about 20 inches of snow on the ground. The Pennsylvania Turnpike was closed to all vehicles with trailers, and traffic was backlogged. On January 15, with temperatures reaching a high of near zero, the wind chills reached negative 50 degrees. Two days later, the county received a foot or more of new snow. The wind chills continued to register at 45 to 55 degrees below zero. On January 19, Governor Robert P. Casey declared a state of emergency as subzero temperatures shattered records throughout the state. That included 32 degrees below zero in Garrett.

Under the declaration, commercial businesses and industries were asked to voluntarily curtail operations, and residents were asked to turn back their thermostats and curtail all nonessential electrical usage to avoid a drain on power. Then on March 3, another storm dropped up to 17 inches of snow on the county. On March 10 the President, on the governor's recommendation, declared 28 counties as disaster areas from January 4 through February 25, making them eligible for disaster relief funds from the Federal Emergency Management Agency (FEMA), but Somerset County was not included. FEMA reversed its decision to exclude Somerset and others after the county filed an appeal, and a total of 44 of 67 counties became eligible. Many municipalities spent two times or more of the amounts budgeted for winter storm costs. The county's communities that participated in the appeal had total winter weather budgets of $623,941 but spent $923,584. The state estimated reimbursement for response to snow and ice storms in the state cost an estimated $80 million, making that winter period one of the top five disasters in the commonwealth.

The Blizzard of 1993, the five-day period in mid-March for which all 67 counties in the state were eligible for funds, cost $28 million.

Chapter Eight

WHEN COAL WAS NO LONGER KING

The editor of the *Windber Era* in 1903 wrote:

> . . . while coal mining is the chief end, it does not imply that when the coal is exhausted the town will decay. Much enterprise is displayed by our people and it will not be many years until Windber will be noted for its manufacturing enterprises as well as its coal mines. Statisticians figure that at the present rate of output of coal the Windber mines will hold out for at least 70 years. By that time manufacturing enterprises will be accordingly great. The present and rising generation has no cause to fear that Windber will decay.

A Windber master plan conducted by Michael Baker, Jr., Inc., consulting engineers from Rochester, Pennsylvania, in 1958 estimated the population of the borough would increase to 9,100 people by 1970. This conclusion was based upon the fact that there were younger people and fewer older people in 1958 because of the high birth rate in 1933 and 1938. It was also expected that the birth rate would be higher than normal for the next decade due to the high birth rate in 1946–1947.

However, the report qualified its estimate by pointing out there would "have to be provisions to supplement employment and diversifying business and industry; otherwise, there was the danger of losing the younger labor force by migration to other communities." Obviously, employment opportunities were not adequate and the 1970 population dropped to 6,332 people—a 21 percent decrease from 1950. The output of coal did not hold out for at least 70 years, as the *Windber Era* editor predicted. It was within 60 years of his writings that Berwind-White closed its last mine in Windber. Rock dumps, or bony piles, are mute evidence of the 65 years of coal mining in the area. This example of Windber is reflective of most areas in Somerset County.

SOMERSET COUNTY

Industrial development efforts in Somerset County, which started to gain momentum in 1951, failed to replace the jobs formerly provided by the mining industry. Some of the younger displaced miners found jobs in steel mills or other regional industries, but these jobs are scarce now. Large parts of the younger generation, with better education, left the area for employment elsewhere. The population of the county has continually dropped, with Somerset and Windber being the two largest boroughs in the area.

But the pride of ownership is very evident in the upkeep of private homes and small businesses, which number close to 300 in each of the towns. For example, Leone's Market, in the 1900 block of Graham Avenue, was opened in the early 1920s by Tony Leone, a native of the L'aquilia Province in Italy, the son of a school teacher and a local magistrate. He was joined in time by his three brothers—Frank, Alphonse, and Ottavio. "Ottavio means 'eighth child,' " explains Rhoda Clyre Leone, who continued the family business after the death of her husband Harry, Ottavio's son, in 1973. Leone's specializes in "very good cheeses," ravioli and shells, and gourmet cakes. "I am very proud to have married into the Leone family," Rhoda Leone says. She continues:

> In the old days we did fantastic business. People couldn't get Italian products anywhere, but we had them. We made our own cheese, drying 100 pounds at a time in a wire cage as big as a piano. When the mines were here, old Mr. Leone would open at 5 a.m. so customers could stop in before work. We also sold coal, kerosene and carbide for the miners' lamps.

Today Leone's continues to be one of the most popular Italian sub shops in the entire area, with people driving several hours for its specialties. The area's educational opportunities, health industry (such as the first rural Hospice Program in the state), and involvement in technology, especially defense contracts, have been the highlights of the larger industrial development. Recent trends also show that many natives and former residents are seeking homes in Windber for their retirement years. The natural beauty of the surroundings and attractive building sites provide the incentives to relocate here.

When Coal Was No Longer King

Meanwhile, tourism has become the latest hope for a revival of the region's economy. In 1988, Congressman John Murtha got Congress to appropriate millions of dollars to promote industrial heritage and tourism projects in a depressed nine-county region in central and southwestern Pennsylvania, which includes all of Somerset County. For example, with this money Windber built a new coal-mining museum and has plans to develop an interactive tour of the Mine 40 area.

One of the best success stories of the area, and one of the largest employers, is Seven Springs Mountain Resort in Somerset County. The story of Seven Springs dates back to the early 1930s when Adolph Dupre, who arrived in the United States several years earlier after leaving his native Bavaria, worked as a groundskeeper on a Pittsburgh businessman's estate in Ligonier, Pennsylvania. Adolph and his new bride, Helen, in 1932 purchased 2.5 acres of land at a tax sale for $13, which was their entire savings. Recognizing that his newly purchased land was similar to his "old country" origin, Adolph rebuilt an aging farmhouse and dubbed it the Bavarian Cabin. What followed were years of hard work by Adolph, Helen, and their growing family of three children: sons Philip and Herman and daughter Luitgarde.

In the next 20 years, he built 28 cabins with the native stone and wood, all in plentiful supply on Seven Springs' land. He designed these cabins himself with unique beauty and style. Many of them are still in use today. His years as groundskeeper in Ligonier convinced him that business people from the Pittsburgh area yearned to relax, hunt, and fish in a beautiful, natural environment. So Adolph would rent the cabins, either by season or by the year. As the stream of visitors to Seven Springs grew, Adolph built the Tyrol House, a combination clubhouse and dining hall, complete with guest rooms. The Tyrol House became the center of social activity on Seven Springs Farm.

Through all of this, Helen Dupre had a desire of her own—a desire to ski. "I always wanted to ski, and when I saw the land where we built our first home, I wanted it to be my ski area," she said. Added to Helen's desire to ski was the fact that Seven Springs was a natural snow bowl, blanketing the hills from early December through March. "Early on, " Helen said, "we realized we couldn't move all the snow we got, so we decided to take advantage of it." Helen convinced Adolph to build a mechanical rope tow, powered by an old Packard automobile engine that was held stationary on wooden blocks. It was the first rope tow outside of Vermont, and by 1935, winter enthusiasts with wooden plank skis and leather bindings traversed the Seven Springs slopes. The popularity of skiing at Seven Springs Farm grew like wildfire.

In 1937, the Dupres opened Seven Springs Farm to the public with runs such as Suicide Hill, Nose Dive, and Hell's Highway. The ski slopes boasted three lifts and even had lights for night skiing. By 1948, the Seven Springs Farm had grown to almost 5,500 acres and, while skiing still attracted the largest number of visitors, summertime activity also grew. More and more, the rustic atmosphere of Seven Springs Farm began to take on the appearance of a resort, and the entire Dupre family worked daily to fulfill the recreational needs of their guests.

The year 1960 saw new guest rooms being built to accommodate more and more skiers. Trophies for special skiing events were awarded by the resort, and such events as giant slalom races began to be regular features in the winter. Between 1960 and 1990, Seven Springs enjoyed phenomenal growth. Seven Springs Mountain Resort replaced Seven Springs Farm. The first section of what is now the resort's Main Lodge, with a formal dining area, 37 sleeping rooms, and a new indoor swimming pool, was completed in 1965. Seventy-three new guest rooms were added to the Main Lodge in 1967 and the Seven Springs 18-hole golf course was finished in 1969. The Convention Hall was built in 1972 and continues to provide meeting attendees with the most up-to-date facilities available. In 1974, the 331-room high-rise hotel and new hotel lobby were opened. Throughout the 1970s and 1980s, many improvements and additions to the resort were completed. Then in September 1987 came the groundbreaking for 800 condominiums and town homes.

Another tourism success story is Indian Lake, the youngest community in Stonycreek Township, which was originated after the incorporation of Allegheny Mountain Lakes Inc. in the summer of 1960. Aerial photographs helped prove the feasibility of a man-made lake covering 750 acres of approximately 20 miles of mostly wooded shoreline and over 2,000 acres of bordering land for residential housing and sports facilities. The development was based upon the concept of rustic resort living either as permanent residents, or for vacation type "second" homes—and it worked.

Construction of the lake began in the spring of 1962 and its completion in May 1963 signaled the active development and building of the present 400 homes in Indian Lake. A water system and road lacing through the entire area were substantially complete about the same time. New residences are still going up today at a slower but steady rate. It is expected to continue by the number of lot acquisitions regularly recorded at the Somerset County Courthouse. Indian Lake boasts its own privately owned air park with two lighted, paved runways, the longer being 5,000 feet in length. A flight school and a fuel and maintenance service center are operated there. It is the only airfield known to be enclosed by the back nine of a championship 18-hole golf course. Two marinas operate on Indian Lake shores to service and fuel the several hundred motor boats that ply its water from May to November each year. Water skiing and fishing attract hundreds of devotees come summer. A ski slope has been constructed descending to the very edge of the south shore of the lake.

Even though over 200 years has passed since the founding of Somerset County, many historic buildings and traces of the past remain in the area. Harmon Husband's farm, called Coffee Springs Farm, is just east of Somerset along Route 31. The very first school in Somerset County was probably located on the farm of Harmon Husband in 1777. James Kennedy was the first schoolmaster. Kennedy was an indentured servant of Husband's and was given the position of schoolmaster after he was dismissed from serving in the Husband household. Kennedy, an Irish Catholic, had run away from home in Ireland and sold himself as an indentured servant to pay passage to America. It is believed that Kennedy served two months as schoolmaster and was then released from the position when it was found out that he was illiterate. Husband's farm building now houses a business. The farm got its name from the chicory found growing wild around the springs.

The present Somerset County Courthouse was erected in 1904. The earliest court in the county was held on December 21, 1795, in a room at the Webster Tavern in Somerset. The first courthouse was built in 1798 and completed in 1801. Construction of the second building, a two-story brick structure, was started in 1851 and finished one year later. It was used until 1904. The present building, considered architecturally significant, was built between 1904 and 1906 and was named to the National Register of Historic Places in 1980.

The present courthouse was built by the firm of Caldwell and Drake of Columbus, Ohio, for $247,440. The basement of the courthouse is made of native sandstone, and the superstructure of the building is constructed of large blocks of Indiana limestone, which were raised, shaped, and marked in the quarries at Bedford, Indiana, before they were transported to Somerset and fitted into place without any further hammering or dressing. The interior of the courthouse is finished in marble paneling. Soon after the completion of the courthouse, funds were raised by popular subscription to defray the expense of placing the clock on the dome of the new edifice. For many years, the clock was operated by heavy weights that dropped from the clock to the basement and were rewound each week by a hand-operated switch. In April 1941, the operation of the clock was changed to short-run weights automatically rewound by electric motors. In the spring of 1952, by public demand and authority of the grand jury, the commissioners installed a spotlight system for the night illumination of the courthouse dome.

Jeremiah Sullivan Black (1810–1883) was born near Brotherton. A marker stands just east of the town along Route 31 near the Brotherton Pike Cemetery. Black served as chief justice of the Pennsylvania Supreme Court and under President James Buchanan as U.S. attorney general and secretary of state. There is a historic marker at the site where Frederich Goeb, the printer of the first bible west of the Allegheny Mountains, built a log cabin at 151 W. Main Street in Somerset.

Five principal Indian trails criss-crossed the county. The Raystown Path ran completely across the county, bisecting it in half, taking much the same direction as present-day Route 30. The Conemaugh Path cut across the northeastern corner from Pleasantville in Bedford to Ogletown and Windber and through to Johnstown. The Fort Hill Path ran from Salisbury to Fort Hill through still-wild country over Negro Mountain. The Turkeyfoot Path entered the southeastern corner of the county near Pocahontas, running by Engles Mill in Salisbury, south of the highest peak of Mount Davis and north of Listonburg to Harnedsville. Nemacolin's Trail cut across the southwest corner near Addison.

The Lumber Railroad Tunnel dates back to 1883 when Andrew Carnegie and William H. Vanderbilt planned the South Pennsylvania Railroad through Somerset County to break the Pennsylvania Railroad's strangle-hold on Pittsburgh freight rates. But when Carnegie went to Europe, Vanderbuilt sold the railroad to the opposition and it was only half-built. Later, six of the nine tunnels that had been constructed for the railroad were used by the Pennsylvania Turnpike, including one through Laurel Hill about 3 miles west of Somerset. That tunnel is the only one ever used by a railroad, the Pittsburgh, Westmoreland, & Somerset, principally a lumber line developed by Andrew and Richard B. Mellon in 1906. Also along the turnpike is Tunnel Spring, a popular spot for refreshment from the time the turnpike was opened until a second tunnel was cut at the east end of Allegheny Tunnel. The spring sends a flow of water down a concrete trough about 100 feet farther down the mountain, emptying into a drain under the road. It is at the eastern portal of Allegheny Tunnel on the turnpike. The water is visible from the south side of the road.

The Somerset Historical Center, located 4 miles north of Somerset along Route 985, was started in the late 1960s with the state's purchase of 16 acres of property from the late Dr. and Mrs. Earl O. Haupt to start a historical society. Included was a log cabin built in 1804 in Brothersvalley Township, which had been purchased by the Haupts to be used in the 1954 sesquicentennial celebration. The center also displays a bridge used in the 1850s at Walters Mill, a maple sugar camp of 1840, and a lean-to barn.

Also in Somerset is the Zimmerman Mansion at the top of a hill along Route 601 north of Somerset. The brick Georgian Revival style mansion is open as a bed and breakfast. It was built from 1915 to 1918 by Daniel B. Zimmerman, a coal and cattle baron. Beam's Reformed Church, made of brick, was built in 1847, and now is called Mount Laurel United Church of Christ. The Beam flax and gristmill was at one time located nearby. The church is located a mile from Gray at the junction of legislative routes 55072 and 55107, south of Jennerstown. Also in Jennerstown area is the Rauch House, built in 1806 and now an antique shop. Located along Route 30 in the borough, the brick residence was the home of Squire Henry Rauch, who conducted a hearing there on charges against the Nicely brothers, who were charged and hanged for killing Herman Umberger in February 1889.

The Kline Gristmill, located at the base of Laurel Hill on Forbes Road near Sequanota Centre west of Jennerstown, was built in 1801, and operated by Joseph Kline from 1896 to 1930, along with a blacksmith shop. It is privately owned. Also at Jennerstown is the historic Mountain Playhouse and Green Gables Restaurant, built in 1927 by the Stoughton family on the old homestead owned by their family since 1795. The Cronin-Grover log gristmill was purchased in 1938 and moved to the Jennerstown property to become the playhouse. The gristmill dates back to 1805 and was in use until 1918. The playhouse is open from May to October and the restaurant is open daily. The playhouse also includes the Jenner Art Gallery.

SOMERSET COUNTY

The Johns House is just outside Davidsville (along East Campus Avenue). It is the last home of Joseph Schantz (Johns), a Swiss Mennonite who came to America in 1769 at the age of 20. He moved in 1806 to this site. Behind the house is the Johns family cemetery, enclosed by a picket fence. Johns was the founder of Johnstown. Also in Davidsville is the Lohr barn, which has Pennsylvania Dutch round louvers decorated with cut-out hearts and stars on both sides, and is similar to the barns of the early German settlers in this area. It was built about 1875 and sits along West Campus Avenue near the high school.

The Turkeyfoot Regular Baptist Church is the oldest of its sect in the county. It was also known as the Jersey Baptist Church, since a group of Baptist settlers from New Jersey organized it on June 14, 1775. The first house of worship was built in 1788, the second in 1838, and the present structure in 1877. It is on two-mile legislative route 55021 from the junction with Route 281 in Ursina (on Jersey Road to Ohiopyle). The Great Crossings Bridge, now under the Youghiogheny Dam, spanned the river at Somerfield near Confluence. It was built in 1818 and dedicated by President James Monroe. The structure is 375 feet long and has three stone arches, which can be seen during the dry season when the water is low. This is the point where George Washington crossed the Youghiogheny River on November 18, 1753, as discussed earlier.

The National Road Tollhouse in Addison, a two-story, seven-sided structure joined to a one-story wing, has a historical marker listing the significance of the Great Crossings Bridge. The only other existing tollhouse is Searights in Fayette County. The National Road Tollhouse is operated by Great Crossings Chapter of the Daughters of the American Revolution. Also in the Addison area is a marker for Braddock Road along Route 40, as well as the National Road, located southeast of Addison.

Mount Davis, the highest point in the state at 3,213 feet with Negro Mountain at its base, is marked by a column of rocks with a brass plate. In general, high elevations are consistent throughout the state. Compton's Grain Mill was operated by Samuel Compton in 1872 as a flour mill. It is near St. Paul's, about 2 miles on Route 55047, half way between St. Paul's and Route 669 to Springs. Also in Salisbury is the 1795 House, easily recognized for the construction date, which is written in bold letters across one gabled end of the house. Across the street is the Keagey House, built in 1815 by John Keagey.

When Coal Was No Longer King

Springs Museum houses collections of thousands of items depicting early life in the Casselman Valley. Founded in 1957 and established on an abandoned poultry farm in 1964, the Springs Historical Society operates the museum. The community of Springs was settled between 1760 and 1775 and is the state's highest unincorporated village. It is at the foot of Negro Mountain at Mount Davis. The museum is in Springs, halfway between Salisbury and Grantsville, Maryland.

In Meyersdale, Maple Manor is the oldest house in the borough, built about 1785. It serves as headquarters for Festival Park and has a cobbler's shop, doctor's office, country store, and collection of antiques. Built as a log cabin, two or three additions have resulted in the present structure. Pius Spring, located along Main Street in Berlin, is the landmark on a tract of land laid out by the Lutheran and Reformed congregations of Brothersvalley Township. In 1784, the members established the town with the stipulation that residents built their homes with frontages of at least 22 feet and with stone chimneys so there would be no danger of fire. The town's largest industry until the Civil War was the manufacture of hats for southern markets. In Berlin, the Trinity Reformed Church, now the United Church of Christ, was built in 1883.

In New Baltimore, located east of Berlin, St. John the Baptist Catholic Church, served by the Carmelite Monastery of the Franciscan Order of Monks, was organized in 1824, and the present building was dedicated in 1890. The church sits high on a hill overlooking the village and can be seen from the turnpike. The monastery now is closed. Worshipers can park along the turnpike and walk to the church. The Stoystown Lions Club operates a historical park at the intersections of Route 30 and 281, with an old schoolhouse and covered bridge on the property.

The Windber Museum is located in what was the Shaffer residence, built in 1869. Its photos and displays offer a nostalgic look back at the mining town once operated by Berwind-White Coal Mining Co. The former company store, Eureka Store, is at 15th Street and Somerset Avenue. The ten remaining covered bridges in Somerset County are listed on the National Register of Historic Places. Seven of them are owned and maintained by Somerset County and six are open for light automobile traffic.

Shaffer Covered Bridge was built in 1879 to connect the road leading to the Somerset and Johnstown Pike across Benscreek. It is owned and maintained by

141

Somerset County and is open to light traffic. It is in Conemaugh Township, off Route 985 near the village of Benscreek. Trostletown Covered Bridge was built in 1873 over Stonycreek River near Daniel Trostle's Mill. It is open to foot traffic only. Barronvale Covered Bridge spans Laurel Hill Creek near Laurel Hill State Park along Route 653. Another bridge built around 1845 is nearby King's Covered Bridge along Route 281. Lower Humbert Covered Bridge is located close to Jersey Church, following Route 281. Bollman Bridge–Wills Creek Railroad Bridge is located from Meyersdale viaduct south along Route 219. It was moved from its original location on the railroad crossing Wills Creek around 1910. It carries vehicular traffic. Burkholder Covered Bridge is located west of Main Street in Berlin traveling south on Route 219, then right on Burkholder Bridge Road. It was built in 1873 to span Buffalo Creek on the road leading to the Berkleys Mills in Summit Township. It is open to light traffic. New Baltimore Covered Bridge is located on Town Hall Road in New Baltimore. It was built in 1878 to carry the public road from New Baltimore over the Raystown branch of the Juniata Creek to the Stonycreek area. Glessner Covered Bridge is located near Shanksville by following Route 160 on Covered Bridge Road. Packsaddle Covered Bridge is built over Brush Creek and is located along Route 31 east of Brotherton.

The people of Somerset County also celebrate the coming of spring, the harvest from summer, and the history of culture of the area each year with a variety of events. Some of the biggest, drawing visitors from within as well as outside the county, are the Pennsylvania Maple Festival, Somerfest, the Somerset County Fair, Mountain Craft Days, Farmers' and Thresherman's Jubilee, and now the Whiskey Rebellion. The Maple Festival was organized in 1947 after the Myersdale Chamber of Commerce sent national radio star Kate Smith a gallon of pure syrup. Members of the community felt Meyersdale needed something to boost its economic climate and also needed a program to conserve the vanishing maple trees, whose lumber was bringing top prices. On April 17, 1947, Smith said she hoped she could come to Meyersdale some time to see the syrup being made. The Chamber of Commerce then decided to buy 200 gallons of syrup with $1,000 provided by Joe F. Reich, a local businessman, and sent the syrup to people from a dozen states. The first festival was held on a budget of $67 and Pennsylvania Lieutenant Governor Daniel B. Strickler proclaimed Meyersdale the capital of "Mapledon."

The first Somerset County Fair, a three-day event, was held at Berlin in 1808. The first Agricultural Society was founded in 1828. The Somerset County Fair is held each year at the Meyersdale Fairgrounds at the end of August, and the Somerset Historical Center, north of Somerset along Route 601, presents Mountain Craft Days the weekend after Labor Day. The purpose is to preserve and interpret the life, times, and culture of Pennsylvania's Laurel Highlands region. Mountain Craft Days is held in a wooded setting, which shows off the variety of displays—pottery, broom-making, gunsmithing, butter churning, drying apples and corn, shingle making, leather working, and hickory furniture making.

For more than 40 years, the Farmers' and Threshermen's Jubilee has educated visitors on the life and times of farmers and theshermen. Demonstrations include a steam-powered cider mill, a ground hog thresher, flailers, horse power with tumbling shaft machines, tread power threshing, self feeder threshing, and bailing straw.

The 100th anniversary of the Whiskey Rebellion was celebrated in Berlin in 1994. The historic event created interest from all over the county and members of the Whiskey Rebellion Committee decided to make it an annual affair.

Chapter Nine

THE NATION LOOKS TO "AMERICA'S COUNTY"

The year 2002 brought major challenges to the people of Somerset County—challenges that showed the character of the people living in this area to the world.

The tranquility of Shanksville, Pennsylvania was shattered on September 11, 2001, when United Airlines Flight 93 crashed in the community. In the days before September 11, the narrow road passing Roxanne Sullivan's Shanksville-area home carried only a handful of cars per day. But now, from dawn to dusk, campers and vans compete with hulking buses and overloaded cars for space on Skyline Road, a main route to the United Flight 93 temporary memorial. "We've been bombarded," Sullivan said, pointing across her wide, sloping yard to the roadway above. "You can't even go to the mailbox without someone asking for directions." But at the same time, Sullivan feels drawn to the crash site and volunteers there every week, answering questions from hundreds of visitors. She talks passionately about building a place in history for Flight 93 and watching over its legacy. "It's a need in me to take care of this," Sullivan said. "I feel that this is what I need to do at this point in my life."

Not everyone who lives on Shanksville's 128 acres or in the wide expanses of surrounding countryside has chosen to volunteer or keep a thick September 11 scrapbook, as Sullivan does. But nearly everyone talks about the same conflicting feelings of frustration, devotion, doubt, and pride. The changes here since September 11 are complex and, in some ways, still unclear even though more than two years have passed since the violent crash of a jetliner carrying 44 people. Most residents have continued to live quietly and serve selflessly despite deep and lingering concerns about where their hometown may be headed. "I don't think we can say for sure," said the Reverend Sylvia Baker, pastor of Shanksville Assembly of God. "We're still caught up in the events of the world."

The world has, for the most part, looked on Shanksville with more than a little curiosity. National reporters and politicians have marveled at a tiny town with one store and no traffic lights, a place where people often welcome visitors into their homes with a smile. But this is no idyllic Norman Rockwell portrait, and that feeling of security and relative isolation was heavily damaged, if not shattered, when Flight 93 fell from the sky on a sunny morning.

A steady parade of strangers arriving since then has served only to further unnerve some locals. "We need to lock our doors and lock our cars, and that's new," Baker said in an interview at her Main Street home just across from Ida's Country Store. "We are feeling more vulnerable to the world than we did before." With 40 innocent people killed in a field just off Lambertsville Road, and with more than 90 percent of their remains deemed unrecoverable, there can no longer be a sense of distance from the world's problems. "Terrorism was something we used to read about in the newspaper— read the headlines and move on," Bridge Street resident Kim Friedline said.

There have been few normal days in Shanksville since September 11, so the heavily promoted notion that things simply should get back to normal rings hollow. The physical changes, too, have been startling. For two weeks in 2002, rural Stonycreek Township hosted a federal crime scene still marked by a long fence that encircles the crash site. While much plane debris has been collected and federal agents are long gone, an increasing number of pilgrims—sometimes thousands each week, rain or shine—are visiting the temporary memorial site.

On any given day, license plates from around the country can be seen at the temporary memorial's two small parking lots. As one car leaves, another appears on the horizon. Instead of recoiling from the clamor, though, some Shanksville-area residents set up a volunteer "ambassador" program. They each spend hours at the site, making presentations and trying to answer inquiries that can be simply factual or morbidly curious. "It's our duty to care," Sullivan said. It is that role that has allowed many to say Shanksville, far from losing its identity, has in fact found itself in the aftermath of the disaster. It is apparent in the bonds local residents have forged with those who lost loved ones on Flight 93. "If there's a good part of this at all, it's just connecting with the people in Shanksville," said Carole O'Hare of Danville, California, whose mother, Hilder Marcin, died on Flight 93. "They took us under their wing like we were part of their family."

The Nation Looks to "America's County"

In Friedline's yard in Shanksville, there's a flowering pear tree planted by Mary White of Port St. Lucie, Florida, who lost her daughter, Honor Elizabeth Wainio, on Flight 93. White has visited Friedline twice and plans to return. Residents say they feel a new pride in their community, a sense of appreciation that has helped place a flagpole on every street corner and gifts of thanks in the hands of emergency workers. Some objected strongly to what they felt were negative or overly simplistic portrayals of Shanksville as some sort of backward, backwoods community. And some others are not without entrepreneurial spirit—there are at least four spots near the crash site where visitors can pick up Flight 93 memorabilia. Reverend Alphonse Mascherino turned his tiny, empty church into a Flight 93 Memorial Chapel, drawing visitors from around the country, as well as donated material and labor worth at least $150,000 for the nondenominational place of worship. A visitor's center and a "memorial depository and library" also are in the works, but it is not yet clear when those plans may become reality.

Just ten months after September 11 and the enormous attention brought to Shanksville and Somerset County, another trauma occurred. Shortly after 1:30 a.m. on Thursday, July 25, 2002, a dairy farmer in Somerset County named Bill Arnold and his wife, Lori, were startled from sleep by the insistent yelping of their dog, Pitch, who had fixed on some commotion outside. Arnold stepped to the bedroom window and looked out into the dark. In the distance, he saw two pickup trucks parked at the edge of his property and nearby, men with flashlights. Arnold quickly dressed, grabbed a .45 automatic he kept in the house, and hurried outside. One of the men, spotting the gun in his hand, shouted, "Don't shoot, Billy!" Arnold recognized the man as Sean Isgan, a local engineer who had done survey work around the Arnold farm. Randy Musser, also an engineer and a competitor of Isgan's, was with him. Both men seemed agitated.

Isgan explained that there had been an accident at the Quecreek coal mine, just up the state road—a sudden, terrible flood. "Nine guys are missing." If the missing miners were alive, they were trapped somewhere underground. Their last known location was a spot in the far corner of the mine, more than a mile from the entrance, which would put them 240 feet beneath the Arnold farm. Drilling was the only way to reach them, and that was what had brought the two engineers to the Arnolds' lower pasture—each man was running a survey to pinpoint the drilling target. They explained the drilling might disturb some of the Arnolds' property. "Take down my house, if you have to," Arnold answered. Using his cell phone, he called his wife, who was watching from the kitchen with their daughter, Roann. "I can remember standing at the window and grabbing Roann's hand and saying, 'We've got to pray,' " Lori Arnold recalled. "I remember praying for God's mercy. And making coffee. I knew it would be a long night."

Arnold climbed into his backhoe and leveled a spot in the lower pasture where the drillers could set up. By 3:15 a.m., the first rig was drilling through the topsoil and into the rock below. The drill bit was a relatively small one, 6-and-a-half inches in diameter, but it was capable of quick work, and time was everything. The rescuers' first priority was to establish communication with the trapped men, by lowering a camera or a microphone down through the hole and into the mine.

By dawn, the Arnold's 6-acre lower pasture had become a crowded, frantic emergency scene. Scores of rescue workers commanded a vast tonnage of great machines—drill rigs and excavators, compressors and cranes—that continued to arrive through the day. As miners at other mines came off their shifts, they went to the Arnold's farm and to Quecreek to join the effort, hopeful, but with a certain measure of dread. Mine disasters rarely end happily, and at Quecreek the odds strongly indicated a dire outcome. Just in Western Pennsylvania within 2002, three coal miners had been killed on the job.

The missing miners had apparently breached a wall into an adjacent mine, long abandoned, loosing an inundation of water that quickly filled their own mine to the point of overflow and beyond. So much water poured in from the breach—tens of million of gallons—that it came spilling out the mine's entrance, and it kept coming. When a coal-company employee at the rescue scene that first night asked Randy Musser for a professional assessment of the miners' chances, Musser was grimly candid. "From an engineering viewpoint, I'd have to say that none of them are alive," Musser said. "If any of them are alive, it's a miracle." Trapped 24 stories below ground, the nine miners were already running short on air.

And that is how the world came to know the miners of the small town of Quecreek in Somerset County—as the "Miracle Nine." They were a veteran crew working the "One Left" section of the new mine. The youngest miner was 31-year-old Harry Blaine Mayhugh Jr. (Stinky to his co-workers, Blaine to his family), a former high-school football player who had gone into the mines five years earlier after serving in the navy. The oldest was Mayhugh's father-in-law, Thomas Foy, a 52-year-old grandfather, who had 29 years in the mines. All of the men could perform any of the tasks, but operating the continuous-mining machine was a bit of an art, and some were better at it than others. When the shift began, the man running the machine was John (Flathead) Phillippi, 36, who was the son of a coal miner. He backed out of the No. 1 entry and moved the mining machine all the way across the section to the No. 7 entry, where he took out 20 feet. After a few more cuts, Phillippi yielded the continuous miner to another crew member, Mark Popernack, for the remainder of the shift.

At 41, Popernack had spent 21 years in the mines—more than half his life. Squatting now, with the remote-control box strapped around his neck, he worked the big machine into the coal face in the No. 6 entry. His mind captured an image from that moment which he later replayed, in some amazement. Quecreek had wet places all over, but the floor and the wall in the space that Popernack had just cut in the No. 6 entry were dry. An instant later, the deluge came. The wall of coal in front of Popernack burst open, and water came rushing through. "It was an instant flood—two seconds, one second, an instant flood," Popernack said later.

It was immediately clear that this wasn't the usual mine rain, or anything like it. This was something fierce, a torrent that lifted the huge mining machine and washed it aside. The water was orange, colored by the sulfur and iron. Somehow, the crew had cut too close to the Saxman mine, shearing what was supposed to have been a 300-foot-thick wall so thin that the weight of the Saxman water (nearly 100 million gallons, by some reckonings) simply pushed through it. Now it was up to a group of people above ground to imagine a way to get the nine miners out.

The first big decision to be made that night was where to drill. That meant guessing where the miners were. By midnight, water was approaching the entrance of the mine, which meant that the mains were already filled. If the miners were dead, their bodies could be anywhere in the mine, and would not likely be recovered until the water was pumped out days or even weeks later. If some or all of them were alive, where would they be? The owners decided there was only one possibility—up in the far reaches of "One Left," at or near the very spot where they had broken through into the Saxman mine.

The crew boss, Randy Fogle, assured them that a serious rescue operation was probably underway, and he promised them that they would all be rescued, somehow. They heard drilling and hoped it meant that help was on the way. In the meantime, Fogle told them that they needed to start building barricades, constructing walls with the cinder blocks that were in plentiful supply around them. It seemed unlikely that cinder blocks could hold back a rising flood—the miners who had escaped from the mains already knew that it couldn't—but building the barricades gave the men something to focus on besides their despair.

Then, just after 5 a.m., the roof of the mine opened above their heads, and the 6-inch steel drill burst through, almost hitting John Unger. The drill created a terrific noise and something more welcome—a fierce whirl of fresh air, forced down the cylindrical steel casing by the drill's air compressor. The miners suddenly felt that they could breathe again. The miners now say that they feel this "air hole" was one of the most important parts of the 77-hour rescue—it managed to stop them from throwing up due to lack of oxygen.

There is a protocol for trapped miners trying to communicate with people on the outside—they must bang on the roof three times, and then once for each miner who is alive. The Quecreek miners had been banging on the roof all night, to no avail. Now Foy stood at the drill steel and hit it with his hammer three times and then nine times to indicate that they were all alive. The miners repeated that routine several times, and heard a response from above. Then they saw the water. It was still rising. If anything, it seemed to be approaching faster than before. The men were now very cold and were constantly shaking.

On the surface, the rescuers weren't sure what they were hearing. Somebody thought he heard five bangs on the drill and then two more. Joe Gallo thought that meant that five were alive, two were missing, and two were dead. Others were certain that they heard nine distinct taps. In any case, they knew that someone was alive.

By now, the plight of the trapped miners had become a huge news event; reporters from around the world were arriving in Somerset and clamoring for information. The air-bubble theory was a compelling angle, and, the more rescue officials talked about it (and the number of officials at the scene was also swelling by the hour), the more convinced they seemed. "This is the way we've got to go," Joe Sbaffoni said. "We've created an air pocket that is providing them a safe haven." John Urosek told a reporter, "If it wasn't for that air pocket, they would have drowned."

By midday on Thursday, the water had seeped out of the mine and was beginning to fill the huge pit, 100 feet wide and 300 feet long, at the mine's entrance. The water inching up the sides of the pit was a direct measure of the trapped miners' mounting peril. The elevation at the mine entrance was 1,836 feet, several feet higher than the spot in One Left, at the intersection beneath the drill hole, where the miners had last been heard from. That morning, the water had risen more than 3 feet from the floor of the pit. That meant that if the miners were still in their last known location they would already be underwater. The water was rising at a rate of more than a foot an hour. The frazzled, dispirited group at the command center hoped that the miners would somehow get to higher ground, although no one knew whether high ground existed or where it might be.

By Saturday afternoon, as the ordeal neared the end of its third full day, the mines were being de-watered and the big drill had been allowed to inch to within 20 feet of the roof of the mine. Finally, at 10 p.m. Saturday, it was declared that it was safe to bore through the mine. If the calculations were right, the atmosphere inside the mine would be normal, and there would be no sudden decompression when the drill broke through. Still, elaborate precautions were taken. The special air lock was readied to be placed over the drill steel, and a pressure gauge was rigged alongside the bore hole so that the pressure in the mine could be measured quickly. The rescue team had practiced all afternoon, getting in and out of the yellow capsule.

Finally, the go-ahead signal was given, and John Hamilton bored through the last few feet of rock. He was nervous, but the final cut was quick and clean. There was a familiar sensation when the drill hit the mine void and then went into a 4-foot free fall to the mine floor. Hamilton had been told to keep drilling into the floor, to create a cradle for the capsule.

Down below, the miners had long since forsaken their contemplation of death for more temporal imperatives; they were wet, cold, and hungry. They had somehow found Denny Hall's lunch pail floating in the water and, opening it, had been surprised to find the corned-beef sandwich his wife had made neatly wrapped and still quite dry. They shared the sandwich and a Pepsi that was in the pail, and, on a scavenger hunt through the mine, they found a couple of cans of Mountain

Dew. The most severe pangs they endured, perhaps, were those of the nicotine addict suffering withdrawal—they'd gone through all their snuff. As the water receded, they had been taking turns going back to the 6-inch pipe, and they heard the big drill coming through (and had wondered, during the 18-and-a-half-hour hiatus, whether the rescuers had given up). On one such reconnaissance mission, Foy and Hileman looked at the mine roof and saw the big hole that John Hamilton had just made. "We got a hole!" Hileman shouted to the others. "Everybody get down here!"

Once the rescuers were assured that the mine was decompressed, the 6-inch drill steel was withdrawn from its hole, and they prepared to make contact with the miners. The world underground has its own landscape, and there is no particular reason for a miner to associate his location in the mine with specific features of the surface above. When the rescued miners reached the surface and saw the open sky, for the first time in 72 hours, they had no idea where they were. Even if they had known that they had reached a corner of the Arnold's farm, just up the state highway from Casebeer Lutheran Church—a place they had all passed a hundred times—they wouldn't have recognized the scene. Besides a cheering crowd of hardhat rescue workers, politicians, and military personnel, the site was crowded with machines—cranes, bulldozers, drill rigs, air compressors, decompression chambers, ambulances, police cars, and two Chinook helicopters. The miners blinked in the glare of the floodlights and nodded numbly in response to questions from medical workers, who stripped them nearly naked and quick-washed them.

That was just the beginning of their disorientation. News coverage did not end with the recovery and continues today. The Windber Coal Heritage Museum beat out the Smithsonian Museum for the honor of having the rescue capsule on display, Disney made a television movie about the event and the miners released a book called *Our Story*. Today nine trees are planted in a circle on the site of the rescue and regular prayer meetings and events are held there. One year after the event, state investigators and the Department of Environmental Protection released a final report on the disaster blaming faulty maps and a lax reading of state laws. Some of the miners continue to pursue legal action against the mine operator Black Wolf Coal Co. Some also continue to have medical and emotional problems associated with the tragedy and one of the men involved with the engineering side of the rescue committed suicide, apparently in relation to the pressure caused by the event. Overall, Somerset County and the nation continue to remember the hope and positive feeling generated by the rescue—even hosting major musicians and personalities in the area.

Both the Quecreek and Flight 93 sites have plans for major memorials and traveling exhibits to commemorate the events and the people who helped with them. Both events were challenges to Somerset County—an area that has long been challenged—yet the pride and character of the area shined through to the nation, taking the positive out of each event. In summer 2003, Somerset County officials registered the name "America's County" for the rural region as a tribute to locals who rose to the occasion during trying times—a tribute to their values. The people of Somerset County are truly proud of their past and present.

BIBLIOGRAPHY

PRIMARY SOURCES

ARCHIVAL MATERIALS

The Historical Society of Western Pennsylvania's Library and Archives
Indiana University of Pennsylvania, Special Collections & Archives, "Coal Dust" and
   "Windber Miners" Collections
Windber Coal Heritage Center's Archive

ORAL INTERVIEWS

Millie Beik, Atlanta, GA
Mr. & Mrs. Danel, St. Michael, PA
Dr. James Dougherty, Indiana, PA
Ed Kozdron, Mine 40, PA
Gatch Gahagan, Windber, PA
Mary Hostetler, Friedens, PA
Dwight Hostetler, Friedens, PA
Rhoda Leone, Windber, PA
Dr. Irwin Marcus, Indiana, PA
Mr. & Mrs. Ohler, Windber, PA

SECONDARY SOURCES

BOOKS AND ARTICLES

Alcamo, Frank Paul. *The Windber Story: A 20th Century Model Pennsylvania Coal Town.*
   Windber: Baylor Memorial Charitable Trust, 1983.
Beik, Mildred Allen. *The Miners of Windber: The Struggles of New Immigrants for
   Unionization.* University Park: The Pennsylvania State University Press, 1998.

Berlin Borough. Berlin, PA: Pius Spring Publications, 1980.

Chew, Paul A. *George Hetzel and the Scalp Level Tradition*. Greensburg: Westmoreland Museum of Art, 1994.

Coleman, Jeanne M. and Kenneth Davis. *Images of Our Past*. Somerset: Historical Society of Somerset County, 1880.

The Daily American. Somerset County, Pictorial History. Marceline, MO: Vintage Publications, 1999.

Doyle, Fred C. *50th Anniversary*. Windber: Windber Anniversary Committee, 1947.

Gorn, Elliott J. *Mother Jones: The Most Dangerous Woman in America*. New York: Hill and Wang, 2001.

The Historical and Genealogical Society of Somerset County. *'Mongst the Hills of Somerset*. Somerset: Historical Society of Somerset County, 1868.

Historical Data Committee. *Sketches of Somerset*. Somerset: Somerset Sesquicentennial Association, 1980.

Hooversville Sesquicentennial Committee. *Hooversville, PA*. Hooversville: Hooversville Sesquicentennial Committee, 1986.

Hovanec, Evelyn A. *Common Lives of Uncommon Strength: The Women of the Coal and Coke Era of Southwestern Pennsylvania*. Uniontown, PA: Coal and Coke Heritage Center, 2001.

Kline, Benjamin F.G. *"Steamwinders" in the Laurel Highlands: The Logging Railroads of Southwestern Pennsylvania*. Somerset, 1973.

McCollexter, Charles. "Pennsylvania's mine rescue was inspiring, but the real story was corporate greed." *The Nation* 17 March 2003: 21–23

Meyersdale Centennial Souvenir Book. Meyersdale: Meyersdale Centennial, Inc., 1974.

The New Republic Newspaper. A Town Remembered: Celebrating the 125th anniversary of Meyersdale, Pennsylvania. Meyersdale: *The New Republic Newspaper*, 1999.

The New Republic Newspaper. A Town Remembered: A Pictorial History of Meyersdale, Pennsylvania. Meyersdale: *The New Republic Newspaper*, 2000.

The New Republic Newspaper. A Town Remembered: Berlin Memories. Berlin: *The New Republic Newspaper*, 2001.

The Official Bicentennial Souvenir Committee. *Generation upon Generation*. Somerset: The Somerset County Bicentennial, 1995.

Rockwood Area Historical & Genealogical Society. *Down the Road of Our Past, Book I*. Rockwood, 1985.

Rockwood Area Historical & Genealogical Society. *Down the Road of Our Past, Book II*. Rockwood, 1987.

Rockwood Area Historical & Genealogical Society. *Down the Road of Our Past, Book III*. Rockwood, 1988.

Bibliography

Statement of Facts and Summary to Investigate the Labor Conditions at the Coal Mines in Somerset County, P.A. Board appointed by Honorable John F. Hylan, Mayor of the City of New York, December, 1922.

Stonycreek-Shanksville-Indian Lake Bicentennial Committee. *Reflections of Stonycreek.* Stonycreek: Bicentennial Committee, 1985.

NEWSPAPERS

The Altoona Mirror
The Daily American
The Johnstown Tribune-Democrat
The New Republic Newspaper
The Pittsburgh Tribune-Review
The Windber Era
The Windber Journal

INDEX

LET'S PREPARE
FOR THE NEW YORK STATE
GRADE 4
ENGLISH LANGUAGE
ARTS TEST

DONNA C. OLIVERIO
DEBORAH S. WHITING

BARRON'S

Dedication

To all students and children
whose curiosity and spirit are truly inspirational

All inquiries should be addressed to:
Barron's Educational Series, Inc.
250 Wireless Boulevard
Hauppauge, New York 11788
http://www.barronseduc.com

International Standard Book No.: 0-7641-2470-6

Library of Congress Catalog Card No.: 2003040399

Library of Congress Cataloging-in-Publication Data
Oliverio, Donna C.
Whiting, Deborah S.
   Let's prepare for the New York State Grade 4 English Language Arts
   Test / Donna C. Oliverio, Deborah S. Whiting.
      p. cm.
   ISBN 0-7641-2470-6
    1. Language arts (Elementary)—Ability testing—New York (State)
   2. New York State Grade 4 Englsih Language Arts Test—Study guides.
   3. Fourth grade (Education)—New York (State) I. Title.

LB1576.W486286 2003
372.6—dc21   2003040399

Printed in the United States of America

9 8 7 6 5 4 3 2 1

Contents

ACKNOWLEDGMENTS

A Universe of Thanks to:

- all the children and their families, who have enriched my life throughout the years

- the wonderful students at Sag Harbor and Riverhead Public Schools

- my colleagues and administrators at Sag Harbor

- Wendy Sleppin at Barron's

- my loving family and friends

Donna Christina

1 INTRODUCTION FOR STUDENTS

It was late January. Everyone at Moosehead Elementary School was wondering why the students in Mr. Antler's fourth-grade class were celebrating. After all, this was around the time that fourth graders would be taking the important test with the long name: The New York State English Language Arts (ELA) Assessment. The name alone is enough to get you nervous or make you want to snooze.

Why, then, did the children in Mr. Antler's class look so cheerful and relaxed? Like you, they have been preparing for the ELA test ever since they first entered school many years ago. They have been listening to their teacher and practicing their language arts skills, so they're actually looking forward to the test. And, so can you! By following your teacher's instructions and doing the practice exercises in this book, you will be able to show everyone, especially yourself, how well you are able to read, write, listen, and think. So, like the students in Mr. Antler's class, get ready to celebrate the test!

The ELA is given over a three-day period. Each day is outlined below.

Day 1: 5-6 reading selections, 28 Multiple-choice Questions, 45 minutes

Day 2: Part 1—Listen to a passage read aloud, write 2 short answers and 1 long response, 30 minutes
Part 2—Write a composition (story, letter, journal entry, article, or essay), 30 minutes

Day 3: Read 2 selections, write 3 short responses and one long response, 60 minutes

We hope you enjoy the interesting stories and activities in this book. They were written to help you improve your language arts skills and to help you become familiar with the types of questions asked on the ELA test.

Think of yourselves as the eager students in Mr. Antler's class. With practice and a positive attitude, you can rise to the challenge and celebrate the ELA test!

In this review book, you will find

- a separate chapter for each section of the ELA test
- two complete practice tests, along with detailed answers
- appendices at the back of the book, which give you a summary of important information

SYMBOLS AND GRAPHICS

The symbols and graphics shown below are used throughout the book to help guide your learning.

TIME MANAGEMENT TIPS

The ELA exam is a timed test. You must plan your time so that you are able to finish the test. Don't worry: Most students are able to finish the test within the time allowed. Look for the clock symbol to give you tips on managing your time.

KNOW THE TASK

Learn about each section of the ELA.

TAKE A CLOSER LOOK

Understanding the questions and what is expected is very important. Learn how questions can be broken down to understand them better.

TIPS TO KEEP YOU ON TARGET

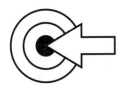

Tips are given throughout the book to help you understand what it takes to be successful.

GET READY TO LISTEN

This is a reminder that you need to do certain things to be ready to listen effectively.

CHECK YOUR WORK

This symbol lets you know that you must look over your work and check it carefully.

2 OVERVIEW FOR FAMILIES AND TEACHERS

FREQUENTLY ASKED QUESTIONS ABOUT THE ELA

The chart below gives you an overview of the exam.

WHAT ARE THE DIFFERENT SECTIONS OF THE ELA TEST?

The chart below outlines each day and section of the test.

New York State English Language Arts Test		
Day 1	Day 2	Day 3
Session 1 45 minutes Multiple-Choice Section ■ Read 5-6 selections. ■ Answer 28 questions.	Session 2—Part 1 30 minutes Listening Section ■ 2 short answers ■ 1 long response Session 2—Part 2 30 minutes Writing ■ Write a story, letter, journal entry, article, or essay.	Session 3 60 minutes Reading and Writing ■ Read 2 selections. ■ Write 1-2 short answers based on the first selection. ■ Write 1-2 short answers based on the second selection. ■ Write a long response based on both selections.

WHAT SKILLS ARE NEEDED TO BE SUCCESSFUL ON THE FOURTH-GRADE ELA EXAM?

Day 1—Reading Comprehension Section

- Read for main idea and details.
- Remember information from reading.
- Quickly reread to locate information to help answer questions.
- Think about information, draw conclusions, and make predictions.

Day 2—Listening Section Skills

- Remember information you hear.
- Take notes and organize information.
- Write answers to question using information from the listening selection.

Day 2—Writing Skills

- Write from a prompt, picture, or story starter.
- Write a story, letter, journal entry, article, or essay using some ideas from the prompt and some of your own.

Day 3—Reading and Response Writing Skills

- Read 2 selections and write a response(s) related to each.
- Write a response that includes details from both reading selections.

WHEN IS THE FOURTH-GRADE ELA GIVEN?

The assessment is scheduled in the winter of fourth grade (late January or early February), depending on state guidelines and your school district calendar. Please check with your child's teacher for exact dates and times.

HOW IS THE ELA SCORED?

To help ensure that all students across the state are graded uniformly, the New York State Education Department provides scorers (teachers) with rubrics (scoring guides) and scored sample answers. See the Appendix (pages 228–231 and 242–243) for examples of rubrics, which will give you an idea of how student work is to be assessed.

HOW IS THE ELA DIFFERENT FROM OTHER TESTS?

- Every student in New York State will take the exam.
- The test is timed.
- The tests are scored by a group of teachers using state guidelines.

WHAT TESTING MODIFICATIONS ARE AVAILABLE FOR STUDENTS WITH SPECIAL NEEDS?

Testing accommodations are being reviewed by the New York State Education Department. Modifications such as having directions read aloud may be indicated on a student's Individualized Education Program (IEP) and approved by the Committee on Special Education (CSE). If your child has an IEP, you should check with his teacher or Special Education Director for information regarding eligibility for testing accommodations.

WHEN WILL I KNOW MY CHILD'S ELA SCORE?

The scores are usually released to school districts in late spring. Districts then send students' individual scores to parents.

WHAT DO THE SCORES MEAN?

- Scores on the assessment range from 1 to 4.
- A score of 4 indicates that the student's performance on the assessment exceeds state standards.
- A score of 3 indicates that the student's work meets state standards and is on track to meet standards in grades 8 and 11.
- A score of either 1 or 2 is below state standards. A score of 2 might mean that your child is struggling in one or more areas and may require some extra support. A score of 1 indicates that your child's work is below the standards set for fourth-grade students in New York State. Additional instruction and intervention services will be needed to reach standards.

WILL MY CHILD BE HELD BACK IN FOURTH GRADE IF SHE RECEIVES A LOW SCORE?

The ELA assessment alone should not determine whether your child is retained in fourth grade. Classroom performance and other factors play an important role in the decision to promote or retain a child.

WHAT CAN A PARENT/GUARDIAN DO TO HELP A CHILD PREPARE FOR THE ELA ASSESSMENT?

The learning process is triangular in nature: Research shows that student achievement is greatly improved when the student, teacher, and parent/guardian work together. Although we strongly believe that the practice exercises in this review book will enhance student performance on the assessment, no single resource could ever replace the cumulative learning experiences that have shaped your child.

Please check with your child's teacher to see if there are any special instructions regarding testing procedures. Be sure your child has a good night's sleep on the nights before the assessment, and a healthy breakfast on the mornings of the exam. If your child appears nervous, explain to him that most people experience some degree of test anxiety. Try to be as reassuring and positive as possible. Send your child off to school with a message to simply do his best.

TO THE PARENT OR GUARDIAN

In fourth grade, your child will take the New York State English Language Arts (ELA) Assessment. The test is designed to measure how well students can read, write, listen, and think.

Let's Prepare for the New York State Grade 4 English Language Arts Test contains exercises that mirror tasks students are expected to perform on the actual ELA assessment. It familiarizes children with test format and the different types of questions asked, thereby helping to improve student levels of confidence. When combined with an overall effective education program, this review book is likely to enhance student performance on the test.

Research has repeatedly shown that parental involvement is crucial to student success. There are several things you can do to improve children's language and literacy experiences:

1. Encourage your child to read a wide variety of material daily, such as books, magazines, and newspapers. Set aside time each day to read with her, and make it a pleasurable experience for both of you. Discuss story elements such as title, setting, characters, conflict, and resolution.

2. Make frequent, regular visits to the library. Bring home plenty of books for both you and your child. Encourage children to select reading material that interests them. Volunteer to read aloud to children material that is too difficult for them to read on their own. Ask the librarian and/or your child's teacher about book clubs, which give children an opportunity to share and discuss literature.

3. Promote good conversational and listening skills. Have frequent discussions with children about their studies. Play imaginative reading and vocabulary word games with synonyms/antonyms, facts/opinions, sight vocabulary, adjectives, and so forth. Emphasize to children the importance of paying attention when you or others speak to them.

4. Monitor the amount of time that children spend watching television or playing computer/video games. Discuss story elements after watching an age-appropriate movie or show together. Note the types of television programs your child likes to view and try to find reading material that reflects her television interests. Help your child understand the difference between fantasy and fact on television.

5. Promote a positive attitude toward written expression. Write notes to children at home, or send them off to school with a note from you in their lunch boxes. Encourage children to keep a journal, correspond with a pen pal, write a letter to the author of a favorite book, and write thank-you notes for gifts.

6. Provide a quiet place in the home for children to complete assignments. Emphasize the importance of homework completion. To improve children's spelling and vocabulary abilities, keep a child-friendly dictionary and thesaurus on hand.

7. Be patient. The growing and learning process take time. Praise children as they acquire new literacy skills. Don't compare your child with others, but respect him as a special individual.

8. Overall, your behavior and attitude should convey to children that you value literacy and learning in general. Aim to create an environment that is rich in both print and the spoken word. When children see you reading and writing daily for meaningful purposes, they begin to understand the connection between their schoolwork and real life. They are then more likely to put forth greater effort into their studies.

TO THE TEACHER

We know firsthand the various challenges inherent in teaching fourth grade. It certainly seems as though much of the year is spent teaching difficult content information and preparing students for the rigorous state assessments. At times, our creativity feels stifled and we may even question our role as caring, effective educators.

This resource is designed to reflect current educational practices in language arts classrooms and to improve student performance on the ELA. By emphasizing effective language arts strategies, we believe we can provide students with appropriate, quality instruction while simultaneously preparing them for the test. Because the last thing we want to do is increase your workload, extra time and emphasis have been placed on scaffolding students' learning and providing responses with detailed explanations. Our goal is to make the ELA experience and language arts learning a positive one.

Each section of the ELA is represented by its own chapter in this review book. The reading selections are educational, engaging, and varied—including such topics as the environment, the Statue of Liberty, teddy bears, animals, and the history of roller coasters.

The Student Checklist at the end of Chapters 4 and 5 uses a graphic organizer to simplify the rubric concept. The Appendix contains two examples of more detailed rubrics, which are offered as samples and guides.

We believe your students will enjoy and learn from the original, rubric poem in Chapter 6. You may want to enlarge the poem for classroom display.

The Appendix is packed full of useful information. It contains an extensive list of important terms (e.g., fact/opinion, main idea, literary elements, transition words), complete with student-friendly definitions and examples. These words comprise the language and concepts of the ELA and of fourth grade in general; they are used in context throughout this resource. The Appendix also contains, among other items, an overview of the various genres, including strategies for understanding the different types of literary forms.

We know that you'll continue to do your best, and we wish you and your students all the best as you guide them through this milestone year in their lives.

3 READING/MULTIPLE CHOICE

OVERVIEW: SESSION 1

The shaded column of the chart below shows what you will be asked to do on Day 1.

New York State English Language Arts Test		
Day 1	Day 2	Day 3
Session 1 45 minutes Multiple-Choice Section ■ Read 5-6 selections. ■ Answer 28 questions.	Session 2—Part 1 30 minutes Listening Section ■ 2 short answers ■ 1 long response Session 2—Part 2 30 minutes Writing ■ Write a story, letter, journal entry, article, or essay.	Session 3 60 minutes Reading and Writing ■ Read 2 selections. ■ Write 1-2 short answers based on the first selection. ■ Write 1-2 short answers based on the second selection. ■ Write a long response based on both selections.

TIPS ON ANSWERING MULTIPLE-CHOICE QUESTIONS

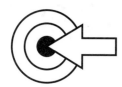

- Read the question very carefully.
- Look back in the selection to find information that may help you answer the question.
- Read *all* answer choices, even if the first answer choice seems correct.
- Eliminate answer choices you know are wrong.
- Choose the best answer from the remaining choices, or make a good guess.
- Be very careful about skipping questions that you are unsure of. If you decide to skip a question and return to it later, you *must* remember to skip the matching number on your answer sheet.

TYPES OF QUESTIONS ASKED

There are different types of questions asked in the multiple-choice section of the assessment. Below you will find examples of the types of questions asked, followed by a list of what the questions expect you to be able to do.

Literal Comprehension Questions

- Recall or locate information from the selection.
- Understand information from the reading/listening selection.

Thinking and/or Reasoning Questions

- Think about the author's purpose.
- Identify the main idea of a selection.
- Make predictions.
- Compare and contrast.
- Use figurative language to understand text.
- Draw inferences and conclusions.

Vocabulary Questions

▪ Use vocabulary strategies, such as determining the meaning of words from their context in the selection.

Note: Remember that some words have more than one meaning. Read the sentence containing the vocabulary word and the surrounding sentences for clues to the word's meaning in the selection. Pay attention to hints or clues that may be given in the details of a selection.

GUIDED PRACTICE

The guided practice section of this review book contains five selections. You will not be timed during the guided practice.

Directions: Read this poem about the wind. Then answer questions 1 through 6.

Wind Song

Anonymous

Here comes the wind, with a noise and a whirr,
Out on the streets he is making a stir.
Now he sends flying a fine, stiff hat,
Tosses and leaves it all muddy and flat.
Turns an umbrella quite inside out,
Tears up stray papers and scatters about,
Makes big balloons out of ladies' long capes,
Skirts into sails, then the queerest of shapes.
The wind is an enemy, often we say:
"We never quite like it—a windy day!"

The wind blows the seeds from their close little pods
And scatters them far away—rods upon rods;
He plants them where never an eye could see
Place for their growing and blooming to be.
He blows away rain, and scatters the dew,
He sweeps the earth clean and makes it all new.
He blows away sickness and brings good health
He comes over laden with beauty and wealth.
Oh, the wind is a friend! Let us always say:
"We love it! We love it!—a windy day!"

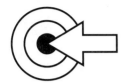

Personification

Personification is a figure of speech in which an animal, object, or idea is given human qualities. In "Wind Song," the wind is given human qualities: He "plants," "sweeps," and "tears up stray papers."

Personification is one tool authors use to make their writing more lively and interesting. Think of ways you can use personification to improve your own writing.

MULTIPLE-CHOICE GUIDED PRACTICE

Directions: Choose the best answer for each question. Then check yourself with the answers provided below each question.

1. What information does the author use to support the opinion that the wind is an enemy?

   A the wind blows seeds around

   B the wind blows the rain away

   C the wind blows sickness away

   D the wind turns umbrellas inside out

This question asks you to recall details from the poem. Skim (look quickly through) the poem to find the section containing the details needed to answer the question. Then, reread that section carefully. Choices **A**, **B**, and **C** are all ways that the wind is a friend. Choice **D** is the only possible answer because a friend would not turn umbrellas inside out.

2. This poem is probably trying to

    F share the good and bad things about the wind

    G teach the reader about our enemy, the wind

    H entertain the reader with stories about the wind

    J remind people to be careful with their umbrellas

In the poem, the wind is described as *both* a friend and an enemy. The only answer that reflects both is **F**.

3. The author uses the pronoun "he" in the poem to refer to

    A the man who lost his hat

    B the wind

    C the gardener who plants seeds

    D the friend

The poem begins with a description of the wind: "Here comes the wind, with a noise and a whirr, / Out on the streets he is making a stir. / Now he sends flying a fine, stiff hat" (lines 1–3). Wind can be noisy and it can blow things such as hats around. The correct answer is the wind, choice **B**.

4. According to the poem, what does the wind leave all muddy and flat?

    F hat

    G balloons

    H umbrella

    J papers

Skim the poem to "find and recall the details" to answer this question. The correct answer, which is choice **F**, is found in lines 3 and 4 of the poem.

5. How does the wind bring good health?

    A it blows away the rain

    B sweeps the earth clean

    C blows away sickness

    D blows seeds around

Skim the poem. Then find and reread the section of the poem containing the answer: "He blows away sickness and brings good health" (line 17). The correct answer is **C**.

6. When the author states that "the wind is a friend," he probably means

    F the wind blew the hat back

    G the wind can be helpful

    H the wind is usually noisy

    J the wind blows papers around

In the second stanza, the author describes some of the good, helpful things that the wind may do. Choices **F**, **H**, and **J** describe the wind as more of an enemy. The correct answer is **G**.

Directions: Read the American tale about two old friends. Then answer questions 7 through 12.

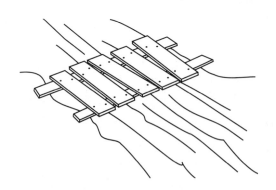

Old Joe and the Carpenter

An American Tale

Old Joe lived in the country. His lifelong neighbor was his best friend. Their children were grown and their wives were gone; they had only each other and their farms.

One day, they had a serious disagreement over a stray calf. It was found on a neighbor's land and both of them claimed it. The two men were stubborn and would not give in. They went back to their farms and stayed there. Weeks went by without a word between them.

Old Joe was feeling poorly when he heard a knock at his front door. At first, he thought it was his neighbor. When he opened the door, he was surprised to see a stranger. The man introduced himself as a "carpenter." He carried a toolbox and had kind eyes.

He explained that he was looking for work. Old Joe said he had a job or two for the carpenter. He showed the man his neighbor's house. There was a new creek running between the two pieces of property, freshly dug by Old Joe's neighbor, to separate their property.

Old Joe asked the carpenter to build a fence on his property so that he would not have to look at the creek. He helped the carpenter get started and then went to get more supplies for the fence. The carpenter worked without rest and finished the job all by himself.

When Old Joe returned and saw what the carpenter had built, he was speechless. The carpenter hadn't built a fence; he had built a bridge. The bridge reached from one side of the creek to the other.

Old Joe's neighbor crossed the bridge; he was quick to apologize for their misunderstanding. He told Old Joe that he could have the calf. They shook hands and thanked the carpenter for his work. Both of them suggested he stay and complete other jobs they had for him.

The carpenter declined the work and said he had to leave; he had more bridges to build.

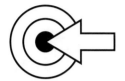

Symbolism

A symbol is a word or object that stands for something else. Writers sometimes use a symbol when they want to suggest a deeper meaning, a meaning beyond what the words themselves seem to say. Think of symbols we see every day, such as a flag, rose, and heart. The American flag itself is just a piece of cloth, but it makes us think of our country, America. A rose is a type of flower, and a heart is an organ, but they frequently stand for love. The tale "Old Joe and the Carpenter" uses the symbols of the fence and the bridge.

MULTIPLE-CHOICE GUIDED PRACTICE

7. Whom did Old Joe expect to see or think he would see when he heard a knock at the door?

A his neighbor

B his children

C a carpenter

D his wife

Skim the tale until you find the answer. Reread the section containing the answer (paragraph 3). This question is tricky. Old Joe thought that he would see his neighbor, but he saw a carpenter instead. The correct answer is choice **A**.

8. The last sentence of the tale begins as follows: "The carpenter declined the work…" What does the word "declined" mean in that sentence?

   F showed

   G expected

   H refused

   J was grateful for

A clue to the word's meaning is found in the rest of the sentence. Reread the last sentence of the tale. After declining more work, the carpenter told Old Joe and his friend that he had to leave. The answer is **H**. The word "decline" means to refuse or turn down.

9. What happens "right after" both Old Joe and his neighbor claimed the stray calf?

   A the neighbor dug a creek

   B both men stopped speaking to one another

   C they met a carpenter

   D Old Joe decided he needed a fence

This question asks you to recall the sequence of events in the tale. The "sequence of events" refers to the order in which things happen in a selection. All of the events happened after Old Joe and his neighbor claimed the calf. Reread the tale to find the event that happened "right after." The correct answer is **B**.

10. Why was the disagreement over the calf so serious for the two men?

   F their wives were gone

   G they both needed the calf

   H they wanted to be right

   J they had only each other

All of the choices listed are possible reasons for a disagreement, but you need to choose the best answer based on information and details provided in the tale. The best answer for this question is **J**.

11. When the carpenter built a bridge rather than the fence that Old Joe had requested, why wasn't Old Joe upset?

   A he changed his mind

   B he got his friend back

   C he didn't have enough materials for a fence

   D he liked the better view of the creek

Old Joe was pleased because he did get his friend back, so the answer is **B**. There is no information in the tale to support the other letter choices.

12. What do you think the carpenter meant when he said that he had more bridges to build?

   F he has more friendships to build

   G he doesn't like to do other jobs

   H he doesn't like to build fences

   J he has more creeks to cross

You need to think about the fence and the bridge as symbols. Fences separate people and things, but bridges connect. The correct answer is **F**. This carpenter is building or repairing (fixing) a relationship.

Directions: Read the poem about Mr. Nobody. Then answer questions 13 through 17.

Mr. Nobody
Anonymous

I know a funny little man,
As quiet as a mouse,
Who does the mischief that is done
In everybody's house!
There's no one ever sees his face,
And yet we all agree
That every plate we break was cracked
By Mr. Nobody.

'Tis he who always tears our books,
Who leaves the door ajar,
He pulls the buttons from our shirts,
And scatters pins afar;
That squeaking door will always squeak,
For, prithee, don't you see,
We leave the oiling to be done
By Mr. Nobody.

The finger marks upon the door
By none of us are made;
We never leave the blinds unclosed,
To let the curtains fade.
The ink we never spill; the boots
That lying round you see
Are not our boots—they all belong
To Mr. Nobody.

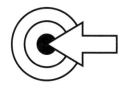

Imagery

Writers sometimes use "images" (mental pictures) to help the reader see pictures or feel sensations without actually experiencing them. In "Mr. Nobody," the poet creates a picture of a house where many things happen and no one takes responsibility.

Similes

Authors use similes to make their writing more descriptive and entertaining. A simile is a figure of speech that compares two different things using the words "like" or "as." In "Mr. Nobody" (lines 1 and 2), the poet compares the funny, little man to a quiet mouse. Try to use similes in your own writing so that it will be "as amusing as a carnival ride" (another simile).

MULTIPLE-CHOICE GUIDED PRACTICE

13. What is the main idea of the poem?

A a stranger keeps sneaking into everyone's house

B Mr. Nobody is a strange neighbor

C a funny little man gets into mischief

D everyone blames Mr. Nobody instead of taking the blame themselves

The main idea is the big idea: It's what a selection (a poem in this case) is mostly about. Read the poem carefully. Choices **A**, **B**, and **C** do not indicate the main (most important) idea of the poem. The correct answer is **D**.

14. According to the poem, what does Mr. Nobody do?

   F oils a squeaky door

   G leaves finger marks

   H repairs torn books

   J sews buttons on shirts

Read the question, answer choices, and poem carefully. Mr. Nobody does not oil the door; it will always squeak so choice **F** is incorrect. He tears books and pulls buttons off shirts so choices **H** and **J** are also incorrect. The correct answer is **G**: Mr. Nobody is blamed for leaving finger marks.

15. The next time something is broken or misplaced, everyone will probably blame

   A the littlest member of the family

   B Mr. Nobody

   C everybody else

   D a mouse

This question asks you to predict what will happen next in the poem. The details given in the poem, including the poem's title, provide clues that will help you make a good guess. According to the poem, no one takes responsibility for the things that happen in the house. Mr. Nobody must be responsible. The best answer is **B**.

16. According to the poem, Mr. Nobody does all of the mischief that is done. What does mischief mean?

  F kindness

  G goodness

  H trouble

  J niceness

Mr. Nobody is responsible for all of the "trouble" that happens around the house, so letter choices **F**, **G**, and **J** are incorrect. A synonym (a word that means the same as or nearly the same as) for *mischief* would be the word trouble, choice **H**.

17. The author of the poem tells us that Mr. Nobody is unknown to everyone because

  A he is as quiet as a mouse

  B he is a funny little man

  C no one ever sees his face

  D he always tears our books

All of the letter choices are details given in the poem. The only one that shows he is unknown would be that "no one ever sees his face," choice C.

Directions: Read the story about teddy bears, and then answer questions 18 through 22.

Who Put the "Teddy" in Teddy Bear?

Source: *The Washington Post*, Clifford K. Berryman, 1902.

In 1902 America's then-president, Theodore "Teddy" Roosevelt, visited Mississippi to settle a disagreement between Mississippi and its neighboring state, Louisiana. While in the south, he went bear hunting with some of his friends and aides. His hunting party was joined by a group of newspaper reporters.

Members hunted for a few days, but they didn't capture any bears. Finally, on the last day of the hunt, Roosevelt's friends cornered a bear cub and presented it to the president as a sitting target. Teddy Roosevelt chose not to shoot the helpless animal: "Spare the bear. I will not shoot a tethered animal!" he exclaimed. A cartoonist, Clifford Berryman, either heard about or witnessed the president's act; he drew a black and white cartoon showing how the president refused to shoot the bear. This cartoon appeared in newspapers all over the country.

One married couple, the Michtoms, from Brooklyn, New York, saw the cartoon and was inspired by the president's action, or lack of action. Morris Michtom's wife created a stuffed bear with movable arms and legs. She and her husband placed the bears in the window of their candy store with a copy of the cartoon. The "Teddy" bears were a hit. The Michtoms wrote the president and received permission to use his name. The popularity of the teddy bears spread and soon they were being created in Germany as well.

Teddy bears are over 100 years old and are still popular with many children and adults. They are collected by many people; stamps and coins are the only items collected more.

MULTIPLE-CHOICE GUIDED PRACTICE

18. According to the article, Teddy Roosevelt became famous for something he did not do. What was it?

    F go bear hunting

    G like cartoons

    H become president

    J shoot a small bear

Read the question carefully. Teddy Roosevelt was famous for NOT shooting the little bear. The correct answer is **J**.

19. After seeing the cartoon, people thought that President Roosevelt was

    A lucky

    B kind

    C frightened

    D mean

The President chose not to shoot the bear. Most people would think he was kind for making that choice. The correct answer is **B**.

20. Which detail from the story is proof of the teddy bear's popularity?

   F there was a cartoon drawn

   G the president went hunting for bears

   H teddy bears were stuffed, with moveable arms

   J teddy bears were copied by other toy makers

When something is "liked" by most people, then that something is considered to be popular. Answers **F** and **G** are about real bears. Answer **H** refers to construction of the bears. The only answer that is proof of popularity is **J**.

21. When did the events described in this story take place?

   A more than 200 years ago

   B about 60 years ago

   C about 30 years ago

   D about a century ago

President Roosevelt went on his now-famous bear hunt in Mississippi in 1902, which is about 100 years ago. Therefore, choices **A**, **B**, and **C** are not correct. A century equals a period of 100 years, so the correct answer is choice **D**. If you did not know the meaning of the word "century," you could have still figured out this answer by eliminating the other choices, which you knew were obviously incorrect. That's what "making a good guess" is about.

22. The story states that the Michtoms were *inspired* by the cartoon.
What does the word *inspired* mean?

F influenced

G taught

H able

J chosen

Read the sentence in the third paragraph containing the vocabulary word "inspired." Also, read the sentence "before" and the sentence "after" the word to decide which of the letter choices makes sense. After seeing the cartoon, Mrs. Michtom created a stuffed bear. The word "inspired" means to influence someone to do something (make teddy bears in this case). The correct answer is **F**.

Directions: Read the Chinese tale below. Then answer questions 23 through 28.

The Nightingale

A Chinese Tale

Long ago, in the far-off land of China, deep in the forest, there lived a nightingale. The nightingale sang a song so beautiful that the other animals of the forest would stop to listen to her sing.

Nightingale: Tra-la-lee! Tra-la-lee! La-la-tra-la-lee!

Emperor: Who is that singing? That is the most beautiful singing I have ever heard! Servants come here at once!

Servant 1: Yes, mighty emperor?

Servant 2: What can we do for you?

Emperor: Do you hear that singing?

Nightingale: Tra-la-lee! Tra-la-lee!

Servant 1: Yes, it is lovely.

Emperor: Well, I must have it! Please find whoever is singing and bring him or her to me. We will dine together.

So the servants went off to find the singer. They listened to every animal they met. They listened to the cow, "Moo." They listened to the frogs, "Rib-bit." They walked deeper and deeper into the forest until at last they heard," Tra-la-lee! Tra-la-lee!"

Servant 1: There she is, a small gray bird.

Servant 2: I don't believe it. Such beautiful music from such a plain-looking bird.

Servant 1: Miss Nightingale, our emperor loves your singing. He has sent us to invite you for dinner.

Nightingale: It would be a pleasure. Tra-la-lee. Let's go to the palace.

They arrived at the palace. The emperor had a special feast prepared and many people came to hear the nightingale's song.

Emperor: My dear nightingale, please sing for us.

Nightingale: Tra-la-lee! Tra-la-lee!

The emperor did enjoy the song. He loved it so much that he decided to keep the nightingale guarded in a beautiful cage. Soon, the nightingale grew homesick. One day, the emperor received a golden toy bird as a present. It was encrusted in diamonds and was the most beautiful thing he had ever seen. It would sing a beautiful song when it was wound up. Everyone was so interested in the toy bird that the nightingale was able to open her cage and fly away.

encrusted: covered or coated in

Emperor: Don't worry; we have a new bird to sing songs.

Servant 1: But the toy bird sings the same song.

After a year, the toy bird broke. The emperor became very sick in his quiet palace.

Emperor: I need music to help me feel better. I think I hear music coming from outside.

Nightingale: Tra-la-lee! Tra-la-lee!

Emperor: You have returned to sing to me! Nightingale, I have missed you! How can I ever repay you?

Nightingale: Your smile and good health are payment enough. You can do one more thing for me.

Emperor: Anything!

Nightingale: I cannot live in the palace. I need to live in the forest, my home. I will visit you often.

The emperor promised, so the nightingale returned nightly to sing to the emperor.

No one ever knew the nightingale was the best medicine.

MULTIPLE-CHOICE GUIDED PRACTICE

23. Why did the emperor need to find the bird?

   A he wanted to fill the cage

   B he wanted to stop the singing

   C he wanted to keep healthy

   D he liked the songs of the nightingale

 Skim the poem to find and recall the details to answer this question. Reread those details carefully. As Servant 1 says in the poem, "Miss Nightingale, our emperor loves your singing." The correct answer is **D**.

24. What surprised the servants when they located the nightingale?

   F it sang a beautiful song

   G it lived deep in the forest

   H it was a plain bird

   J it was the most beautiful bird they had ever seen

 As Servant 2 stated, "I don't believe it. Such beautiful music from such a plain-looking bird." The correct answer is **H**.

25. How did the nightingale feel about singing for the Emperor "at first?"

   A the nightingale liked to make the emperor smile

   B the nightingale liked living in the beautiful palace

   C the nightingale liked the beautiful cage

   D the nightingale didn't like being in the palace

This is a question about the sequencing of events in the tale. Read the question carefully. Pay attention to the words "at first." The nightingale's feelings changed. In the beginning, she enjoyed making the emperor smile with her songs. The correct answer is **A**.

26. What was the most likely reason that the emperor had the nightingale guarded?

    F   he needed to hear the songs of the nightingale

    G   he cared for the nightingale

    H   he wanted to be sure the nightingale stayed in the cage

    J   he wanted to keep the nightingale happy

The best answer to explain why the nightingale was "guarded" is choice **H**. The other choices do make some sense, but they do not explain the most likely reason for having the nightingale guarded.

27. What lesson do you think the emperor learned from his experience with the nightingale?

    A   never try to keep a bird in a cage

    B   songs will keep you healthy

    C   you need to treat someone well if you care for him or her

    D   it is better to have a toy bird than a live bird

Lessons taught by tales are usually life lessons or important lessons to live by. All of the above choices are lessons that may have been learned. The most important "life lesson" learned is letter choice **C**.

28. Why did the nightingale fly away from the palace?

    F she was jealous of the toy bird

    G the door of the cage was open

    H she didn't like the song of the toy bird

    J she wanted to return to the forest

According to the tale, the nightingale was homesick and wished to return home to the forest. The best answer is **J**.

4 LISTENING

OVERVIEW: SESSION 2—PART 1

The shaded box in the chart below shows what you will be asked to do in Part 1 of Session 2 on Day 2 of the test.

New York State English Language Arts Test		
Day 1	Day 2	Day 3
Session 1 45 minutes Multiple-Choice Section ■ Read 5-6 selections. ■ Answer 28 questions.	Session 2—Part 1 30 minutes Listening Section ■ 2 short answers ■ 1 long response Session 2—Part 2 30 minutes Writing ■ Write a story, letter, journal entry, article, or essay.	Session 3 60 minutes Reading and Writing ■ Read 2 selections. ■ Write 1-2 short answers based on the first selection. ■ Write 1-2 short answers based on the second selection. ■ Write a long response based on both selections.

The practice listening exercises in this book are designed to help you become a better listener, note taker, and writer. Listening is a skill you will use throughout your life. In the world around you, people perform tasks that require good listening skills. Doctors listen to their patients to heal them. Mechanics listen to customers to fix their cars. A waitress listens to customers' orders to serve the correct food.

You listen every day to directions and information presented in your classroom. You also listen to carry on conversations with your friends. Sometimes, a conflict arises between people simply because someone was not listening properly.

Being a better listener requires more than good hearing. You must remember information and be able to think about what you have heard.

LISTENING TIPS

- You will have 30 minutes to complete this part of the exam.
- Take no more than 1–2 minutes after the selection is read to complete your notes.
- Take 5–10 minutes to write the two short answers.
- Use the last 15–20 minutes to write the long response.
- Write about what you have listened to and read.

Your writing on the ELA will be scored on:

- how well you organize and communicate your thoughts
- how completely and correctly you answer all parts of the question
- how clearly you use details and examples to fully support your ideas
- how pleasurable and interesting your writing is
- how accurately you use spelling, grammar, punctuation, and paragraphing

Use one or both of the following to check your writing:

- the Student Checklist on page 66 (last page of this chapter).
- the more detailed Listening/Writing Rubric, which can be found in the Appendix on pages 228–231.

LISTENING TIPS TO KEEP YOU ON TARGET

- Prepare for listening by removing distractions (such as scraps of paper).
- Stop moving, touching, and talking.
- Tune out distracting sounds.
- Focus on the speaker (eye contact).
- Think about what is being said.
- Try to form a picture in your head of what the speaker is saying.
- Pay very close attention to both readings.
- During the second reading, take notes on the most important details.

If the selection read aloud is a story, listen for and try to write down the following story elements in your notes:

1. title/author

2. setting

3. important characters

    —what do they look like?

    —how do they act?

    —why do they act a certain way?

4. conflict (problem in the story)

5. sequence of main events (beginning, middle, and end)

6. resolution or lesson learned

If the passage read aloud is not a story, listen for and try to write down the following:

1. title/author

2. important ideas and details

3. why the author is writing the selection (example: to describe or explain something, to convince)

4. people, animals, and places

- Use single word notes and phrases, abbreviations, and/or pictures/symbols to save time.
- You may want to organize details in a graphic organizer such as a chart, diagram, story map, or list.

PART 1: LISTENING

Directions: In this section of the test, a selection will be read aloud to you twice. Please listen carefully each time you hear the selection because you will then be asked to answer specific questions about the selection.

You will listen to the story twice. **Do not take notes during the first reading.**

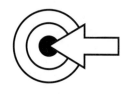

During the first reading, listen carefully for main ideas and details. Think about the story elements: title, setting, characters, conflict (problem), sequence of events to solution, and resolution (solution).

You may take notes during the second reading using the space provided.

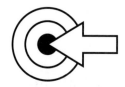

Between the first and second reading, you may want to create some type of graphic organizer to help you organize your notes.

During the second reading, begin to take notes about the most important details in the selection. Write only key words or phrases to remember the details. When taking notes, do **not** write in complete sentences. Your notes should answer questions about the story elements.

You may refer back to your notes to answer the questions that follow. **Your notes will not count toward your end score.**

When the second reading is finished, fill in the necessary details. Don't spend too much time on your notes page. Refer back to your notes during writing. You will need to use details from the selection in your writing.

GUIDED PRACTICE
LISTENING PRACTICE 1

Directions: In this section of the test, a story called "A Village of Listeners" will be read aloud to you twice. Please listen carefully each time the story is read because you will then be asked to answer specific questions about the story.

During the first reading, listen closely but do not take notes. You may take notes during the second reading. Please use the space provided below for your notes. You may refer back to your notes to answer the questions that follow. Your notes will *not* count toward your score.

Notes

A Village of Listeners

There once was a village where no one listened. Everyone talked and everyone could hear, but no one listened. When villagers ordered pancakes at the local restaurant, the waitress brought them chocolate cake instead. Often, firemen and policemen went to the wrong address because they didn't listen carefully to the address of the emergency. Things were usually in a state of confusion in this rural community.

At village meetings people talked, but sadly no one listened. Everyone wanted to share personal ideas and opinions, but didn't want to listen to anyone else's. There was always more fighting than cooperation. Nothing ever seemed to get accomplished in this village.

One day, a wise man visited and spoke to the hearts of the villagers. He advised them to clear their minds, focus on the other people around them, and value what others had to say. The wise man asked people to work together and have real conversations that required more listening than talking.

Soon, the village buzzed with cooperation. People were happier and safer; problems were solved. The villagers taught their children to be better listeners so that the village would continue to be wiser for generations to come.

NOTE TAKING

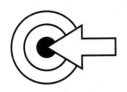

Write down key words or phrases, which summarize the order of events in a selection. Do **not** try to write down every word you hear. Take notes on only the most important details.

You can save time and write down more information if you use abbreviations and symbols during note taking. Think about and practice using abbreviations and symbols that will work for you, such as "bec." to stand for *because,* or a * to show that the information is super important.

Like the athlete who needs to practice for an upcoming sports events, you can improve your skill in note taking by practicing. A good time to practice taking notes is when your teacher is giving a lesson.

The sample response below uses the following abbreviations and symbols: choc. for *chocolate* and & for *and.* It is written using words and phrases, rather than complete sentences.

SEQUENCE OF EVENTS

How many of these details did you record during listening?

village
no one listened
pancakes—choc. cake
firemen & policemen—wrong address
confusion
meetings—no one listening
fighting
nothing gets done
wise man—spoke to hearts
focus on others
listen
cooperating
happier, safer, problems solved
teach children to listen
brighter future

GRAPHIC ORGANIZER FOR UNDERSTANDING STORY ELEMENTS

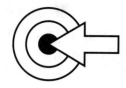

Simple notes can be arranged in a story web using details from the story.

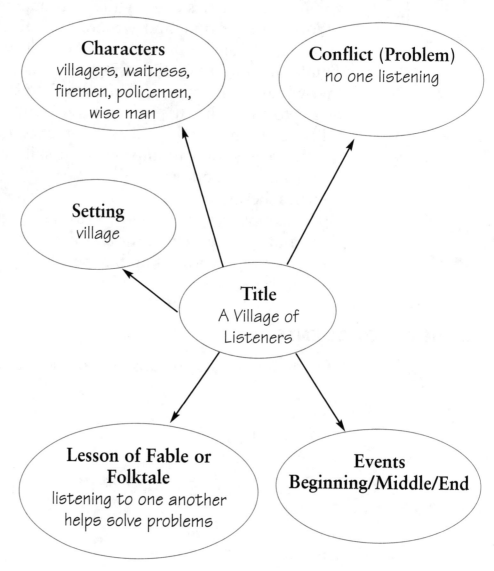

Characters
villagers, waitress,
firemen, policemen,
wise man

Conflict (Problem)
no one listening

Setting
village

Title
A Village of
Listeners

**Lesson of Fable or
Folktale**
listening to one another
helps solve problems

**Events
Beginning/Middle/End**

Use at least 2 to 3 details from the story in your answer. You need to show that you are a good listener and that you understood the story.

BEGINNING, MIDDLE, AND END ORGANIZER

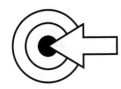

Directions: Use your notes to help you complete the chart below.

SETTING Where and when the story takes place	
BEGINNING What happens at the beginning of the story? Readers meet the characters. The conflict begins.	
MIDDLE What happens in the middle of the story? The characters and the conflict are described in more detail.	
END What happens at the end of the story? The problem is somehow solved.	

Remember that the beginning of the story introduces the problem. The end of the story should tell the resolution of the problem.

Sample Completed Chart

SETTING Where and when the story takes place	in a village, a long time ago
BEGINNING What happens at the beginning of the story? Readers meet the characters. The conflict begins.	Villagers do not listen to one another.
MIDDLE What happens in the middle of the story? The characters and the conflict are described in more detail.	Waitress served the wrong food. Firemen and policemen go to wrong address. Wise man visits village. He tells people to start listening to one another.
END What happens at the end of the story? The problem is somehow solved.	Villagers start to listen to one another. They begin to solve problems and are happier. They teach their children to be good listeners so they can solve future problems.

What caused most of the problems in the village?

Planning Space

Answer

_____

_____

_____

_____

_____

_____

_____

_____

CAUSE AND EFFECT

When one event makes another event happen, the first is the cause and the second is the event.

The cause-effect chart below shows what happens in the village as a result of people not listening to each other.

Cause (event that happened first)	Effects (event that happened second)
People in the village do not listen to one another.	The entire village was in a state of confusion. Many problems could not get solved. A waitress served the wrong food. Firemen and policemen go to wrong address.

Sample Response

The response below includes a **topic sentence** that reflects or restates the question. A topic sentence states the main (big) idea of a paragraph. The response also includes 3 examples from the selection that support the answer given.

Most of the problems in the village were caused by people not listening to one another. The waitress in the restaurant served the wrong food to customers because she did not listen carefully. She served chocolate cake, but the customer had ordered pancakes. Firemen and policemen went to the wrong addresses for emergencies because they didn't listen carefully. The problems were caused and could not be solved because no one listened to anyone else.

WRITING ABOUT CHANGE

Describe how the village changed from the beginning to the end of the story. Write your answer using details from the story.

In your answer, be sure to:
■ describe the village at the beginning of the story.
■ tell what caused the village to change.
■ explain how the village is different at the end of the story.
■ use specific details from the story.
■ check your writing for correct spelling, grammar, capitalization, and punctuation.

Planning Space

_____

_____

_____

_____

_____

_____

_____

_____

_____

_____

_____

_____

_____

Did you use a graphic organizer to help you plan your answer?

T-CHART

Below is a two-column list known as a T-chart. The list helps organize details to show how the village changed. It shows you the differences between the village at the beginning of the story and the village at the end of the story.

Sample T-Chart

Village at beginning of story (before the wise man)	Village at end of story (after the wise man)
People talk; no one listens	People have conversations
Things confused—	More listening than talking
restaurant orders,	People happier
emergency addresses	Taught children to listen
More fighting than teamwork	Problems solved
Could not solve problems	

Sample Response

The village changed greatly from the beginning to the end of the story. It changed for the better, thanks to the visit from a wise man.

At the beginning of "A Village of Listeners," the villagers did not listen to each other. The whole community was in a state of confusion. Restaurant orders were not made correctly, and the firemen and policemen sometimes went to the wrong address because they did not listen carefully. This village had more problems than a math book. Problems could not get solved because everyone was talking a mile a minute all at the same time.

One day, a wise man visited the village. Surprisingly, the villagers stopped talking long enough to listen to the wise man. He told the villagers to listen to others. They followed his advice, and began to talk less and listen to each other more. Problems could now get solved, and children would be taught the importance of listening. The community was now a more cheerful place.

LISTENING PRACTICE II

Directions: In this section of the test, a story called "A Little, Big Man" will be read aloud to you twice. Please listen carefully each time the story is read because you will then be asked to answer specific questions about the story.

During the first reading, listen closely but do not take notes. You may take notes during the second reading. Please use the space provided below for your notes. You may refer back to your notes to answer the questions that follow. Your notes will not count toward your score.

Notes

A Little, Big Man

Once there lived a little man. He wished he would grow to be taller, but he did not grow at all. As the years passed, the only thing that grew was his disappointment. He decided to ask others for advice.

One day the little man approached a bull. He asked the bull how to become bigger. The bull tossed his head and said, "Eat lots of grass and hay and spend all day lying down. That is how I became as big as I am."

The little man went home and ate lots of grass and hay and spent the day lying around. He did not grow. He got a stomachache from the hay and grass, and a backache from lying down all day.

The little man decided to ask the horse for advice. The horse suggested he eat oats and straw, and get plenty of exercise running around.

The man went home and followed the horse's directions. He didn't grow an inch. He got sick from the oats and straw and his legs were sore from all the running.

The little man was ready to give up when he decided to consult the wisest creature in the forest. When he asked the owl for advice to grow taller, the owl wanted to know why he wanted to be taller.

The man explained that he wanted to see more. The owl suggested he climb a tree. The man was surprised by the idea and embarrassed that the solution could be so simple.

He thanked the owl and, as he was about to leave, the owl left him with this thought, "If a man has a brain and uses it, it doesn't matter what size he is; he is big enough for anything."

TIPS FOR UNDERSTANDING THE MEANING OF QUOTATIONS

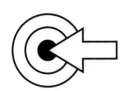

■ Review your notes for any information that may help explain the quotation.
■ Name the character(s) involved.
■ Restate the quotation using different words.

Complete the chart below using details from the story.

Quotation	Meaning
As the years passed, the only thing that grew was his disappointment.	
If a man has a brain and uses it, it doesn't matter what size he is; he is big enough for anything.	

Sample Completed Chart

Quotation	Meaning
As the years passed, the only thing that grew was his disappointment.	For a long time, the little man wished he would grow taller. He was very sad that he couldn't grow and he became sadder and sadder.
If a man has a brain and uses it, it doesn't matter what size he is; he is big enough for anything.	The owl's advice was that if people think with their brain, then they can solve any problem. They can overcome being small by using their brain power.

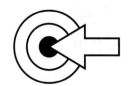

Why do you think the horse and the bull gave the little man the advice they did?

- Begin with a topic sentence. A topic sentence tells what the rest of the paragraph is about.
- Then give at least 3 details to answer the question and to show your understanding of what you heard.

_____

_____

_____

_____

_____

_____

_____

_____

Sample Response

The horse and bull gave the little man advice about growing taller. The advice they gave was what had worked for them. The bull knew that he grew when he ate grass and hay, and spent the day lying down. The horse knew that he grew when he ate oats and straw, and ran around. Their advice didn't work for the little man.

ANSWERING ALL PARTS OF THE QUESTION

■ Read the question carefully.
■ Pay attention to each bullet.
■ Put a check next to each bullet answered.
■ Read your writing to be sure you have answered all parts of the question.

Tell how the little man changed from the beginning to the end of the story.

In your answer, be sure to:

■ describe the little man at the beginning of the story.
■ tell what caused him to change.
■ explain how he is different at the end of the story.
■ use specific details from the story.
■ check your writing for correct spelling, grammar, capitalization, and punctuation.

Planning Space

LISTENING PRACTICE III

Directions: In this section of the test, a story called "Dr. Jane Goodall" will be read aloud to you twice. Please listen carefully each time the story is read because you will then be asked to answer specific questions about the story.

During the first reading, listen closely but do not take notes. You may take notes during the second reading. Please use the space provided below for your notes. You may refer back to your notes to answer the questions that follow. Your notes will not count toward your score.

Notes

Dr. Jane Goodall

Jane Goodall loved and cared for animals from the time she was a young girl. One of her favorite toys was a stuffed chimpanzee, which was given to her by her father. Her favorite childhood books were about animals. She was fond of Tarzan books and dreamed of adventures in Africa.

Her animal research can be traced back to her childhood. Jane was curious about how chickens are able to lay eggs. She waited quietly for hours in the hen house to witness a hen laying an egg. This curiosity and patience would later be helpful in her study of chimpanzees.

In her early twenties, Jane went to Africa to work, first as a secretary for a documentary film company. Next, she worked as an assistant for the famous Dr. Louis Leakey. He was impressed by her knowledge of Africa and its animals. Dr. Leakey gave her the opportunity to live her dream of

studying and working with animals. Jane lived with, played with, and studied the chimpanzees. She made many new discoveries about chimpanzees. She watched them make a tool from a branch to catch termites. Dr. Goodall wrote books and helped produce documentaries to share her discoveries with others.

Jane Goodall's childhood love has become a lifelong passion. Today, she speaks to children around the world about caring for the environment and the creatures living in it.

TIME ORDER WORDS

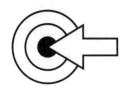

Look for clue words or phrases that will help you understand the events of a selection in the order in which they happened. Below are some time order words from "Dr. Jane Goodall":

- from the time she was a young girl
- this curiosity and patience would "later" be helpful
- in her early twenties
- today

TIMELINE CHART

Dr. Jane Goodall is a famous humanitarian and scientist. Create a timeline with information from the selection.

Time in the Life of Dr. Goodall	Event
Childhood	
When she was in her twenties…	
Today	

Time in the Life of Dr. Goodall	Event
Childhood	She watched a chicken lay an egg.
When she was in her twenties…	She went to Africa to study chimpanzees.
Today	She speaks to children around the world about caring for the environment and the creatures in it.

Time Order Words and Phrases

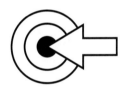

Time order words and phrases help you understand the events of a selection in the order in which they happened.

in the beginning (middle, end)	shortly	earlier
first	soon	when
second	as soon as	while
then	before	at the end
next	later	finally
after	during	at last
after a while	now	until
after that	by the time	in the meantime
afterward	at that time	meanwhile
	immediately	in the past

Exact time order words and phrases, such as:

days of the week—on Wednesday, after Monday, before Saturday

months—last February, next October

hours—at noon, by six o'clock

dates and years—July 4, 1776

In the article about Dr. Jane Goodall, the author wrote, "This curiosity and patience would later be helpful in her study of chimpanzees." What do you think this statement means?

Sometimes it helps to break a question into parts.

■ This curiosity and patience—Dr. Goodall was always curious and patient.
■ Would later be helpful—She was curious and patient as a child and would later use those skills in her work. She would question and search for answers in her research.

Sample Response

Ever since she was a little girl, Dr. Jane Goodall was always curious and patient. She would use both of these traits in her work, later in her life.

When she was young, Dr. Goodall was very interested in learning how chickens laid eggs. She spent hours waiting in the hen house to see the event take place.

In her adult life, Dr. Goodall was curious about chimpanzees. She spent years patiently observing their behavior in the wild. Her curiosity made her question the things around her and search for answers. Dr. Goodall's patience would help her spend much time trying to find the answers.

Your answer may be correct if you have at least 3 details from the story to support your answer.

1. She was curious about chickens laying eggs.

2. She waited patiently in the hen house to observe the hens laying eggs.

3. As an adult she was curious about chimpanzees.

4. She patiently observed chimpanzees' behavior and made discoveries.

5. She watched chimpanzees make tools to catch termites.

Dr. Goodall's lifelong love could be traced back to her childhood.

1. What was that love?

2. How did it change over time?

3. Be sure to include examples from the article.

_____

_____

_____

_____

_____

_____

_____

_____

_____

_____

_____

Sample Response

Dr. Goodall's lifelong love of animals can be traced back to her childhood. She loved and cared for animals even as a young girl. Her favorite books were about animals and African adventures. During her childhood, Dr. Goodall was interested in how chickens were able to lay eggs.

As an adult, she lived in Africa doing chimpanzee research. Today, she speaks to children around the world about caring for the environment and animals.

Details from the listening selection:

1. Her favorite toy as a child was a stuffed chimpanzee.
2. She liked Tarzan books.
3. She observed animals as a child.
4. She watched a hen lay eggs.
5. She was always curious about animal behavior.
6. As an adult, she studied animals in Africa.
7. She made new discoveries about chimpanzees.
8. She wrote books about animals.
9. She still shares her love of animals with children today.
10. She writes and speaks about caring for animals and their environment.

Your answer should have at least 3 details that show her lifelong love of animals and how it changed over time.

STUDENT CHECKLIST

Meaning

> Did you complete the task by answering all the bulleted items in the question?
>
> Did you make connections and show you thought about the text read aloud?

Development

> Did you use specific examples and important details from the selection to support your ideas?
>
> Did you explain your answer fully?

Organization

> Did you begin with a topic sentence, an introduction to your writing?
>
> Did you use signal words to help with the direction of your writing?

Ideas and Language Use

> Did you write with a purpose (to inform, entertain, persuade, describe) in mind?
>
> Did you use interesting language?

Conventions

> Did you check your spelling, punctuation, and grammar?
>
> Did you start every sentence with a capital and end every sentence with the correct punctuation?

5 WRITING

OVERVIEW: SESSION 2—PART 2

The shaded box in the chart below shows what you will be asked to do in Part 2 of Session 2 on Day 2 of the test.

New York State English Language Arts Test		
Day 1	Day 2	Day 3
Session 1 45 minutes Multiple-Choice Section ■ Read 5-6 selections. ■ Answer 28 questions.	Session 2—Part 1 30 minutes Listening Section ■ 2 short answers ■ 1 long response Session 2—Part 2 30 minutes Writing ■ Write a story, letter, journal entry, article, or essay.	Session 3 60 minutes Reading and Writing ■ Read 2 selections. ■ Write 1-2 short answers based on the first selection. ■ Write 1-2 short answers based on the second selection. ■ Write a long response based on both selections.

WRITING A STORY OF YOUR OWN

In this part of the test, you will be asked to write a story of your own. Do NOT include information from the listening stories in your writing.

PLANNING YOUR WRITING

There will be a space provided for you to plan your writing; it is called the Planning Page. Do not write your final answer on the Planning Page because your writing on the Planning Page will not count toward your final score. Write your final response on the page(s) following the Planning Page.

WRITING TIPS

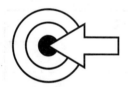

Before Writing:

Think about your topic, purpose, and audience (your readers).

Use a pre-writing tool, such as a graphic organizer or simple notes, to help focus and organize your writing.

During Writing:

Choose a title that captures the reader's attention and relates to your writing piece.

Write interesting topic sentences that tell the main idea of a paragraph.

Add many details to support the main idea—details, details, details!

There are many types of details you can add to support the main idea, such as examples, reasons, facts, and sensory descriptions. The type of details you add will depend on the writing genre.

Vary your sentence beginnings and sentence lengths. Do not begin every sentence the same way.

Use interesting language.

Try *not* to use overused words such as good, great, happy, and nice. Use vivid synonyms instead, such as excellent, outstanding, cheerful, and pleasant.

Use figures of speech, such as similes, to create mental pictures for the reader.

After Writing:

Reread and check your writing for correct spelling, grammar, punctuation, and paragraphing.

Use one or both of the following to check your writing:

- the Student Checklist on page 102.
- the more detailed Writing Rubric, which can be found in the Appendix on pages 240–241.

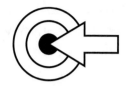

Use the Planning Page to organize your writing if you wish. Simple notes or graphic organizers work well. Do not take the time to write complete sentences on this page. Write only key words and phrases. Do not spend too much time on the Planning Page.

Type of Writing (Genre)	Beginning	Middle	End
Story	Setting Character(s) Conflict begins	Details about character(s) and conflict Events leading to the resolution	Resolution of the conflict
Letter	Date, greeting, and introduction	Supporting details	Conclusion Closing
Journal entry	Date of the entry Introduction	Supporting details	Conclusion
Article/News story	Introduce important facts and thoughts about the topic	Supporting details (add more facts and thoughts)	Conclusion
Essay	Introduction of purpose	Supporting details	Conclusion

Notice the importance of supporting details to the development of your writing.

GUIDED PRACTICE

During the Writing section of Session 2, Part 2, you are going to read the directions and information given to you and then write a story using your own ideas. The directions may include a picture, document, or a story starter. Read the directions carefully.

PICTURE PROMPT

Begin by listing at least 4 to 5 details from the picture.

1. **Setting**—where and when the story/picture takes place.

2. **Mood**—the feelings readers get about a story or picture. The mood must fit the story or picture. For

example, if you were reading a mystery story, the mood might be exciting or suspenseful. On the other hand, if you were reading a biography filled with sad events about the person's life, the mood might be sad or upsetting. Moods can be scary, funny, lonely, silly, cheerful, dark, bright, and so forth.

3. People/Animals—how many and who; describe people/animals.

4. **Add at least 3 events from your imagination.**

List details from the picture prompt.

_____

_____

_____

_____

_____

_____

_____

_____

_____

SAMPLE LIST OF DETAILS FROM PICTURE PROMPT

Answers may differ slightly, but they must reflect the picture prompt.

1. Setting

- Tropical island with sandy beach and rain forest plants
- During the day

2. Mood

- Mostly friendly, curious

3. People/Animals

- The main person could be either an explorer, scientist, tourist, or tour guide.
- The other people could be family members, tourists, or fellow scientists.
- A strange creature

4. Other Details

- Camera worn by person; creature has rhino head with a horn, hooves, webbed feet, small ears, long tail
- Creature has a wagging tail; one person looks curious, another looks frightened, as another stares

The same picture prompt may be used to write a story, article, or journal entry. Use a graphic organizer to help you organize your writing.

Directions: Pretend that you are the main person in the picture prompt above. Write a story about your discovery and experience.

Your story should include

■ a title
■ a beginning, middle, and end
■ details to make your story colorful and interesting

Planning Space: What type of graphic organizer will you use to plan your story?

Sample Graphic Organizer for Planning a Story

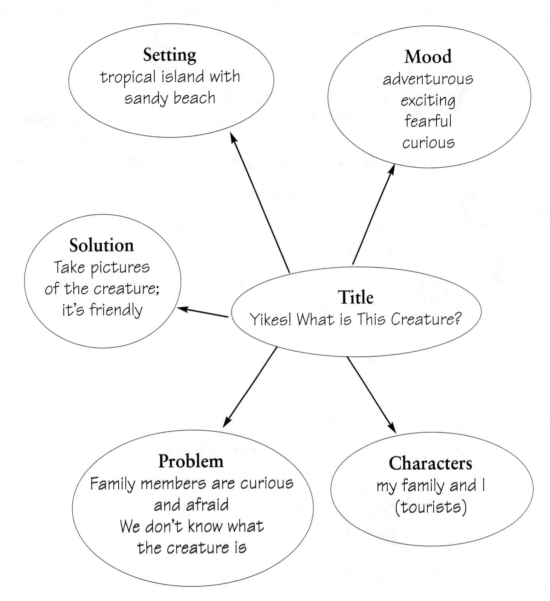

Setting
tropical island with
sandy beach

Mood
adventurous
exciting
fearful
curious

Solution
Take pictures
of the creature;
it's friendly

Title
Yikes! What is This Creature?

Problem
Family members are curious
and afraid
We don't know what
the creature is

Characters
my family and I
(tourists)

Directions: Pretend that you are the main person in the picture prompt on page 71. Complete the graphic organizer below, and then write a story about your discovery and experience.
Be sure to include

■ a title for your story
■ a beginning, middle, and end
■ details to make your story colorful and interesting

Another Sample Graphic Organizer for Planning a Story

PLOT **Beginning** Characters Setting Beginning of problem	
Middle Details about characters and problem	
End Resolution of problem	

Title: _____

_____

_____

_____

Directions: Pretend that you are the main person in the picture prompt on page 71. Complete the graphic organizer below, and then write a story about your discovery and experience.
  Be sure to include

- ▪ a title for your story
- ▪ a beginning, middle, and end to your story
- ▪ details to make your story colorful and interesting

Sample Graphic Organizer

PLOT **Beginning** Characters Setting Beginning of problem	My family and I
	Tropical island, rain forest plants,
	sandy beach
	Plenty to do: scuba dive, build sand
	castles, explore unknown areas
Middle Details about characters and problem	Hear odd noises
	Discover very strange but friendly
	creature
	Try to take pictures of creature to
	show friends
End Resolution of problem	Have mental photo of creature
	Talk about our discovery for years
	to come

Sample Response

An Adventure to Remember

When my family and I packed our bags and flew to a distant tropical island, we never expected the summer vacation of a lifetime.

There was something for each of us to do on this beautiful island. As a family, we agreed to take turns planning the day's activities so that each of us got a chance to do what we liked best. Dad organized the first day of our vacation, which we spent building sand castles as big as the state of Texas. On the second day, which Mom had planned, we enjoyed scuba diving in the sparkling, blue waters. I was the leader on the third day of our vacation. And that was when the real adventure began.

Like an eager explorer, I wanted to travel around every inch of the magnificent island. I led my family into an unknown area of the island filled with gigantic rain forests plants. Suddenly, we heard a noise, which sounded like the purring from a kitten, only louder. We all stopped to listen. At first, we couldn't tell where the sound was coming from. Then, a strange-looking creature with four legs appeared on the path in front of us. It had a head like a rhinoceros, front hooves, back webbed feet, and a long, thin tail.

My family and I could not believe our eyes. Just as I was wishing for this creature to be friendly, it began to wag its tail back and forth. Then I lifted my camera and click, it was gone.

Even though I was not able to get a picture of the creature, my family and I have a permanent picture of it in our heads. We will discuss this amazing discovery for many years to come.

PERSUASIVE WRITING—ARGUING FOR

The task below asks you to write a persuasive article. In persuasive writing, writers try to convince (get) readers to agree with their opinion. First, writers give an opinion. Then, they give details or reasons to support their opinion. Finally, they conclude by restating the opinion.

Directions: Write an article persuading (encouraging or convincing) people to visit a tropical island.
   Be sure to

- create a title for your article.
- convince others to visit a tropical island.
- include details from the picture.

Hint: Think about the following. How can you get people to want to visit a tropical island? Should you tell them about how much money it might cost to get there? No! That might make some people not want to go. Or, should you give your opinion (thoughts) about a tropical island in such a way that the place sounds like a beautiful dream come true? Yes!
   Your writing purpose, then, is to make the island sound so fantastic and magical that your readers will be most eager to arrive there.

Planning Space

ANSWERING THE FIVE W'S AND ONE H

Have you answered the following questions with your planning?

Sample Graphic Organizer

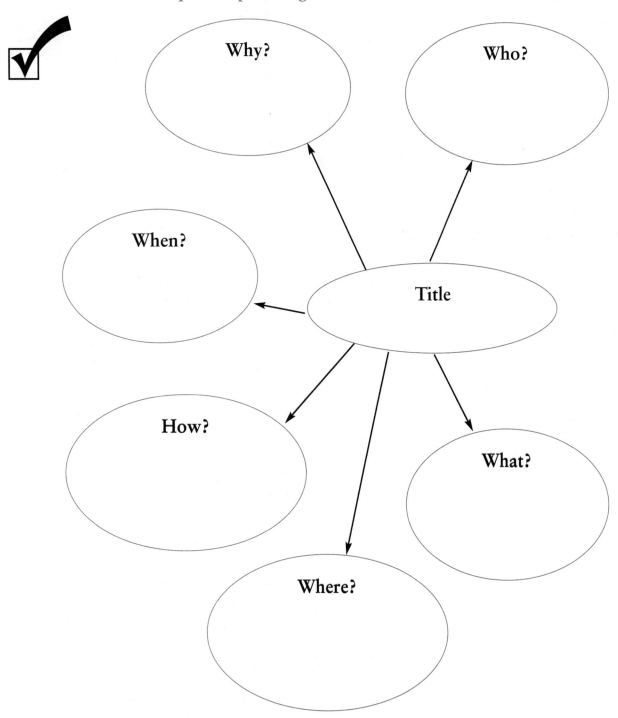

Title: _____

_____

_____

_____

_____

_____

_____

_____

_____

_____

_____

_____

_____

_____

_____

_____

Directions: Write an article persuading (encouraging, convincing) people to visit a tropical island.
Be sure to

■ create a title for your article.
■ convince others to visit a tropical island.
■ include details from the picture on page 71.

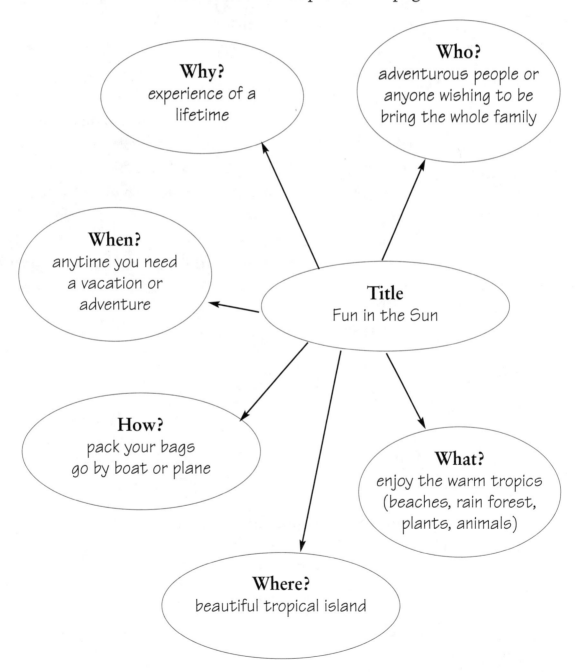

Sample Response

Fun in the Sun

Are you in need of a vacation or some excitement in your life? If so, it's time to pack your bags, leave your homework behind, and journey to a tropical island. Bring the entire family because there's an adventure for everyone.

Whether you wish to spend your day reading in a hammock, building a sand castle, or touring the island, you never know what you will discover in the tropics. Be sure to have a camera with you, along with plenty of film. There are many interesting sights to photograph, such as the beautiful beaches, rain forest plants, and different animals that live on the island. If you're adventurous enough, you may even discover something such as a friendly, strange creature that would amaze both you and your friends back home.

Don't waste another second. Tell the family, start packing, and let the adventure begin. Get ready to have fun in the sun!

Your answer should include

Who?
What?
Where?
When?
Why?
How?

Your answer should also include

Details from the picture prompt

Your answer should be:

Interesting
Convincing

PERSUASIVE WRITING—ARGUING AGAINST

Now, let's pretend that the above task had asked you to write an article that would make people NOT want to visit a tropical island. The focus of your writing, then, would be to describe the negative (bad) points about a possible visit.

Directions: Write an article that would make people *not* want to visit the tropical island known as Creature Crawly Island.

Be sure to

■ create a title for your article.
■ convince others to stay away from Creature Crawly Island.
■ include a beginning, middle, and end.

Title: _____

_____

_____

_____

_____

_____

_____

_____

_____

Sample Response

Do Not Visit Creature Crawly Island!

If you want to have an excellent and safe vacation, then Creature Crawly Island is not the place for you.

This strange tropical island is filled with many weird plants and creatures. The weather there is sizzling hot and humid, making the island a breeding ground for all sorts of biting insects. You'll spend your whole vacation scratching yourself with special backscratchers that you've been forced to buy on the island at a cost of one hundred dollars each. This money will be in addition to the thousands of dollars you'll have to spend for travel and hotel expenses. Also, food on the island is very expensive because it has to be brought in by boat or plane from other places.

Whatever you do, for your own safety, do not visit Creature Crawly Island!

JOURNAL ENTRY

Directions: Write a journal entry that the person might have written on the day he encountered (met) the interesting creature.

Be sure to include

■ a title for the journal entry
■ how the discovery was made
■ details about the creature discovered

Planning Space: Choose a graphic organizer to help you get ready to write.

Date

Title: _____

_____

_____

_____

_____

_____

_____

_____

_____

_____

_____

_____

_____

_____

_____

Sample Graphic Organizer

PLOT **Beginning** Setting Characters Beginning of problem	area with large palm leaves
	I saw footprints, but not the creature
	making them.
Middle Tells more about the characters and problem	heard loud, purring noise
	finally saw the strange-looking creature
	was friendly, wagged tail
End Resolution of problem	Will send photo of creature to fellow
	scientists to help identify it

Sample Response

November 7, 2003

A Day to Remember!

Today was a day I will always remember.

Here I was, on a tropical island known as Sand Castle Isle, simply trying to do my job as a scientist and study the rare rain forest plants found here. During the last few days, I had noticed unusual footprints in the sand in the area surrounding the gigantic palm trees. The footprints were very large and strange. Until today, I had not seen the creature leaving the prints.

But today, I heard a rustling in the palm leaves and a purring sound. Suddenly, I saw the creature. I stayed hidden and observed it for a long while. The creature had a horn on its head like a rhino. It had hooves on its front feet. The animal also had webbed feet on its back legs, small ears, and a long tail like a donkey.

The creature appeared to be friendly and it was wagging its tail. Still, I approached the animal very carefully. I took several pictures and will show them to fellow scientists when I get home.

You never know what you may discover on a tropical island. I discovered that even though I'm a scientist, I will need help from other people to identify the strange creature I saw today.

LETTER WRITING

Directions: The United States (U.S.) Postal Service issues stamps to honor people, animals, or special occasions/events. Write a letter to the U.S. Postal Service to nominate a person, animal, or occasion to be celebrated on a stamp.

Look at the parts of the task given.
Be sure to answer all parts of the task:

1. Write a letter to the U.S. Postal Service.

2. Choose a person, animal, occasion, or event.

3. Include at least 3 details to support your choice for the nomination. Be persuasive (convincing).

Planning Space

_____
Date

Dear United States Postal Service,

_____

_____

_____

_____

_____

_____

_____

_____

_____

_____

_____

_____

_____

Sincerely,
A New York Fourth-Grade Student

Sample Graphic Organizer

> **BEGINNING**
>
> U.S. Postal Service issues stamps to honor people, animals, or special occasions.
> My letter will nominate dogs—Labs.

> **MIDDLE**
>
> Labs—smart, gentle, & loving
> Guide dogs for the blind
> My pet lab

> **END**
>
> The animals on stamps are often symbols. Labs are symbols for improving people's lives.

Sample Reponse

October 26, 2005

Dear Members of the United States Postal Service,

Today, in my fourth-grade classroom, I learned that the United States Postal Service issues stamps in honor of people, animals, or special events. The reason for my letter is to ask you to design a stamp celebrating the wonderful breed of dogs known as Labrador Retrievers (Labs).

Labs are smart, gentle, and loving. They are easily trained to help the blind so they are often guide dogs. I have read nonfiction books about how Labs have even saved people's lives.

I have a Yellow Lab named Buffy for a pet. She is like a member of my family. Buffy improves my life just by being in it. She greets me when I arrive home from school with as much excitement as I would welcome a brand-new bicycle.

Some United States presidents have owned Labs. Like me, they know that Labs are true friends. Please design a stamp honoring them for all they do for people.
Bow wow for now,
One of Many Lab Lovers

STORY STARTER

Directions: Pretend you find the treasure map below. Write a story about your discovery and what you plan to do after studying the map.

In your story, be sure to include

- 5 details from the map
- where you found the map
- what happens next

Treasure Map

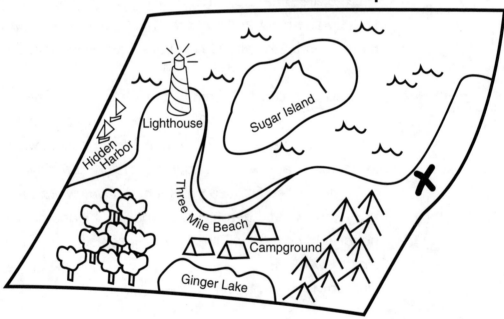

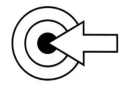

Be sure to include 5 details from the map and follow the other task directions.

1. ————————————————————————

2. ————————————————————————

3. ————————————————————————

4. ————————————————————————

5. ————————————————————————

6. ————————————————————————

7. ————————————————————————

How will you organize your details so that your story has a beginning, middle, and end? Use the space below to plan your story.

Planning Space

Title: _____

_____

_____

_____

_____

_____

_____

_____

_____

_____

_____

_____

_____

_____

_____

_____

_____

Sample Graphic Organizer

BEGINNING

Camping at Three Mile Beach

Digging to build a sand castle

Find a box with a treasure map inside

MIDDLE

Explore the area and find the treasure

Go over the mountains or rent a boat at Hidden Harbor to
sail to the spot

END

Went to the spot on the map

New hotel on the spot named "The Buried Treasure"

Your answer should include

- 5 details from the map
- Where you found the map and what happens next
- Story elements such as setting, characters, and problems

INDEPENDENT PRACTICE

PERSONAL NARRATIVE

American poet John Greenleaf Whittier was born in 1807 in Haverhill, Massachusetts.

He once wrote

"For all sad word of tongue or pen,
The saddest are these: It might have been!"

He meant that it's better to try something than to give up and wonder later if you might have succeeded.

Write about a time in your life when you tried something and succeeded, or didn't try and wondered about how the situation would have turned out.

- This story should be about you.
- Be sure your story relates to the quotation.
- Refer to (use) the quotation in your answer.

Use the Student Checklist on page 102 to check your writing.

Planning Page

STUDENT CHECKLIST

Meaning

> Did you complete the task by answering all the bulleted items in the question?
>
> Did you make connections and show you thought about the task?

Development

> Did you use specific examples and important details from the selection to support your ideas?
>
> Did you explain your answer fully?

Organization

> Did you begin with a topic sentence, an introduction to your writing?
>
> Did you use transition words to help with the direction of your writing?

Ideas and Language Use

> Did you write with a purpose (to inform, entertain, persuade, describe) in mind?
>
> Did you use interesting language?

Conventions

> Did you check your spelling, punctuation, and grammar?
>
> Did you start every sentence with a capital and end every sentence with the correct punctuation?

6 CONNECTING READING AND WRITING

OVERVIEW: SESSION 3

The shaded column in the chart below shows what you will be asked to do in Session 3 on Day 3 of the test.

New York State English Language Arts Test		
Day 1	Day 2	Day 3
Session 1 45 minutes Multiple-Choice Section ■ Read 5-6 selections. ■ Answer 28 questions.	Session 2—Part 1 30 minutes Listening Section ■ 2 short answers ■ 1 long response Session 2—Part 2 30 minutes Writing ■ Write a story, letter, journal entry, article, or essay.	Session 3 60 minutes Reading and Writing ■ Read 2 selections. ■ Write 1-2 short answers based on the first selection. ■ Write 1-2 short answers based on the second selection. ■ Write a long response based on both selections.

You will have 60 minutes to finish this part of the exam.

- Reading the two selections should take about 15–20 minutes.
- Writing answers for each of the short responses should take about 5–10 minutes each.
- Organizing and writing the long response should take about 20 minutes.

TIPS FOR SUCCESS

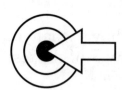

The poem below will help you remember the steps needed for success on the ELA test.

RUBRIC

R is for **reading carefully twice,**

>   That is certainly the best advice.

U is for **understanding the question asked.**

>   Once you do, you are ready to start the task.

B is for **beginning with a topic sentence,** number one.

>   Be sure it answers the question when done.

R is for **real examples** you choose.

>   They're from the story and support ideas you use.

I is for **interesting, insightful connections.**

reflections:
thoughts

>   Think about important facts during reflections.

C is for **concluding sentence** and organization that's clear.

>   **Correct** spelling, grammar, and punctuation; you have nothing to fear.

The chart below further explains the poem "RUBRIC." In some of the pages that follow, you will be asked to place a check next to each lettered section of the word rubric to show that you have completed the task required for that section.

R	Reading carefully	Read all information on the page: directions, captions, as well as the selection. READ AT LEAST TWICE.
U	Understanding the question	Read the question carefully. Be sure you understand it.
B	Beginning with a topic sentence	A topic sentence will get your answer started and focus the supporting details.
R	Real examples from the selection	Search the selection you have just read for examples that will support your answer.
I	Interesting, insightful connections	Think about what you have read. Make connections and build on the examples you use from the selection.
C	Conclusion and corrections	End with a concluding sentence. Then, go back and check your work for spelling, grammar, and punctuation. See the Appendix for more information.

GUIDED PRACTICE

R IS FOR READING CAREFULLY

Read all information carefully: introduction, headings, title, captions, and directions.

Directions: Below you will find the beginning part of a magazine article titled "Friendship." Read the article and then complete the Venn diagram.

Friendship

One day after swimming, nine-year-old Sammy Long found a bottle washed up on the beach near his home. When he discovered this note inside, he had no idea it would lead to a 10-year friendship.

Hello, Finder of This Bottle,

   Thank you for discovering this bottle and reading my note. I am an eleven-year-old girl, who lives on the island of Grand Turk in the Atlantic Ocean. Grand Turk is southeast of Florida and northeast of Cuba. It is a beautiful, warm, and sunny island. My home is very close to the beach, where I go often to walk and swim in the sparkling, blue ocean.
   I would like to have a pen pal as much as a coach would like to win a championship game. Please write back soon. Kindly send the letter to me at the following address: PO Box 22, Grand Turk, IH2237.

   Cheerfully,
   Helena Canti

Use the Venn diagram below to compare (tell how they are alike and how they are different) Helena and Sammy.

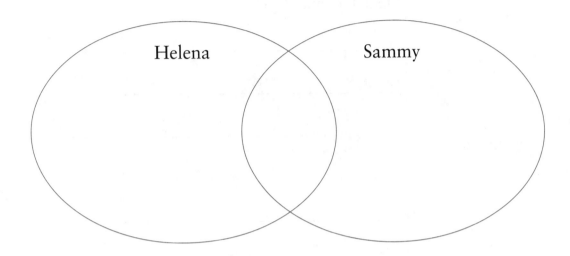

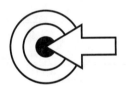
All the information about Sammy came from the introduction. To complete the Venn diagram, you had to read all information carefully.

U IS FOR UNDERSTANDING THE QUESTION ASKED

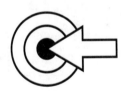
Look for key words in the question to help you understand the task.

Directions: Pretend you are Sammy. You have just found Helena's note and you are now going to write a letter to her. Use details from the article "Friendship" in your letter
   In your letter, be sure to:

- describe your discovery of the note.
- tell about yourself as Sammy.
- use at least 3 specific details from the article.

Date

Dear Helena,

_____

_____

_____

_____

_____

_____

_____

_____

Your new pen pal,
Sammy

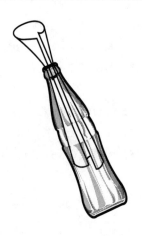

Check your writing.

Did you READ CAREFULLY?	R
Did you UNDERSTAND THE QUESTION?	U
Did you BEGIN WITH A TOPIC SENTENCE?	B
Did you use REAL EXAMPLES FROM THE SELECTION?	R
Did you make INTERESTING, INSIGHTFUL CONNECTIONS?	I
Did you end with a CONCLUDING SENTENCE and make CORRECTIONS?	C

Did you do the following?

- Pretend you are Sammy and just found Helena's note.
- Write her a letter.
- Include details from the article "Friendship."
- Describe your discovery of the note.
- Tell about yourself as Sammy.
- Include at least 3 specific details from the article.

MORE ABOUT UNDERSTANDING THE QUESTION ASKED

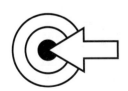

Underline important information in the task as a reminder of the details that must be included in your answer.

Underline key words in the task below. Be sure to use those details in your answer.

Pretend you are Sammy. You are going to write a letter to Helena. Use details from the article "Friendship" to recall how your friendship started more than 10 years ago.

_____
Date

Dear Helena,

_____

_____

_____

_____

_____

_____

_____

_____

_____

Your longtime buddy,
Sammy

Did you **read carefully?**

Did you **understand the question?**

R	
U	
B	
R	
I	
C	

B IS FOR BEGINNING WITH A TOPIC SENTENCE

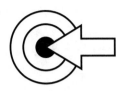

A **topic sentence** is an opening sentence that tells the main idea of a paragraph.

Use clues in the question or task to help you write the topic sentence.

You have just read the magazine article "Friendship" (page 106) about people sending notes in bottles. You are concerned that bottles washing up on beaches around the world may be adding to our pollution problem. You decide to write a letter to the editor of the magazine expressing your concern.

Write only your topic sentence for the letter to the editor you will write.

_____

_____

_____

_____

After reading the magazine article "Friendship," you have decided to write a report about the island of Grand Turk. Use information from the article to start your report.

Write only your topic sentence for your report about Grand Turk.

_____

_____

_____

_____

R IS FOR REAL EXAMPLES TO SUPPORT YOUR ANSWER

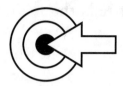

Be sure your examples support your answer and are from the reading.

The article "Friendship" describes two children who become friends.

Compare Helena and Sammy: Write a paragraph telling how they are alike and how they are different. Use details from the article. You may refer back to the Venn diagram activity on page 107.

_____

_____

_____

_____

Use details from the article "Friendship" to write a paragraph describing the island of Grand Turk.

_____

_____

_____

_____

I IS FOR INTERESTING, INSIGHTFUL CONNECTIONS

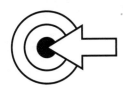

Write about specific details from the story in your own words.

Showing insight means you use your own words and build on the details from the story. It is your own personal stamp on your answer.

The task below has 2 answers attached. Both answers are acceptable. One answer shows more insight. Which answer shows the most interesting, insightful details?

Question: Pretend you are Sammy. You have just found Helena's note and you are now going to write her a letter. Use details from "Friendship" in your letter.

Answer **A:**	The answer is acceptable. There are at least 3 details from the selection included.

Dear Helena,
 	
    I am a nine-year-old boy who found your note in a bottle. You are only two years older than me so we should have things in common. Like you, I live near the beach.
    I would like to be your pen pal. Please write back soon.
 	
                    Sincerely,
                    Sammy	

Question: Pretend you are Sammy. You have just found Helena's note and you are now going to write her a letter. Use details from "Friendship" in your letter.

Answer **B**:	
Dear Helena,	
I am a nine-year-old boy, who was pleasantly surprised when your floating note washed up on the beach near my house. Opening the bottle and reading the message inside was as thrilling as opening presents on my birthday. I have always wanted a pen pal and am very excited about writing to you.	The answer is acceptable. There are at least 3 details from the selection included.
The island of Grand Turk sounds delightful. Enjoy your walks on the beach and have fun swimming, but please don't forget to write me back.	
Hope to hear from you soon.	
Your pen pal, Sammy	

Both are acceptable answers.

Which answer showed more thought and used more interesting language? A   or   B?

Answer B has many more details and shows a more thorough understanding. Notice the simile in Answer B: "Opening the bottle and reading the message inside was as thrilling as opening presents on my birthday." See the Appendix pages on Figurative Language for added ideas on how to make your writing more interesting.

MORE ABOUT INTERESTING, INSIGHTFUL CONNECTIONS

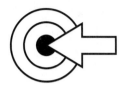

Showing insight means you use your own words and build on the details from the story. It is your personal stamp on your answer.

The task below has 2 answers attached. Both answers are acceptable. One answer shows more insight. Which answer shows the most interesting, insightful details?

Question: Compare Helena and Sammy; tell how they are alike and how they are different. Use details from the article.	
Answer **A:** Sammy and Helena are two friends who met in a very unusual way. Helena sent a message in a bottle and Sammy found it. Sammy was a nine-year-old boy, and Helena was an eleven-year-old girl. They both live near a beach.	The answer is acceptable. Does it show insight or thought? Is it interesting?
Answer **B:** Sammy and Helena are alike, but they are also different. Sammy is a boy, and Helena is a girl. Sammy is nine, and Helena is eleven. They both live near a beach.	The answer is acceptable. Does it show insight or thought? Is it interesting?

Both are acceptable answers.

Which answer showed more thought and used more interesting language? A or B?

Answer choice A is more detailed and complete.

C IS FOR CONCLUDING SENTENCE, ORGANIZATION THAT'S CLEAR, CORRECT SPELLING, GRAMMAR, AND PUNCTUATION

Concluding Sentence

DO

- highlight the main ideas
- provide an ending

DO <u>NOT</u>

- use the same language as in the introduction
- end too simply with no reference or connection to the main idea
- use "in conclusion..."

Clear Organization

- Your writing is easy to understand.
- You are able to make your point.

Correct

Spelling—Look back in the reading selection and the task. Some words you need to write may have been spelled for you in the task. Please see the Appendix (pages 232–236) for a list of commonly misspelled words.

Grammar—Pay attention to how you use words in sentences and sentences in paragraphs. Most of the time you will need to write in complete sentences on the ELA test.

Punctuation—Please see the Appendix for common rules for punctuation.

You be the teacher. Choose the best concluding sentence for each response.

Sample Response

I am very curious about your island. I am writing this letter to request more information about the island of Grand Turk.

Which is the best concluding sentence?

   A That is all.

   B I would appreciate any information you could send to help me learn more about your beautiful island.

   C In conclusion, I am writing for more information.

The best concluding sentence is **B**; it includes related details. Choice **A** is *not* detailed, and choice **C** begins with "in conclusion."

Sample Response

Grand Turk is an island located southeast of Florida and northeast of Cuba in the Atlantic Ocean. The weather here is warm and sunny. There are many beautiful beaches for sunbathing and swimming.

Which is the best concluding sentence?

   A I love going to the beach with my family.

   B That is all I learned about Grand Turk.

   C Its location and weather make it a wonderful place to visit in the middle of winter.

Why do you think choice **C** is the best concluding sentence?

Return to some of your answers on the previous pages. Check them for conclusion and clear organization. Correct any spelling, grammar, and punctuation errors.

UNDERSTANDING INFORMATION FROM TWO SELECTIONS

Directions: In this section, you are going to read 2 articles. One article is titled "Earth Matters" and the other is titled "Kids to the Rescue." You will complete 2 graphic organizers and write about what you have read. You may look at the articles as often as you like.

Earth Matters

Every year, Americans throw away about 50 billion food and drink cans. They dispose of 27 billion glass bottles and jars. Most of it is taken to a dump, also known as a landfill. It can take from 100 to 400 years for some garbage to decompose, after it is covered with dirt. Glass has been found in perfect condition after being buried for 4,000 years.

Communities are running out of places to bury our garbage. It is time to practice the three R's of the environment: reduce, reuse, and recycle. Everyone can buy less, use less, and reuse things. Using a glass cup instead of a paper one each time we take a drink may save thousands of paper cups. We should also recycle as much as possible. To recycle, we need to separate items so that they can be used again to make new things. Paper, plastic, and glass are all materials that can be recycled.

People of all ages can make a difference. We all need to make less garbage and encourage others to do the same. If we follow the three R's, we won't be down in the dumps anymore.

According to the article, there are ways to solve the garbage problem. Write your answers in the boxes below.

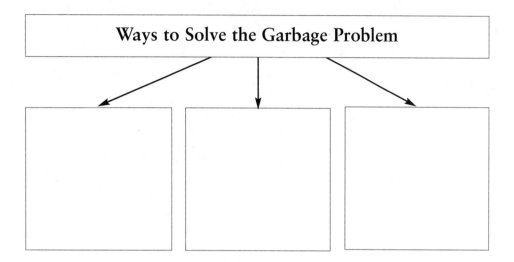

COMPLETING A GRAPHIC ORGANIZER

Are the boxes below filled in correctly?

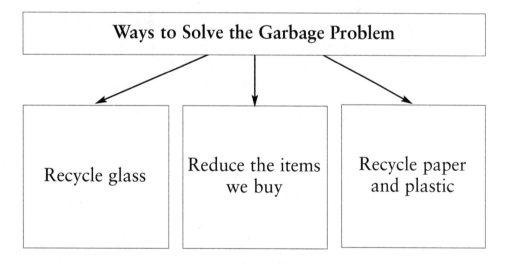

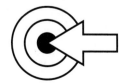

The first and last box are similar. The boxes need to have 3 different answers.

Are the boxes below filled in correctly?

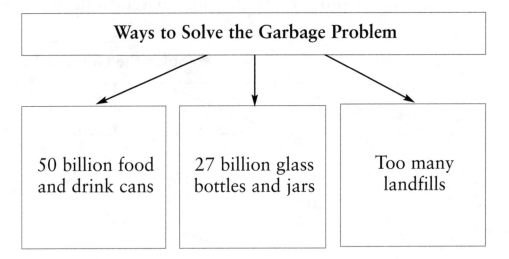

Ways to Solve the Garbage Problem		
50 billion food and drink cans	27 billion glass bottles and jars	Too many landfills

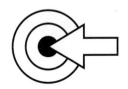

All of these items are problems, not ways to solve problems. None of the answers are correct.

Are the boxes below filled in correctly?

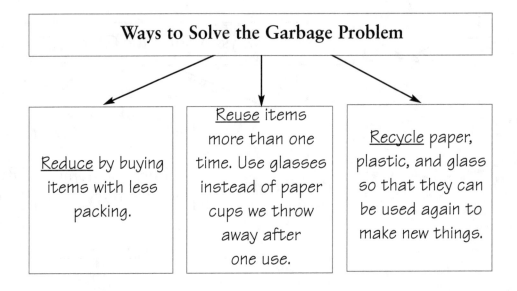

Ways to Solve the Garbage Problem		
Reduce by buying items with less packing.	Reuse items more than one time. Use glasses instead of paper cups we throw away after one use.	Recycle paper, plastic, and glass so that they can be used again to make new things.

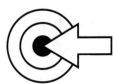

These answers are excellent. They are more detailed and come directly from the reading.

Acceptable Answers = Less Credit or Less Points Earned

- Reduce
- Reuse
- Recycle

Exceptional Answers = More Credit or More Points Earned

- Reduce by buying items with less packaging.
- Reuse items instead of using things and throwing them away.
- Recycle by separating paper, plastic, and glass so that they can be made into something new.

NOT ACCEPTABLE ANSWERS:

- Problems stated, not solutions
- Same answer repeated in more than one box

Kids to the Rescue

environment:
our
surroundings

Taking care of our environment is an important job, and it's not just a job for grown-ups. There is something for everyone, including children, to do. Some things you can do on your own, some with a friend, and others with the help of an adult. Just look around your neighborhood or school, and think about ways to improve the environment. It is never too late to begin. Here are a few ideas to help you get started.

Keep America Beautiful: Never litter. If your parents own a car, make litter bags for them. Keep your yard free of trash. If your school playground doesn't have a garbage can, ask the principal or custodian to put one out. You can make posters reminding other students to put garbage where it belongs. You can also make a bulletin board showing pictures of clean areas and other areas spoiled by litter or trash.

Kids can make a difference by "reducing," "reusing," and "recycling," often referred to as the 3 R's. They need to educate themselves and others about ways to promote the 3 R's. Environmental clubs encourage groups of children to work together to protect our planet. Some clubs sponsor school-wide environmental education programs and events. Others organize clean-up days in the community and at school.

Directions: Complete the graphic organizer below using information from the article "Kids to the Rescue."

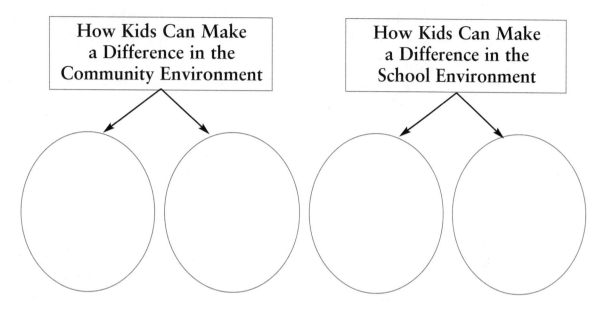

Directions: Look at the graphic organizer below. According to the article "Kids to the Rescue," which item is <u>not</u> correct?

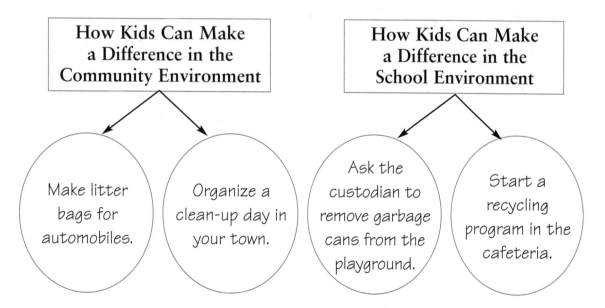

All items are correct except for "ask the custodian to remove garbage cans from the playground." The article suggests that a garbage can should be on the playground. **Information needs to come from the article.**

WRITING TO INFORM

You are a member of your school's environmental club. Your task is to write an article for the school newsletter informing the community about all the ways you are helping your school.

Use details from both articles to help you write your article.

Title: _____

_____

_____

_____

_____

_____

_____

_____

_____

_____

_____

_____

Remember to look for clues in the task or question. In the task below, the underlined words indicate:

Type of writing—ARTICLE

Purpose—INFORM

Audience—COMMUNITY

Source of Information—BOTH ARTICLES

You are a member of your school's environmental club. You need to <u>write an article</u> for the school newsletter <u>informing the community</u> about all the <u>ways you are help-ing your school.</u>
   <u>Use details from both articles to help you write the article.</u>

Sample Response

   Did you know that Americans throw away about 50 billion food and drink cans every year? They are taken to the dump to be covered by dirt. It may take a long time for some things to decompose. Glass can be found in perfect condition after being buried for 4,000 years. Soon communities will run out of places to bury their garbage. As a community we need to reduce, reuse, and recycle. Every person can make a difference.

This answer does not inform the community about ways your club is helping your school. It uses information from just one article. Most items are copied from the article and not written in the author's own words. **The task directions have not been followed.**

Sample Response

The Environmental Rangers at Work

Did you know that Americans throw away 50 billion cans and 27 billion glass bottles every year? Students at Hillside Elementary School became concerned when we learned this disturbing fact. We have started a club called the Environmental Rangers. So far, we have organized a recycling program in our cafeteria. Student volunteers separate items such as glass and plastic, which can be used again to make new items. Club members have made posters and bulletin boards to remind other students about the importance of taking care of our environment. The Environmental Rangers are children who are making a difference.

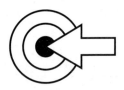

This is an informative response that uses details from both articles. **This answer is acceptable.** An outstanding answer would include even more detail. How did your response measure up?

You are a member of your school's environmental club. You need to write an article for the school newsletter encouraging your fellow students to join the club to help the school.

Use details from both articles to help you write the article.

Title: _____

_____

_____

_____

_____

_____

_____

_____

_____

_____

_____

_____

_____

You are a member of your school's environmental club. You task is to **write an article** for the school newsletter **encouraging your fellow students** to **join the club** to help the school.

Use details from both articles to help you write the article.

Sample Response One

The school's environmental club needs your help. Student members do many things around the school. We could do more if we had more members. If you would like to join our club, come to the next meeting. You need to bring only a smile, ideas for helping our school, and plenty of energy to do a very important job. Even Paul Revere, a hero of the American Revolution, recycled. He melted down and reused old silver. You can join our club and recycle, too!

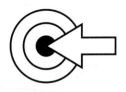

This response does <u>not</u> answer the question. It does not contain information from the articles read. It includes a recycling fact about Paul Revere based on the writer's memory. **Be sure to use information from the articles, even if the topic is familiar to you.**

Sample Response Two

Caring, Creative Students Wanted

The environmental club, known as Planet Protectors, needs creative people like YOU who care about our school environment. If you would like to make a difference and help keep our school beautiful, please join our important club.

Members of Planet Protectors get to do many interesting projects. We help with the school recycling program in the cafeteria, and create bulletin boards to teach students about littering. In the spring, we will be organizing a school clean-up program.

Our club needs your talents and energy. Please come to our next meeting, which will be held tomorrow at 4:00 P.M. in Ms. Wizard's science room. Delicious ice cream sundaes will be served in glass, not plastic, bowls. You will have an exciting time meeting new people and working together to improve our school.

This answer is acceptable. It uses information from both articles and completes the task given. It also includes a title.

7

PRACTICE TEST 1

28 Questions
45 minutes

Directions: In this part of the test, you are going to do some reading and then answer questions about what you have read.

You will be filling in the answers to Numbers 1 through 28 on the answer (bubble) sheet. If you make a mistake, erase it completely.

Do not write answers on the test pages. All of your answers must be marked on the answer sheet. You may make notes or underline in the book as you read. Do not use highlighters.

You will have 45 minutes to read all of the selections carefully and answer the 28 questions about what you have read. On the answer sheet, you will fill in the letter that matches your answer for each question.

Try to answer all questions. Read each question carefully, and make your best attempt at answering the question.

SESSION 1—ANSWER SHEET

1. Ⓐ Ⓑ Ⓒ Ⓓ   15. Ⓐ Ⓑ Ⓒ Ⓓ

2. Ⓕ Ⓖ Ⓗ Ⓙ   16. Ⓕ Ⓖ Ⓗ Ⓙ

3. Ⓐ Ⓑ Ⓒ Ⓓ   17. Ⓐ Ⓑ Ⓒ Ⓓ

4. Ⓕ Ⓖ Ⓗ Ⓙ   18. Ⓕ Ⓖ Ⓗ Ⓙ

5. Ⓐ Ⓑ Ⓒ Ⓓ   19. Ⓐ Ⓑ Ⓒ Ⓓ

6. Ⓕ Ⓖ Ⓗ Ⓙ   20. Ⓕ Ⓖ Ⓗ Ⓙ

7. Ⓐ Ⓑ Ⓒ Ⓓ   21. Ⓐ Ⓑ Ⓒ Ⓓ

8. Ⓕ Ⓖ Ⓗ Ⓙ   22. Ⓕ Ⓖ Ⓗ Ⓙ

9. Ⓐ Ⓑ Ⓒ Ⓓ   23. Ⓐ Ⓑ Ⓒ Ⓓ

10. Ⓕ Ⓖ Ⓗ Ⓙ   24. Ⓕ Ⓖ Ⓗ Ⓙ

11. Ⓐ Ⓑ Ⓒ Ⓓ   25. Ⓐ Ⓑ Ⓒ Ⓓ

12. Ⓕ Ⓖ Ⓗ Ⓙ   26. Ⓕ Ⓖ Ⓗ Ⓙ

13. Ⓐ Ⓑ Ⓒ Ⓓ   27. Ⓐ Ⓑ Ⓒ Ⓓ

14. Ⓕ Ⓖ Ⓗ Ⓙ   28. Ⓕ Ⓖ Ⓗ Ⓙ

Directions: Read this poem about autumn. Then answer questions 1 through 5.

Autumn Fancies

Anonymous

The maple is a dainty maid,
The pet of all the wood,
Who lights the dusky forest glade
With scarlet cloak and hood.

pet: favorite

dusky: dark

The elm a lovely lady is,
In shimmering robes of gold,
That catch the sunlight when she moves,
And glisten, fold on fold.

The sumac is a gypsy queen,
Who flaunts in crimson dressed,
And wild along the roadside runs,
Red blossoms in her breast.

crimson: red

And towering high above the wood,
All in his purple cloak,
A monarch in his splendor is
The proud and princely oak.

monarch: king

1. In the poem "Autumn Fancies," the trees are described as

   A animals

   B insects

   C people

   D towers

2. The largest of all the trees in the forest is the

   F elm

   G oak

   H sumac

   J maple

3. How does the maple affect the woods?

   A it lights up a dull forest

   B it is the favorite

   C it towers over all of the other trees

   D it acts like a queen

4. Of all of the trees mentioned, which one would probably <u>not</u> be chosen to be planted in someone's yard?

   F maple

   G oak

   H elm

   J sumac

5. When the author of the poem describes the maple as the "dainty maid," he or she means that the maple is

   A wild

   B lovely

   C small

   D tall

Directions: Read this article about a famous monument. Then answer questions 6 through 10.

A Proud Lady in the Harbor

Who wears a crown with seven huge spikes, has an index finger longer than the height of a very tall basketball player, and wears a size 879 in women's shoes? The answer, of course, is the world-famous Statue of Liberty. It was the first site that immigrants saw when they arrived in America.

In 1884 France gave the Statue to the United States as a symbol of the friendship these two countries had made during the American Revolution. The huge copper structure was shipped to the United States in 1885 in 214 cases. Over the years, the monument has also come to symbolize freedom under America's free form of government.

The Statue, whose proper name is "Liberty Enlightening the World," stands proudly 115 feet above New York Harbor. It is a tremendous sculpture of a lady, who is dressed in a loose robe. She holds a torch in her right hand, which is raised high in the air. Her left arm holds a tablet containing the date of the Declaration of Independence: July 4th, 1776. People hardly notice the broken shackles underfoot, which represent Liberty destroying the chains of slavery. The seven spikes in her crown stand for either the seven seas or the seven continents.

tablet: book

shackles: chains

Millions of people visit the Statue annually. Many visitors climb 354 steps to reach the crown, which contains 25 windows. The normal waiting time to climb to the crown in the summer is three hours. Some visitors take an elevator to the base of the statue, where there is an observation balcony and view of the city. The original torch, which was replaced when the structure was restored in the 1980s, is now at the base.

restored: repaired

Today, next to the flag of the United States, the Statue is America's most common symbol for freedom.

6. What is the main idea of this article?

   F Lady Liberty has a large foot and index finger.

   G Visitors can either climb many stairs or take the elevator to view different parts of the monument.

   H The Statue of Liberty is a well-known monument and symbol for freedom.

   J Visitors to the Statue of Liberty should take more time and notice the important broken shackles by her feet.

7. The spikes on the crown of the Statue of Liberty look most like

   A the seven continents

   B the rays of the sun

   C the seas

   D windows

8. Which of the following is an *opinion* from the article?

   F France gave the monument to the United States in 1885.

   G The Statue of Liberty holds a torch in her right hand.

   H It was kind of France to give the United States the Statue of Liberty.

   J There are 25 windows in Lady's Liberty's crown.

9. According to the article, millions of people visit the Statue of Liberty annually. What does the word "annually" mean?

A monthly

B weekly

C yearly

D every two years

10. What is the most likely reason that the Statue was shipped to the United States in 214 cases?

F The height of the Statue is 214 feet.

G The cases stood for the 214 battles in the American Revolution.

H The Statue was very large and had to be taken apart before being shipped.

J It took 214 long, hard days to build the monument.

Directions: Read the article about animals' tails. Then answer questions 11 through 15.

A Tail Comes in Handy

Animals use their tails for different purposes. You can learn fascinating information about animals just from observing their tails.

A tail comes in handy for communication. Animals such as wolves and ostrich use their tails to show rank among the group. A timid wolf will keep its tail between its legs, whereas a fearless wolf will raise its tail. The highest-ranking male ostrich will hold his tail pointing straight up to show his dominance. The next-highest male will hold his tail horizontal, while other birds droop their tails down to show they are subordinate.

Deer also use their tails to communicate with each other. A white-tailed deer will lift its tail straight up and wag it, showing the white fur underneath. The white fur acts like an alarm or signal, which warns other deer of approaching danger.

A tail comes in handy for balance purposes. The kangaroo and the squirrel use their tails for balance. A kangaroo's tail acts like a third leg; it allows the animal to prop itself up. The squirrel's bushy tail not only provides warmth on winter days, but it also helps the animal keep its balance when it is leaping and climbing.

A tail comes in handy for movement. Birds use their tails to move around and balance on branches. Most fish have tails that help them with movement and direction.

A tail comes in handy to scare off predators. Many animals use their tails to give a warning that they feel threatened and are ready to defend themselves. To warn would-be attackers, a rattlesnake will rattle its tail and a porcupine will raise its quills and shake

communication: talking

subordinate: lower in rank

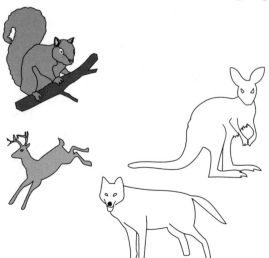

them. A ground iguana scares off its enemies by whipping its tail fiercely. Horses, giraffes, cows, and lions have tails that can swat off the peskiest of flies.

Tails serve many purposes. They can be as useful to animals as a baseball is to a pitcher.

11. According to the definition given in the article, which of the following words is the <u>opposite</u> of *subordinate*?

   A junior

   B higher

   C lesser

   D inferior

12. The main idea of the article is that

   F tails can help protect against predators

   G animals use their tails in many ways

   H some animals could not survive without tails

   J tails come in many shapes and sizes

13. The article suggests that animals use their tails for protection in all of the following ways <u>except</u>

   A warning others to stay away

   B warning before striking

   C warning with smell

   D warning others in the group of approaching danger

14. The word *timid* means

   F powerful

   G brave

   H shy

   J silly

15. Which word from below should be used to complete both blanks in the graphic organizer?

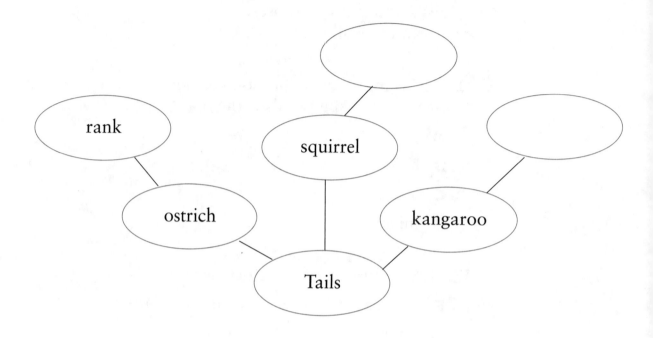

A warmth

B signal

C communicate

D balance

Directions: Read the poem entitled "The Kayak." Then answer questions 16 through 19.

The Kayak

Anonymous

Over the briny wave I go,
In spite of the weather, in spite of the snow:
What cares the hardy Eskimo?
In my little skiff, with paddle and lance,
I glide where the foaming billows dance.

Round me the sea-birds slip and soar;
Like me, they love the ocean's roar.
Sometimes a floating iceberg gleams
Above me with its melting streams;
Sometimes a rushing wave will fall
Down on my skiff and cover it all.

But what care I for a wave's attack?
With my paddle I right my little kayak,
And then its weight I speedily trim,
And over the water away I skim.

skiff: small boat

16. What word would best describe the water being traveled?

   F calm

   G smooth

   H rippling

   J rough

17. How does the kayaker feel about the ocean?

   A he loves it

   B he is afraid of it

   C he hates it

   D he is troubled by it

18. What does the kayaker not see in his travels?

   F snow

   G birds

   H icebergs

   J waterfalls

19. The phrase "foaming billows dance" describes

   A birds flying around

   B Eskimos dancing

   C water bubbling strongly

   D kayak bouncing around

Directions: Read the tale below. Then answer questions 20 through 24.

The Stone in the Road

Adapted Tale

This story took place long ago in the kingdom of a very wise king, who was always attempting to teach people good habits. He often tested others to see if they were thoughtful, good people. He believed that people should do less complaining and solve their own problems.

One night, while everyone slept, he placed a large stone in the road that led past his palace. He hid at the edge of the road to see what would happen.

A short time afterward, a soldier marched casually along the road. The soldier's foot struck the rock, and he sprawled in the road. The soldier rose angrily, waving his sword at the rock. He complained to himself as he continued down the road, blaming lazy people for leaving the rock in the road; never once did the soldier think that he should move the stone himself.

After a few more minutes, a farmer guided his grain wagon around the rock in the road. He was on his way to the mill to have his grain ground to flour, and he did not have time to stop and remove the rock.

"The world is filled with careless, lazy people!" the farmer complained. "Someone should remove the rock from the road so that it doesn't cause an accident."

All day long the king secretly watched people go around the rock and complain about lazy people leaving the rock in the road: yet no one touched the rock to move it.

It was almost evening when a young girl walked past the palace. She was very tired from working at the mill all day. She spotted the rock and thought, "I should move this rock from the road; it is almost dark and someone may trip and get hurt."

She struggled with the heavy rock and managed to move it aside. Beneath the rock was a box. She lifted the heavy box out of the hole it was in. On it was written, "This box belongs to the thoughtful one who moves the stone out of the way for others."

The girl opened the box and discovered it was filled with gold. The news of her find spread throughout the area. The soldier and the farmer and the other passersby went back to the spot in the road to search in the dust for a piece of gold.

The king announced the find: "As we go through life, we often are faced with obstacles and problems. We may complain while we just walk around them waiting for someone else to solve them, or we can take the time to solve the problems ourselves. If we leave problems for someone else to solve, we are usually disappointed."

20. Why did the king bury the gold under the rock?

    F to teach people a lesson

    G to hide it from people

    H to save the gold

    J to keep it safe

21. The farmer did not move the rock because

    A he was in a hurry

    B he drove around it

    C he didn't notice it

    D he thought someone else should take care of it

22. What was the soldier most likely thinking when he passed the rock in the road?

    F it was a trick

    G it was left by the farmer

    H it was left by a lazy person

    J he should move the rock

23. When she saw the stone in the road, the young girl

    A walked around it

    B complained about the careless person who had left it there

    C moved it before someone was hurt

    D went to the king for help

24. What lesson was the king probably trying to teach?

    F everyone has a duty to make changes for the good of all

    G people are careless and leave things lying around

    H sometimes when you least expect it, good things happen

    J you should always watch where you are going

Directions: Read the article about roller coasters. Then answer questions 25 through 28.

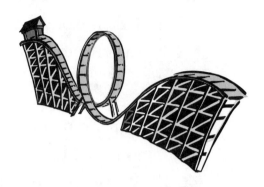

Roller Coasters: Scream Machines

When you think of roller coasters, you probably imagine amusement parks on summer days. If so, your mental picture is very different from their origins in fifteenth-century Russia in the cold of winter.

The first roller coasters earned the nickname "Russian Mountains." They were ice-covered hills, constructed of wood. Children and adults would climb up five stories of stairs (70 feet high) and sit on an ice block for the 50-mile-per-hour ride that would last just a few seconds.

In 1804, the ride "Russian Mountains" was brought to Paris, France. Wheels were added to the sleds. Little was done to make the ride safe, which seemed to attract more riders. It took a number of years for safety measures to be improved.

In 1827, a coal mining company in Pennsylvania opened "Gravity Road" (a converted railway that rolled downhill to transport coal) to the public for amusement purposes. This would be one of the first roller coasters in the United States. Many of the next roller coasters were built in amusement parks on Coney Island in New York. This increased competition led to new, more daring innovations and the required safety improvements.

Today, the roller coaster with the biggest drop is located in California. It is called the "Super Man Escape" and has a drop of 328 feet. The fastest coaster is in Japan; it reaches speeds of 107 miles per hour. The ride of the future will undoubtedly be taller and faster.

25. The author wrote this article to

   A persuade people to ride roller coasters

   B increase the safety of roller coasters

   C learn about all the different roller coasters today

   D review the history of roller coasters

26. According to the article, what happened as roller coasters became more daring?

   F fewer people rode

   G they were made more comfortable

   H safety improvements were needed

   J height and weight restrictions were important

27. One of the first roller coasters in the United States was

   A located on Coney Island

   B made of ice

   C in an amusement park

   D used to transport coal

28. Which is <u>not</u> a nickname for roller coasters?

   F Scream Machines

   G Paris Mountains

   H Russian Mountains

   J Gravity Road

DAY 2, SESSION 2—PART ONE: LISTENING

2 short answers
1 long response
30 minutes

Directions: In this section of the test, a story called "Doing What Comes Naturally" will be read aloud to you twice. Please listen carefully each time the story is read because you will then be asked to answer specific questions about the story.

During the first reading, listen closely but do not take notes. You may take notes during the second reading. Please use the space provided below for your notes. You may refer back to your notes to answer the questions that follow. Your notes will *not* count toward your score.

Notes

Doing What Comes Naturally

An African Tale

Long ago in an African jungle, Monkey and Rabbit were enjoying a meal together. Rabbit was enjoying his bounty of green leaves, and Monkey was dining on bunches of yellow bananas.

During the feast each acted naturally. Rabbit turned his head, first to the left, then to the right, then behind him, and finally in front of him. He was always watching for an enemy. He was not able to stop looking around, even during the meal.

As Rabbit was on the lookout, Monkey scratched. He scratched all over: his arms, legs, chest, and head. He was unable to stop the scratching. Rabbit watched and asked, "Did you sit on an ant's nest? Something is making you scratch."

"I didn't sit on an ant's nest; I scratch naturally," responded Monkey firmly.

"Please stop; it is very impolite," demanded Rabbit.

"You should talk about being impolite; you have been looking around the whole time we have been eating," answered Monkey.

"I will stop looking around, if you stop scratching," replied Rabbit.

"I think I can stop for longer than you can," boasted Monkey.

"The first one to move has to feed the winner for a week," announced Rabbit.

They continued their lunch, with no scratching or looking around. Thirty minutes passed. Monkey wanted to scratch himself more than a person who had a bad case of the chicken pox. And Rabbit was shaking with fear.

Rabbit suggested that the two tell each other stories while they ate. He began: "One night, my mother left me to watch over my brothers and sisters. I was frightened by every sound. I heard a twig snap to my left and then to my right...." Rabbit acted out the story looking to the left and

then to the right. "Then I heard something in the trees above," Rabbit stated as he looked up.

Monkey laughed, realizing that Rabbit was trying to trick him. He began his story, "One day I was separated from my mother in the jungle; I was hit on the head with a branch." Monkey scratched his head. He continued, "Then I discovered a nest of bees and was stung on my chest over and over again." He took the opportunity to scratch his chest repeatedly.

Rabbit stopped Monkey's story; "I guess we can't change what comes naturally to us."

Monkey agreed. "I think you are right."

Today, Rabbit and Monkey continue to eat their meal, looking around and scratching happily.

29. Complete the story chart with details from the tale.

Beginning of the story

Middle of the story

End of the story

30. This story is titled, "Doing What Comes Naturally." What would be another title for the African tale? Use details from the tale to support your answer.

_____

_____

_____

_____

_____

31. This African folktale teaches a lesson. Which lesson does the folktale teach best? Use details from the tale to support your answer.

■ Love your neighbors for who they are.
■ Be yourself; don't try to be something you're not.

_____

_____

_____

_____

_____

_____

_____

_____

_____

_____

_____

DAY 2, SESSION 2—PART TWO: WRITING

Write a story
30 minutes

Directions: In this section of the test, you are going to write a story of your own. Please do NOT include information from "Doing What Comes Naturally" in your writing. You may use this page to PLAN your writing. The work that you do on the Planning Page will *not* count toward your end score.

Write your final answer on the next page(s).

Planning Space

32. Write a story about a time when you learned that it was better to be yourself, rather than trying to be like someone else. Describe how you learned this lesson, and what helped you realize that it's better to be yourself.

In your writing, be sure to include
■ a title for your story
■ a beginning, middle, and end to your story
■ details to make your story interesting to the reader

Check your writing for correct spelling, grammar, capitalization, and punctuation.

Title: _____

_____

_____

_____

_____

_____

_____

_____

_____

_____

DAY 3, SESSION THREE—WRITING

60 minutes
Read 2 selections.
Write one short answer based on the first selection.
Write 2 short answers based on the second selection.
Write a long response based on both selections.

Directions: In this section of the test, you will read a web site called the "Aunt Tillie's Web Site of Alaska," and an e-mail from a class of fourth-grade students from Alaska. Then you will answer some questions and write about what you have read. You may look back at the web site and e-mail as often as you like to help you answer the questions.

AUNT TILLIE'S WEB SITE OF ALASKA

Browse This Educational Site and Learn the Fun Facts About This Fantastic State from an Expert on Alaska: Aunt Tillie

The name Alaska means "great land" or "that which the sea breaks against."

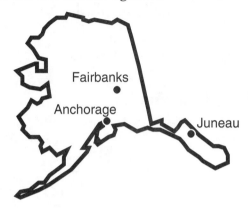

- Capital City is Juneau
- Largest City is Anchorage
- Bordering U.S. States—None
- Bordering Country—Canada

Alaska became our 49th state on January 3, 1959.

FLAG: In 1926, a 13-year-old Native American boy named Benny Benson designed the official Alaskan flag. His flag contained eight gold stars on a blue field. The blue field is for the sky and the wild forget-me-not, the state flower. The star in the upper right stands for the North Star, representing Alaska's northern location. The seven stars stand for the Big Dipper, representing strength.

Fun Facts About Alaska
- On October 18, 1867, the United States purchased Alaska from Russia for 7.2 million dollars.
- In 1880, there was a gold rush.
- Alaska is the largest state in the United States. It is over twice the size of Texas. The state of Rhode Island could fit into Alaska more than 400 times.
- Most of America's salmon and crab come from Alaska.
- The most important source of income (money) for Alaska is the oil and natural gas industry.

Mountains Everywhere
- 39 mountain ranges
- 17 of the 20 highest peaks in the United States are located in Alaska
- Mount McKinley, in Alaska, is the highest point in North America

Official State Symbols
- **flower:** the wild forget-me-not
- **bird:** willow ptarmigan
- **tree:** sitka spruce
- **state mineral:** gold
- **insect:** four-spot skimmer dragonfly
- **fish:** giant king salmon

Alaska's Weather Changes from Year to Year
Following are averages only:
- Average January temperatures range from 8 to 21 degrees
- Average February temperatures 26 degrees
- Average July temperatures range from 51 to 65 degrees
- Annual precipitation is 15.9 inches
- Annual snowfall is 69–71 inches

33. Use Aunt Tillie's web site to complete the boxes below. Your answer must include

■ one fact about mountains in Alaska
■ one fact about the Alaskan flag
■ one fact about Alaskan state symbols

Include facts from the web site only.

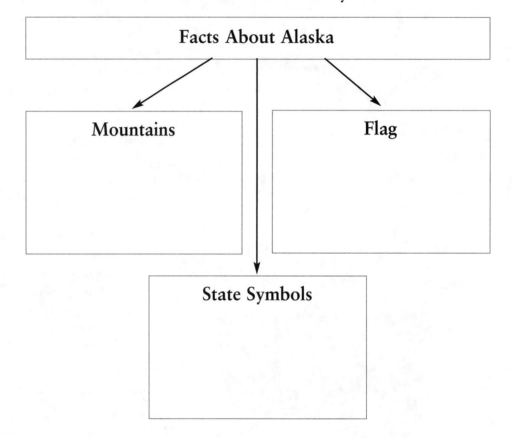

Below is an e-mail sent by Mr. Peabody's fourth-grade students from Anchorage, Alaska. They are interested in becoming e-pals (pen pals corresponding by e-mail) with fourth-grade students in another part of the United States.

To: Fourth Grade Students in New York
From: Fourth Grade Students in Alaska

Re: We Want to be E-pals

Hello E-pals,

  We are interested in becoming E-pals with fourth-grade students. Our class would like to learn about life as a fourth grader in another part of the United States.

  When you think of Alaska, you probably think of igloos and sledding. The truth is, however, that most Alaskans live in modern houses. Many of us also own and drive cars. Sledding is no longer the main transportation in our northern state.

  Alaskans like to participate in outdoor activities including dogmushing, skiing, snowmobiling, canoeing, backpacking, rock climbing, and biking. Dogmushing, or sled dog racing, is the state sport of Alaska. Today, people come to Alaska from all over the world to see the Iditarod Race from Anchorage to Nome. This famous sled dog race lasts for about nine days. Mushers and their loyal, strong, heavily coated dogs race along frozen rivers and icy tundra.

  Alaska is sometimes called the "Land of the Midnight Sun." This is because in the summer, it is light outside until almost 11:00 P.M. The sun appears to circle in the sky rather than set. In some of the villages in the northernmost parts of Alaska, the sun doesn't set for 84 days!

  We hope you have learned some interesting facts about Alaska.

  Please write back soon!
Your Northern Friends

34. Use information from the e-mail to complete the web with dogmushing facts.

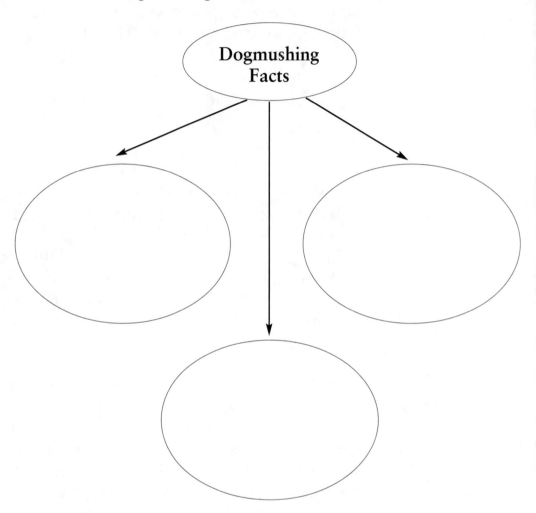

35. Write an e-mail in response to the e-mail sent by the fourth-grade students in Alaska. In your e-mail, be sure to

- include at least 3 interesting details about New York State
- ask questions about the information presented by the Alaskan students in their e-mail, so that you can learn more about life in Alaska

To: Fourth-Grade Students in Alaska
From: Fourth-Grade Students in New York State

Re: Eager to be e-pals

_____
_____
_____
_____
_____
_____
_____
_____
_____
_____
_____
_____
_____

36. Your teacher has encouraged your class to become e-pals with students from another state. You have received many e-mails from around the country. You have decided that you would like to correspond with students in Alaska. It is your job to write a speech to present to your classmates to convince them to vote for writing to Alaskan e-pals. Be sure to use information from both the web site and the e-mail.

_____

_____

_____

_____

_____

_____

_____

_____

_____

_____

_____

ANSWERS AND ANSWER EXPLANATIONS

"Autumn Fancies"

1. **C** The maid, lady, queen, and monarch are words that describe people.

2. **G** In the last stanza, the poet writes that the "oak" is towering high above the wood.

3. **A** According to the first stanza in the poem, the maple lights the dusky forest glade. Dusky was defined as dark.

4. **J** In the third stanza, the poet states that the sumac grows wild along the roadside.

5. **C** The meaning of the word dainty is small.

"The Statue of Liberty"

6. **H** The main idea of the article is that the Statue of Liberty is a famous symbol for freedom. The other letter choices are details about the Statue, but they do not tell the big idea of the paragraph.

7. **B** Be careful: This question can be tricky. The spikes on the Statue of Liberty's crown stand for either the seven continents or seven seas, but they look most like the rays of the sun. The correct answer is choice **B**.

8. **H** A fact is something that can be proven to be true so choices **F**, **G**, and **J** are incorrect because they are facts. An opinion is what someone feels or believes about something: If one thinks it was kind of France to give America the Statue, then that's an opinion. The correct answer is choice **H**.

9. C The word "annually" means yearly. A clue to the word's meaning is given in the question: If millions of people visit the Statue annually, choices **A** (monthly) and **B** (weekly) would not be likely answers.

10. H The huge Statue had to be taken apart before it was shipped. It arrived in America in 214 cases, or crates. The other choices are not supported by information given in the article.

"A Tail Comes in Handy"

11. B The opposite of subordinate (lower) is higher.

12. G The entire article is about the different ways animals use their tails. Choice **F** is a fact from the article, but it is only a supporting detail (not the main idea). Choices **H** and **J** are not mentioned in the article.

13. C The article did not mention that animals use their sense of smell for protection.

14. H Read the entire sentence containing the vocabulary word. According to the article, a timid wolf will keep its tail between its legs, whereas a brave wolf will raise its tail. The word timid means shy. The other word choices (powerful, brave, silly) would not make sense.

15. D The word "balance" completes both empty circles because both the kangaroo and squirrel use their tails for balance.

"The Kayak"

16. J The word "rough" matches the descriptions in the poem: "foaming billows," "ocean's roar," and "rushing wave."

17. **A** Like the sea-birds (second stanza), the kayaker loves the ocean.

18. **J** The kayaker sees snow, birds, and icebergs; he does not see waterfalls.

19. **C** The phrase "foaming billows dance" describes the water; choice **C** is the only choice that describes the water.

"The Stone in the Road"

20. **F** The king wanted to teach people a lesson.

21. **D** According to the tale, the farmer thought someone else should take care of the rock.

22. **H** The soldier thought that the rock was left by a lazy person.

23. **C** The tale states that the girl moved the stone.

24. **F** The king felt that people had a duty to solve problems, rather than wait for others to solve them.

"Roller Coasters: Scream Machines"

25. **D** The article is a review of the history of roller coasters, beginning with their origins in fifteenth-century Russia.

26. **H** The article states that safety improvements were needed.

27. **D** One of the first roller coasters in the United States also hauled coal.

28. G The nickname "Paris Mountains" does not appear in the article.

29. Complete the story chart with details from the tale.

Beginning of the story

Rabbit and Monkey were eating a meal. Rabbit kept looking around and Monkey kept scratching.

Middle of the story

The looking around bothered Monkey and the scratching annoyed Rabbit, so each of them tried to get the other to stop the troubling behavior. It was very difficult for them to change and behave in an "unnatural" way.

End of the story

Both of them decided to act naturally, rather than trying to be something that they were not.

---

30. This story is titled, "Doing What Comes Naturally." What would be another title for the African tale? Use details from the tale to support your answer.

Sample Response

Another interesting title for the African tale would be, "Just Be Yourself." The characters in the tale tried to change each other. Rabbit wanted Monkey to stop scratching himself, and Monkey wanted Rabbit to stop looking around. Both of them learned that they were more content when they were just being themselves, rather than trying to be someone else.

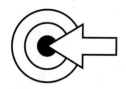

Your answer should include
■ a new title
■ at least 3 details from the tale to support your title

You may have a couple of ideas for a title. Choose a title that is creative and accurate. Be sure you can support it with details in the tale.

Examples of titles:

"The Monkey"—This title is incomplete because the tale is about more than the monkey.

"Lunchtime"—This title identifies the setting, but the tale is about much more.

"The Monkey and the Rabbit"—This title is accurate, but not very creative.

"Act Natural"—This title is accurate and creative, but is too much like the original title.

"Appreciate Being Different" and "Jungle Lessons" are both better titles because they are accurate and creative.

31. This African folktale teaches a lesson. Which lesson does the folktale teach best? Use details from the tale to support your answer.

■ Love your neighbors for who they are.
■ Be yourself: don't try to be something you're not.

Sample Response

There is an important lesson to be learned in the African folk-tale, "Doing What Comes Naturally." The lesson is, "Be yourself: don't try to be something you're not." The monkey scratches and the rabbit looks around, naturally. Each of them tries to stop these behaviors to be more like the other and to please the other. The rabbit and the monkey realize how difficult it is to change. They both decide that it is better to simply be themselves.

Your answer should include:
■ identification of the tale—use the title
■ one of the lessons given
■ details from the tale to support the lesson
■ details to make your story interesting to the reader

32. Write a story about a time when you learned that it was better to be yourself, rather than trying to be like someone else. Describe how you learned this lesson, and what helped you realize that it's better to be yourself.

In your writing, be sure to include
■ a title for your story
■ a beginning, middle, and end to your story
■ details to make your story interesting to the reader

Sample Response

Be Yourself!

Up until today, I had always wanted to be as smart as my classmate, Ed. His amazing brain is like a computer.

Today, our school went on a field trip to Ellis Island. Ed had his camera with him. He takes such excellent photographs that when birds see him, they stop in mid-flight and say, "Cheese!" This morning, however, Ed was upset because his camera wasn't working. I offered to help and fixed the camera quicker than he could have said "Pizza." My classmates were surprised that I was so talented with my hands.

Later that day, when our group could not figure out certain directions, I used the position of the sun and the time of the day to guide us back to where we needed to be. Once again, my classmates were amazed but, this time, by my wonderful sense of direction. They told me one million times that I am super bright.

During that field trip to Ellis Island, I learned that it is much better to be myself. Everyone, including me, is special. I still think Ed is as wise as Einstein, but I am pleased to be me and grateful for the talents I have.

33. Use Aunt Tillie's web site to complete the boxes below. Your answer must include

- one fact about mountains in Alaska
- one fact about the Alaskan flag
- one fact about Alaskan state symbols

Include facts from the web site only.

Sample Response

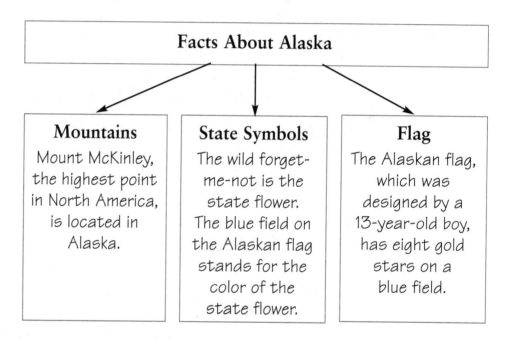

Facts About Alaska

Mountains	State Symbols	Flag
Mount McKinley, the highest point in North America, is located in Alaska.	The wild forget-me-not is the state flower. The blue field on the Alaskan flag stands for the color of the state flower.	The Alaskan flag, which was designed by a 13-year-old boy, has eight gold stars on a blue field.

THERE ARE OTHER POSSIBLE ANSWERS.

Note: All answers must be based on information from the web site. They must be written in the correct box. For example, a correct fact about the Alaskan flag would be considered wrong if it is written in the box labeled "Mountains."

All answers must be based on "facts" given in the web site, rather than opinions. A response "I like the Alaskan flag" or "The Alaskan flag is pretty" is not correct because it is an opinion, not a fact.

34. Use information from the e-mail to complete the web with dogmushing facts.

Sample Response

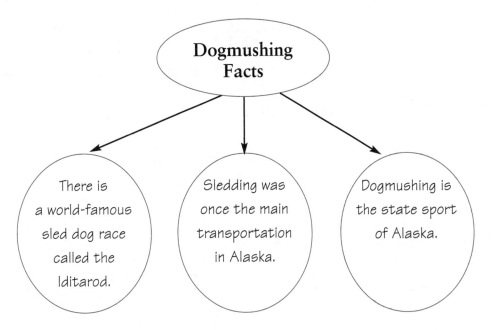

Other acceptable answers to complete the chart above:

- Alaskans participate in many outdoor activities, including dogmushing.
- Iditarod is a famous sled dog race from Anchorage to Nome.
- The Iditarod is a well-known sled dog race, which lasts for about nine days.
- Dogmushers and their faithful, strong dogs race along icy tundra in the Iditarod.

35. Write an e-mail in response to the e-mail sent by the fourth-grade students in Alaska. In your email, be sure to

- include at least 3 interesting details about New York State
- ask questions about the information presented by the Alaskan students in their e-mail, so that you can learn more about life in Alaska

Sample Response

To: Fourth-Grade Students in Alaska
From: Fourth-Grade Students in New York State

Re: Eager to be e-pals

Hello e-pals from the Land of the Midnight Sun,

Thank you for your e-mail, which had many interesting facts about Alaska. My classmates and I would also like to become e-pals with students in another state.

Like Alaskans, New Yorkers enjoy longer days in the summer, but they are only a few hours longer than winter days. I think it would be wonderful to have sunshine until almost 11:00 P.M. My friends and I like to ride our bikes and play soccer in the summer. During the winter, we go sledding and skating. What kind of indoor activities do you like to do?

Dogmushing seems like an exciting sport. Have you ever tried it? Popular sports in New York are hockey, football, and baseball. We do not have a state sport.

Please e-mail me again soon.

Your New Friend from the Empire State

36. Your teacher has encouraged your class to become e-pals with students from another state. You have received many e-mails from around the country. You have decided that you would like to correspond with students in Alaska. It is your job to write a speech to present to your classmates to convince them to vote for writing to Alaskan e-pals. Be sure to use information from the web site and the e-mail.

Sample Response

There are many reasons that we should be e-pals with the class from Alaska.

By choosing Alaskan e-pals, our class would learn interesting information about a place that is both different from, but also similar to, our own state. Did you know that Alaskans do not live in igloos and that the average yearly snowfall in Alaska is 69 inches? That amount of snowfall is less than some parts of New York State might receive in an average year.

Alaskans know how to have fun and enjoy life. They enjoy doing many exciting outdoor activities, such as canoeing, biking, and rock climbing. Wouldn't it be exciting to share information with them about those adventurous sports? We can also learn more about their world-famous sled dog race known as the Iditarod.

Here are a couple of fascinating facts about Alaska. During the summer, in some of the northernmost parts of the state, the sun does not set for 84 days. In other parts of Alaska, there is sunlight until almost 11:00 P.M. Now, we know why Alaska is sometimes called, "Land of the Midnight Sun."

Please join me and vote for Alaskan e-pals. You will <u>not</u> be disappointed, and you'll see why the name Alaska means "great land."

Chart your answers to be sure that you have facts from both selections. This can be done before writing, in the planning stage.

Facts from the Web Site	Facts from the E-mail
"great land" snowfall per year	Land of the Midnight Sun dogmushing hours of sunlight canoeing, biking, and rock climbing

PRACTICE TEST 2

DAY 1, SESSION 1—MULTIPLE-CHOICE

28 Questions
45 minutes

Directions: In this part of the test, you are going to do some reading and then answer questions about what you have read.

You will be filling in the answers to Numbers 1 through 28 on the answer (bubble) sheet. If you make a mistake, erase it completely.
Do not write answers on the test pages. All of your answers must be marked on the answer sheet. You may make notes or underline in the book as you read. Do not use highlighters.

You will have 45 minutes to read all of the selections carefully and answer the 28 questions about what you have read. On the answer sheet, you will fill in the letter that matches your answer for each question.

Try to answer all questions. Read each question carefully, and make your best attempt at answering the question.

SESSION 1—ANSWER SHEET

1. Ⓐ Ⓑ Ⓒ Ⓓ 15. Ⓐ Ⓑ Ⓒ Ⓓ
2. Ⓕ Ⓖ Ⓗ Ⓙ 16. Ⓕ Ⓖ Ⓗ Ⓙ
3. Ⓐ Ⓑ Ⓒ Ⓓ 17. Ⓐ Ⓑ Ⓒ Ⓓ
4. Ⓕ Ⓖ Ⓗ Ⓙ 18. Ⓕ Ⓖ Ⓗ Ⓙ
5. Ⓐ Ⓑ Ⓒ Ⓓ 19. Ⓐ Ⓑ Ⓒ Ⓓ
6. Ⓕ Ⓖ Ⓗ Ⓙ 20. Ⓕ Ⓖ Ⓗ Ⓙ
7. Ⓐ Ⓑ Ⓒ Ⓓ 21. Ⓐ Ⓑ Ⓒ Ⓓ
8. Ⓕ Ⓖ Ⓗ Ⓙ 22. Ⓕ Ⓖ Ⓗ Ⓙ
9. Ⓐ Ⓑ Ⓒ Ⓓ 23. Ⓐ Ⓑ Ⓒ Ⓓ
10. Ⓕ Ⓖ Ⓗ Ⓙ 24. Ⓕ Ⓖ Ⓗ Ⓙ
11. Ⓐ Ⓑ Ⓒ Ⓓ 25. Ⓐ Ⓑ Ⓒ Ⓓ
12. Ⓕ Ⓖ Ⓗ Ⓙ 26. Ⓕ Ⓖ Ⓗ Ⓙ
13. Ⓐ Ⓑ Ⓒ Ⓓ 27. Ⓐ Ⓑ Ⓒ Ⓓ
14. Ⓕ Ⓖ Ⓗ Ⓙ 28. Ⓕ Ⓖ Ⓗ Ⓙ

Directions: Read this poem about dandelions. Then answer questions 1 through 5.

Dandelion

Anonymous

There was a pretty dandelion
With lovely, fluffy hair,
That glistened in the sunshine
And in the summer air
But oh! This pretty dandelion
Soon grew old and gray;
And, sad to tell! Her charming hair
Blew many miles away

1. What stage of the dandelion plant is described in the beginning of the poem?

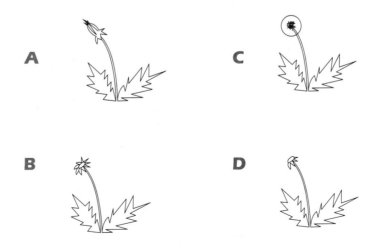

2. The mood in the poem changes from beginning to end; it changes from

   F happy to sad

   G sad to happy

   H excited to scared

   J scared to excited

3. What probably caused the hair to be gone?

   A the sun started shining

   B it started raining

   C it was summer

   D a strong wind blew

4. The season described in the poem is

   F winter

   G spring

   H summer

   J fall

5. In the poem, the word "charming" means

   A pleasing

   B fluffy

   C old

   D gray

Directions: Read the following Chinese tale. Then answer questions 6 through 13.

How to Weigh an Elephant

Adapted Chinese Tale

One day a Chinese emperor received an elephant as a gift from a friend. The emperor was amazed by the size of the creature and wanted to know the weight of the elephant. He commanded his advisors to solve this problem. If they could not tell the weight of the elephant in three days, they would be punished.

The advisors had very small scales, much too small to weigh the immense elephant. They were completely stumped by this challenge. On the third day, a young boy came to share his idea with the advisors. They listened doubtfully, but then decided to give the boy a chance to try his weighing method. They went to the river together.

doubtfully: unsure

First, the boy put the elephant in a boat. Then, he swam around the boat and marked the water line with red paint. He removed the elephant and filled the boat with stones until the side of the boat reached the previous water line, marked with red paint. The boy then weighed all of the stones. He now knew the weight of the elephant. The young boy's creative idea worked, which saved the advisors from punishment. And, the emperor was delighted to learn the weight of his gift.

6. Which is the best description of the young boy in the story?

  F lucky

  G kind

  H clever

  J mean

7. What happened right after the emperor received the elephant?

  A he wanted to know the weight of the elephant

  B he was amazed by the size of the elephant

  C he asked his advisors to weigh the elephant

  D a young boy weighed the elephant

8. The word "creature" refers to the

  F boy

  G advisors

  H emperor

  J elephant

9. What will most likely happen the next time the emperor has a problem to solve?

  A he will call the advisors to help

  B he will call the boy to help

  C he will call his friend

  D he will threaten to punish people

10. This story proves that

  F younger people are always smarter than older people

  G elephants are heavy

  H problem solving sometimes requires creativity

  J scales need to be made larger

11. Which word would best describe the emperor?

  A kind

  B demanding

  C clever

  D helpful

12. The meaning of the word "immense" is

  F small

  G very dangerous

  H tiny

  J very large

13. Which of the following events should fill in the box in the timeline?

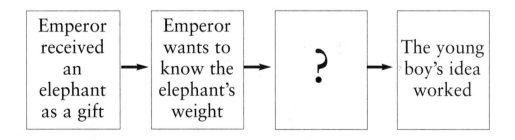

  A Emperor is amazed by the size of the elephant

  B Advisors are not able to weigh the elephant

  C Young boy saves advisors from punishment

  D Emperor was happy to learn the weight

Directions: Read this poem about cobwebs. Then answer questions 14 through 19.

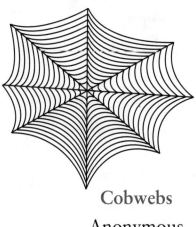

Cobwebs

Anonymous

dainty:
delicate

Dainty fairy lace-work, O so finely spun,
Lying on the grasses and shining in the sun,
Guess the fairies washed you and spread you out to dry,
And left you there a-glistening and a' shining to the sky!

14. The cobwebs described in the poem would most likely be found in a

F field

G barn

H basement

J house

15. According to the poem, the cobwebs were created by

A spiders

B the sun

C fairies

D grasses

16. The speaker in the poem uses the word "you" to refer to the

    F   reader

    G   sun

    H   grasses

    J   cobwebs

17. The poet uses the phrase "lace-work" to describe the

    A   grasses

    B   shining sun

    C   fairies

    D   weaving of cobwebs

18. What may have inspired the poet to write about cobwebs?

    F   a dislike of cobwebs

    G   a fear of spiders

    H   a love of cobwebs

    J   a curiosity of fairies

19. The opposite of "dainty" is

    A   strong

    B   tiny

    C   clean

    D   small

Directions: Read the article about potato chips. Then answer questions 20 through 24.

The Original Potato Chip

Today, potato chips are a very popular snack. The original chips had a very interesting beginning, in Saratoga Springs, New York, in a restaurant called Moon Lake Lodge.

patron:
customer

A famous patron of Moon Lake Lodge ordered a new dish called French fries, which he had first had in Paris, France. The chef at Moon Lake Lodge was not French, but he was able to cook many French dishes. He made the French fries and sent them to the customer. The customer sent the fries back to the kitchen because they were too thick. He insisted he wanted thin fries.

The chef quickly made a batch of thinner French fries. These were still not correct according to the paying guest. The chef became angry and sliced the potatoes so thin that you could almost see through them. He fried them to a crisp, salted them, and served them himself. He was surprised to observe the customer enjoying the chips and was even more surprised to receive a compliment.

version:
variety

Before long, potato chips were such a hit that they were added to the restaurant's menu. In 1887, the American version of the French fry, today known as the potato chip, was included in the White House cookbook.

20. The author probably wrote this article to

   F   teach readers about how to make potato chips

   G   persuade readers to eat chips

   H   explore the varieties of potato chips

   J   inform readers about how potato chips were invented accidentally

21. Which of the following words was <u>not</u> used to identify the visitor to the restaurant?

   A   patron

   B   paying guest

   C   customer

   D. mister

22. According to the article, potato chips were first served in

   F   Paris

   G   New York

   H   the White House

   J   France

23. The customer <u>did not</u> like French fries that were too

   A   thick

   B   thin

   C   small

   D   salty

24. The first potato chips were made in an attempt to

   F   advertise a new restaurant

   G   make a chef angry

   H   create a new French recipe

   J   get back at a "picky" customer

Directions: Read the poem about rain. Then answer questions 25 through 28.

The Rain

Anonymous

"Open the window, and let me in,"
  Sputters the merry rain;
"I want to splash down on the carpet, dear,
  And I can't get through the pane."

"Here I've been tapping outside to you,
  Why don't you come, if you're there?
The windows are shut or I'd dash right in,
  And stream down the attic stair."

"I've washed the windows, I've spattered the blinds
  And that is not half what I have done;
I've bounced on the step and the sidewalk too
Till I've made the good people run."

pane: divided window

25. In the poem, the rain is trying to communicate to the

    A people on the sidewalk

    B windows of the house

    C people inside the house

    D people who are running

26. Why did the people run?

    F they needed to close the windows

    G water was splashing onto the carpet

    H water was streaming down the stairs

    J the rain was splashing on the sidewalk

27. In the poem, the word *dash* means

    A tap

    B rush

    C shut

    D step

28. The rain is responsible for

    F splashing down on the carpet

    G tapping outside

    H streaming down the attic stairs

    J splashing in the window

DAY 2, SESSION 2—PART ONE: LISTENING

2 short answers
1 long response
30 minutes

Directions: In this section of the test, a story called "Doing What Comes Naturally" will be read aloud to you twice. Please listen carefully each time the story is read because you will then be asked to answer specific questions about the story.

During the first reading, listen closely but do not take notes. You may take notes during the second reading. Please use the space provided below for your notes. You may refer back to your notes to answer the questions that follow. Your notes will *not* count toward your score.

Notes

How the Ostrich Got His Long Neck
Adapted African Tale

Introduction to the Tale: Long ago, Ostrich had a short neck, like all the other birds. That was . . . until his encounter with Crocodile.

Ostrich wanted to be friends with Crocodile, even though he was warned that it would be a big mistake.

Monkey gave Ostrich this advice, "Don't trust Crocodile; he has no manners and he's mean. His favorite pastime is scaring all of the animals away from the river."

Then Ostrich asked Wildebeest for his opinion and he received this warning, "Crocodile is lazy; he lies around all day waiting for his dinner to walk past."

Elephant also added his own two cents, "Crocodile would not be a good friend; he thinks only of himself. He will snap at you if he gets a chance."

Ostrich decided to ignore the advice of his friends and play with Crocodile.

One day, Crocodile was hungry. He asked Ostrich to look in his mouth to see what was wrong with his tooth. Crocodile opened his jaws very wide. Ostrich wanted to help a friend so he stuck his head inside.

"You have so many teeth," Ostrich announced with amazement. "How will I know which one is aching?"

"It's the one in the back," Crocodile moaned.

So, Ostrich kept sticking his head further and further into Crocodile's mouth.

Crocodile saw his chance and snapped his jaws shut on Ostrich's head.

Ostrich yelled for help, but no one heard because all the other animals stayed as far away from Crocodile as they could. He started to pull. Crocodile pulled back. They both continued to pull. Ostrich's neck began to stretch.

It stretched longer and L-O-N-G-E-R.

Ostrich continued to pull because he did not want to lose his head.

Crocodile grew tired, stopped pulling, and finally let go. Ostrich jumped back away from shore.

To this day, Ostrich has a long neck to remind him to stay away from Crocodile.

29. Complete the boxes below with Crocodile's character traits from the tale.

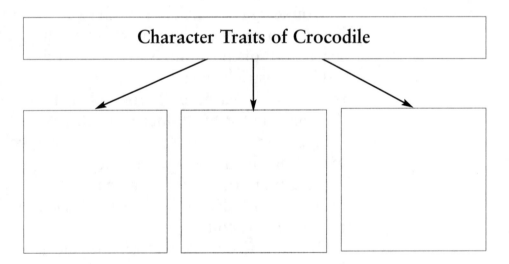

Character Traits of Crocodile

30. In the tale "How the Ostrich Got His Long Neck," the statement "Elephant also added his own two cents" means

_____

_____

_____

_____

_____

_____

_____

_____

_____

_____

_____

Planning Section

You may plan your writing here for the question on the next page. Do NOT write your answer on this page. Writing on this page will NOT count toward your score.
  Write your answer on the next page.

31. In the tale "How the Ostrich Got His Long Neck,"
Ostrich learns a very good lesson. Which lesson below
does the tale best teach? Use examples from the tale to
support your choice.

■ Listen to your friend's advice.
■ Choosing the wrong friends can be bad for you.

_____

_____

_____

_____

_____

_____

_____

_____

_____

_____

_____

_____

DAY 2, SESSION 2—PART TWO: WRITING

Write a story
30 minutes

Directions: In this section of the test, you are going to write a story of your own. Please do NOT include information from "Doing What Comes Naturally" in your writing. You may use this page to PLAN your writing. The work that you do on the Planning Page will *not* count toward your end score.

Write your final answer on the next page(s).

Planning Space

32. Write a story about a time when someone gave you advice. Did you listen to the advice given or did you make your own decision? How did the advice or your decision turn out?

Your story should include
- a title
- a beginning, middle, and end
- many interesting details

Be sure to check your writing for correct spelling, grammar, capitalization, and punctuation.

Title: _____

_____

_____

_____

_____

_____

_____

_____

_____

DAY 3, SESSION THREE—WRITING

60 minutes
Read 2 selections.
Write one short answer based on the first selection.
Write 2 short answers based on the second selection.
Write a long response based on both selections.

Directions: In this section of the test, you are going to read 2 selections. Then you will answer qustions about what you have read.

TECHNOLOGY NEWSLETTER

Health Concerns Addressed

Doctors report seeing increasing numbers of children with computer-related injuries.

Back, neck, and wrist injuries are related to the increase in computer use among younger children.

Experts suggest teaching children good posture and proper techniques early to decrease this trend.

Helping Kids Connect

For years, kids have had pen pals. They have used the mail to correspond with their long-distance friends. Today, kids use the Internet to create new friendships and join cooperative projects.

Some classroom exchange programs offer instant translation, making it easier to have a non-English speaking e-pal. Live chats with experts and monitored e-mail accounts have features that overcome the safety concerns.

Contact *Classroom Exchange.net* for more information.

Video Game Club Forming Based on Popular Demand

All students interested in joining the video game club should report to the cafeteria on Thursday after school.

Members will play games and share game strategies. Games containing violence will not be allowed. Look forward to an exciting, social time!

33. According to the newsletter, what are some of the positive and negative effects technology may have on the lives of children? Write your answer in the boxes below.

Positive Effects of Technology on Lives of Children	Negative Effects of Technology on Lives of Children

Fashions for the Twenty-first Century

functioning:
working

Computer scientists and the clothing makers are working together to produce clothes that are functioning computers. They are called "wearable computers."

Today there are many experimental models being tested. The items range from a hooded jacket with an MP3 player that plays music, to clothes for soldiers that warn of approaching vehicles. One company is working on a sneaker that will tell runners how fast they are moving.

image: picture

Other wearable computers are built into eyeglasses. This eyewear allows an image to be projected onto one eye, while the other eye can still see what is in front of it. Doctors are experimenting with this technology to assist them in surgery.

The makers of this wearable clothing admit that it will be some time before some of these items will be available to the public. Fabrics containing the technology need to be more durable; they are still easily damaged.

In the near future, our computers may be wash and wear.

34. What are "wearable computers?" What are some reasons people might be excited about these new inventions? Be sure to use examples from the article.

_____

_____

_____

_____

_____

_____

35. According to the article, why are we not able to buy all of these inventions in the stores today?

_____

_____

_____

_____

_____

_____

36. Technology is everywhere today. It affects almost
every part of our life. What are some of the ways
that technology influences lives?

Be sure to include examples from both the newsletter on technology and the article on fashions.

_____

_____

_____

_____

_____

_____

_____

_____

_____

_____

_____

_____

ANSWERS AND ANSWER EXPLANATIONS

"Dandelion"

1. **C** In the beginning of the poem, the dandelion is described as having fluffy hair. When a dandelion is fully seeded, its seeds are attached to stems with white fluffy threads (hair).

2. **F** In the beginning of the poem, the dandelion is described as being pretty and having lovely hair. However, the poem ends sadly ("sad to tell") with her hair blowing away.

3. **D** The poem states that the dandelion's hair *blew* many miles away. A gust of wind would cause things such as her hair to blow away.

4. **H** The poem mentions sunshine and "summer air."

5. **A** The poet is "sad to tell" that the dandelion's charming hair blew away. The poet then must have liked her hair or found it "pleasing."

"How to Weigh an Elephant"

6. **H** The boy is clever; his creative idea worked. The other answer choices are not supported by information from the tale.

7. **B** According to the tale, after the emperor had received the elephant, he was amazed by its size. He then wanted to know the weight of the animal.

8. **J** When the emperor received the elephant, he was amazed by the size of the creature. The word "creature" then refers to the elephant.

9. **B** The emperor knows that the young boy was the one who had determined the elephant's weight. He will then most likely ask the boy for help if he has future problems to be solved.

10. **H** The boy's creative idea solved the emperor's problem. Choice **F** is not correct because younger people are not *always* smarter than older people. There is no proof in the tale to support the remaining choices, **G** and **J**.

11. **B** The emperor commanded his advisors to solve his problem. A word to describe him would then be "demanding." The other choices (kind, clever, helpful) would not make sense.

12. **J** The emperor was amazed at the size of the elephant; it was too big for normal-sized scales.

13. **B** The advisors were not able to weigh the elephant. Choice **A** happened right after the emperor had received the gift. Choices **C** and **D** happened after it was discovered that the young boy's idea had worked.

"Cobwebs"

14. **F** The cobwebs were lying on grasses and shining in the sun, so they would most likely be found in a field.

15. **C** The cobwebs are referred to as "fairy lace-work."

16. **J** The "you" in the poem refers to the cobwebs.

17. **D** "Lace-work" describes the "O so finely spun" cobwebs.

18. **H** The poet's choice of language in the poem shows a love for cobwebs: "Dainty fairy lace-work, O so finely spun."

19. A According to the information given, dainty and delicate are synonyms (dainty = delicate). The opposite (antonym) of dainty is strong.

"The Original Potato Chip"

20. J The article was written to inform readers about the accidental invention of potato chips. It does not teach readers how to make potato chips (choice **F**), nor does it persuade us to eat chips (choice **G**). Choice **H** is also incorrect because the article does not explore the different types of potato chips (barbecue, sour cream and onion, etc.).

21. D The word mister was <u>not</u> used to identify the visitor. All other word choices were used.

22. G Potato chips were first served in Saratoga, New York. French fries were first served in Paris, France.

23. A The customer sent the French fries back to the kitchen because they were too thick.

24. J A customer had made the chef angry, so the chef made the potato chips to get back at the customer.

"The Rain"

25. C According to the first few lines in the poem, the rain wants the people inside the house to open the window and let it in.

26. J The rain bounced on the step and the sidewalk, which made people run.

27. B *Dash* means rush. Substitute each letter choice into the sentence, "The windows are shut or I'd dash right in." The word choices "tap" and "shut" would not make sense in the sentence. The poet uses strong words to describe what the merry rain wants to do. The rain wants to splash down on the carpet and stream down the attic stairs. So, the rain would most likely want to rush (a strong word) right in, rather than just "step" in.

28. G The rain has been tapping outside, but it has not been able to do what it wants to do (splash on the carpet, splash in the window, and stream down the attic stairs).

29. Complete the boxes below with Crocodile's character traits from the tale.

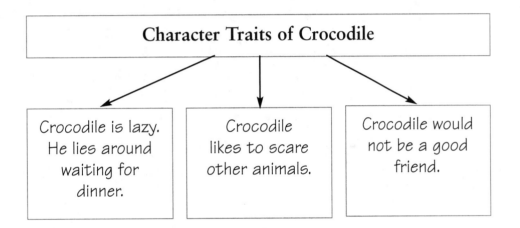

Other acceptable answers:

Crocodile is mean.
He has no manners.
He is not trustworthy.
Crocodile thinks only of himself.
He will snap at you when given a chance.

30. In the tale "How the Ostrich Got His Long Neck," the statement "Elephant also added his own two cents" means

Elephant was very worried about Ostrich wanting to be friends with Crocodile. He "added his own two cents," meaning he gave his advice to stay away from the crocodile. He said that Crocodile thinks only of himself and will snap at others when given a chance.

Tips for understanding quotations:
■ Review your notes for any information that may help explain the quotation.
■ Name the character(s) involved.
■ Restate the quotation using different words.

31. In the tale "How the Ostrich Got His Long Neck," Ostrich learns a very good lesson. Which lesson below does the tale best teach? Use examples from the tale to support your choice.

■ Listen to your friend's advice.
■ Choosing the wrong friends can be bad for you.

Sample Response

In the tale "How the Ostrich Got His Long Neck," Ostrich learns that it is wise to listen to his friends' advice. Because he ignored his friends' warnings about Crocodile, Ostrich finds himself in great danger.

Monkey, Wildebeest, and Elephant agreed that their animal buddy, Ostrich, should stay away from Crocodile. They described Crocodile as a mean, lazy, selfish animal who would not be a true pal. As Elephant had commented to Ostrich, Crocodile "will snap at you if he gets a chance."

Ostrich did not follow his friends' warnings and decided to play with Crocodile one dreary day. Crocodile almost ended up biting Ostrich's head off.

Ostrich has a very long neck, today, because he had to keep pulling his head out of Crocodile's jaws. His stretched neck is a constant reminder to him that he should listen to his friends' advice.

32. Write a story about a time when someone gave you advice. Did you listen to the advice given or did you make your own decision? How did the advice or your decision turn out?

Your story should include
■ a title
■ a beginning, middle, and end
■ many interesting details

Be sure to check your writing for correct spelling, grammar, capitalization, and punctuation.

Note: Below you will find two different sample responses. Please use the Writing Rubric on pages 242–243 in the Appendix to decide how well each response is written. Then, read "A Look at the Sample Responses," which helps break down and explain each piece of writing.

Sample Response One

My Best Friend's Advice

Last month my best friend gave me the book, Holes. She said that it was a good book and I would like it.

At first, I wasn't sure. I had tried to read other books that were recommended to me. I didn't always like the books. After all, not everyone likes the same type of book. I thought I would give the book a chance since the last book my friend recommended was good.

Holes was a great book. I like mystery and suspense. Holes had plenty of that. The next time I won't hesitate to listen to my friend's recommendations.

Sample Response Two

Listen to Lucy

My best friend, Lucy, gave me the book <u>Holes</u> for my tenth birthday, along with the following advice. She told me that I would enjoy the story as much as a hungry ant would like leftovers from a picnic.

At first, I was not excited about her gift because Lucy and I have different reading interests. She likes mysteries and adventure stories, but I prefer biographies. However, because I had nothing to lose, I decided to follow Lucy's advice and read the book <u>Holes</u>.

Much to my surprise, I found the novel as entertaining as a baseball fan would find a World Series game. I am grateful to Lucy for giving me the gift of reading. The next time she recommends a book to me, I will gladly listen to her advice.

A Look at the Sample Responses

Sample Answer One

Overall, the choice of language in the response is not interesting, and the answer lacks lively details. The word "book" is used eight times in a piece of writing that contains a total of 10 sentences. The writer chose words that are commonly overused by elementary school students, such as "good" and "great." Please see the Appendix (pages 237–238) for better synonyms and describing words.

To improve the sample answer, the writer could use a form of figurative language, such as a *simile*. A simile compares two unlike things using the words "like" or "as." Following is a simile: Reading the fabulous book, *Holes,* was as thrilling as a fun-filled day at a water park. The book is being compared to a water park.

Similes help the reader form a clear mental picture of what is happening in the selection. Use similes in your writing, but don't overuse them; otherwise they may lose their effect.

Sample Answer Two

This response is well written; it contains colorful language and vivid details. Try to find the similes and descriptive words in this sample answer. Also, note the specific details given, such as the following: the name of the writer's best friend (Lucy); the reason why the writer received the book (birthday present); and the concerns the writer had regarding the differing reading interests (mystery/adventure stories and biographies). The writer also tries to limit the use of the word "book" and uses synonyms for it, such as novel and story.

33. According to the newsletter, what are some of the positive and negative effects technology may have on the lives of children?

Positive Effects of Technology on Lives of Children	Negative Effects of Technology on Lives of Children
Children can meet and get to know other children from faraway places.	Children can have neck injuries from sitting at the computer with poor posture, for long periods of time.
Children can have chats with experts to get information.	Sometimes children may not be safe; e-mail should be monitored.

Other Positive Effects (+)	Other Negative Effects (−)
Children enjoy playing video games. Communication is improved; different languages can be translated. Children can join cooperative projects.	Back injuries Wrist injuries Some games may be violent

34. What are "wearable computers"? What are some reasons people might be excited about these new inventions? Be sure to use examples from the article.

Sample Response

   Wearable computers are clothes with computers built into them. Some wearable computers will be used for entertainment purposes, such as a hooded jacket that plays music. Others are designed to improve safety, like the clothes for soldiers that will warn them of approaching danger. Doctors are experimenting with projection glasses, which would help them during surgery. Wearable computers will someday be used for many exciting purposes, and they may make our lives better and more interesting.

Note the 3 examples from the article.

35. According to the article, why are we not able to buy all of these inventions in the stores today?

Sample Response

Many of the wearable computer inventions are not in the stores yet. Some models are being tested, like the computers in sneakers that tell how fast a runner is moving and the projection glasses for doctors doing surgery.

The wearable computers need a fabric that will last over time. Presently, the fabric holding the technology is not strong enough, but new fabrics are being tested. When such problems are solved, the wearable computer inventions will be sold to the public.

Note the 3 examples from the article.

36. Technology is everywhere today. It affects almost every part of our life. What are some of the ways that technology influences lives?

Be sure to include examples from both the newsletter and the article.

Sample Response

Technology is a major part of our world today. It affects almost every area of our lives.

Technology influences our military and doctors. Computer experts are working together with makers of clothing to help protect our soldiers. Their goal is to invent a "wearable computer" that would warn soldiers of approaching vehicles. Some doctors are experimenting with projection glasses, which would help them during surgery.

Children use the computer for many reasons. They enjoy playing video games and e-mailing friends in faraway places. Technology is also making it easier for children and adults to find and learn information.

Technology affects our safety, health, pleasure time, and learning. Each year, new inventions make the influence of technology in our lives even greater.

Did you use examples from both reading selections?

Information from Newsletter Technology	Information from Article
Kids play video games. Kids make long-distance friends.	Soldiers use technology. Doctors use technology. New inventions are coming.

APPENDICES

APPENDIX 1—WORDS YOU SHOULD KNOW

Below you will find a list of important words, their meanings, and some examples. You may already know some of them. The words are used throughout this book and are important for understanding the language and tasks of the ELA. Reviewing the list below will also help you in your language arts classroom.

adjective—describes a noun or pronoun by telling what kind, how many, or which one

Examples: large, empty, kind, smooth, six, some, these, that

Use adjectives in your writing to paint clearer descriptions and details for your readers: "Like *multicolored* paints on a *white* sheet of *drawing* paper, adjectives can turn a *colorless*, *lifeless* piece of writing into a *delightful* work of art."

alliteration—repeating the beginning or middle sounds in words

Example: Try to write stories that have *b*rilliant *b*eginnings, *m*arvelous *m*iddles, and *e*xcellent *e*ndings.

Alliteration is a tool often used by poets to help create the beautiful sounds of language and to make readers remember the words.

antonyms—words with opposite meanings

Examples: happy/sad and big/little

article—a piece of writing, usually about one topic and usually nonfiction captions—words found next to a picture or illustration that help explain it

character(s)—the people and animals in a story
    Pay attention to:

■ the names of characters
■ what they look like
■ what they say, do, think, and feel
■ how characters react to each other.

Note: Pay special attention to how character(s) grow and change.

climax—the most exciting and interesting part of a story
    Readers wonder what will happen next.

compare—to show how persons or things are alike and how they are different

concluding sentence—a reworded topic sentence
    It restates the main idea of the paragraph in different words.

conflict—the problem in the story
    Every story has a conflict.
    The conflict leads to all the action and keeps the reader interested in the story.

contrast—to show how persons or things are different

dialogue—the talking that takes place between characters in a story

essay—a short piece of nonfiction work, which supports a main idea with details and examples

event—a specific action or happening in a selection

fact—a thing known to be true
Example: The beaver is the state animal of New York.

fiction—writing that is made up or invented
Examples: fantasies, adventure stories, mysteries, science fiction, historical fiction

figurative language—words used out of their usual meaning to create a special effect, such as in poetry
It is made up of words that do not mean what they first seem to mean.
Example: "Michelle wrote so much that she wore her fingers to the bone." The sentence is trying to state in an imaginary way that Michelle wrote for a long period of time. It does not mean that Michelle actually wore her fingers to the bone. Figurative language, then, is a special use of words. It is descriptive language that helps readers form a word picture in their minds.

figures of speech—the different ways to use figurative language
Examples: simile, metaphor, personification, and hyperbole
Good writers use figures of speech to create strong word pictures.
When used correctly, figures of speech can greatly improve your writing.
Use figures of speech in your writing, but do not overuse them.
Look for figures of speech in your reading. Pay attention to how writers use figures of speech.

genre—a kind or type of book form
Examples: historical fiction, picture book, fantasy, folktale, biography

graphic organizer—something that organizes information and helps readers understand information at a glance
Examples: chart, diagram, web, story map, picture

homophone—a word that sounds like another word with a different meaning and spelling
Examples: their, there, and they're

hyperbole—saying more than is true to create an effect; exaggerating or stretching the truth
Example: Uncle Johnny has so many pennies that instead of saving them in a jar, he stores them in a wheelbarrow.

literal language—language that means exactly what it seems to mean
Example: "Marilyn wrote for one hour." The words are used in their usual meaning, without stretching the truth.

metaphor—figure of speech that compares two unlike things
A metaphor often uses some form of the verb "to be" (is, are, was, were) to compare and link the different things
Example: She is a cuddly bear.

mood—the feelings readers get from a story or picture
Examples: fear, sadness, danger

moral—the lesson an author is trying to teach, usually in a fable or tale

nonfiction—written material about true people, places, and events

noun—the name of a person, place, thing, or idea
Examples: boy, woman, tent, hat, happiness

opinion—what a person thinks, believes, or feels
Example: New York is the best state in the country.

paragraph—a group of sentences that work together to create a main idea

The topic, or opening, sentence states the main idea.

The main (middle) part of the paragraph contains the details that support the topic sentence.

The closing or concluding sentence restates the main idea in a new and different way.

A paragraph usually begins on a new line that is indented.

passage—a piece or section of a written work

personification—giving *human* qualities to things

Example: The building invited me in with open arms.

plot—the action in a story or play; how the order of events in a story or play is arranged

A plot usually involves conflict.

point of view—a position from which angle the story is being told (who is telling the story)

pronoun—part of speech used in place of a noun

Examples: I, you, he, she, him, her, we, they, them, someone, mine

purpose—the reason that the author is writing the piece

Some possible reasons for writing are to describe or explain something, to convince someone to do something, or to tell a story.

resolution—the end of the main problem; the solution

selection—a short piece of writing such as a story or article

sensory details—details that come to us through the senses: sight, sound, smell, taste, touch

Sensory details help readers see, hear, smell, taste, and feel what the writer's describing.

Examples:

- the vivid colors of the leaves (sight)
- the rush of the wind and crunching of the leaves (sound)
- the fresh smell of springtime flowers (smell)
- the taste of berries Mother picked (taste)
- the branches brushing against my arms and leaves (touch)

sequence of events—the order in which things happened

Example: *First* Steven played basketball, *then* he went swimming.

setting—when and where the events of a story happen

Settings can help create the mood of a story.

Stories can be set in the past (history), present (now), or the future (tomorrow).

A setting can be as simple as an afternoon in the park, or as detailed as a year in the busy life of the president.

simile—figure of speech that compares two unlike things using the words "like" or "as"

Examples:

Monica and her best friend, Christina, belong together like popcorn and butter.

Mark jumped up and down like an excited kangaroo when I invited him on our family trip to the mountains.

Ryan's hands are as warm as towels that have just come out of the dryer.

stanza—an arrangement of lines in a poem

story—a written work, either true or made up, which tells the order of events in the lives of characters

A story has a beginning, middle, and end.

A story has a conflict, or problem, to be solved.

story elements—important details about stories

Examples: genre, title, characters, setting, mood, theme, point of view, plot, conflict, climax, and resolution

supporting details—the details (reasons, examples, facts, sensory descriptions) that help writers make a point or develop their stories

synonyms—words that have almost the same meanings

Example: Giant and huge are synonyms for big.

Our language is rich in words. Synonyms can improve your writing because they give you more words to choose from and more ways to say exactly what you mean.

theme—the main idea or meaning in a piece of writing

topic sentence—an opening sentence that gives the main idea of a paragraph

transitions—words and phrases that are like "bridges"; they help connect thoughts and ideas, making it easier for readers to understand a writing piece

Examples: first, then, next, later, before, after, during

verb—a word that shows action or connects two ideas in a sentence

Examples: Mary *sings* and *dances* whenever she *hears* music.

J.J. *is* always helpful.

APPENDIX 2—UNDERSTANDING GENRES

NONFICTION

	Features of Genre	Strategies for Success
Informational Article from a Magazine or Newspaper	Gives factual information about a topic. Organizes facts in a way that helps readers learn about the topic. Photos, illustrations, graphs, charts, and/or diagrams may be used to help support the text. Headings tell about each section in the article.	Underline important text while reading. Read captions carefully: information given in captions is important. Pay attention to the extra information provided by graphic organizers. Note how the information is organized into sections because it helps the reader's search for details. Note the Five W's and One H: who, what, where, when, why, and how.
Editorial	Article is written to express an opinion about a news topic. Article tries to persuade others to agree. Evidence (proof) is given to support the opinion and to defend against other people's arguments.	Think about why the author has written the article and what the author wants readers to believe after reading it. Make connections between the information given; compare and contrast the information being presented.
Interview	An interview with a real person gives factual information about the person's experience.	Pay attention to the questions asked and answers given. Think about the point of view of the person being interviewed.

	Features of Genre	Strategies for Success
Biography	It is the factual story of a person's life, written by someone else.	Pay attention to the events that have shaped the person's life. Chart the person's life in a time line. Note how the person grows and changes over time.

FICTION

	Features of Genre	Strategies for Success
Mystery	The plot includes a problem or puzzle to be solved. Clues are given to keep the reader in suspense. The mood is filled with suspense, danger, and excitement.	Use clues or hints given by the writer to gather details, solve the puzzle, and discover "who done it" (whodunit). Note the use of suspense to hold the reader's attention.
Realistic Fiction	Characters are fictional, but the story is based on situations that could really happen. The setting is a place that readers know or can recognize. Story elements are all present.	Chart the story elements: title, setting, character(s), conflict, events leading to resolution.
Historical Fiction	Setting is a time and place in the past (in history). Some of the characters and events are from history; some are created (made up) by the author.	Compare/contrast the factual (facts) and fictional parts in the story.

	Features of Genre	Strategies for Success
Fable Fables, myths, legends, and folktales began as storytelling and were later written down.	A short tale that usually teaches a lesson or moral. Characters are often animals or non-living things which talk and act like human beings.	Look for animals that act like humans. Note the story elements, the lesson or moral learned, and how the lesson was learned.
Myth Myths and legends often explain how and why things happened in nature.	A myth is a fantasy; it is not based on facts in history. Myths include heroes and heroines who perform amazing acts. Animals in myths play important roles. Often, in myths, good is rewarded and evil is punished.	Note the story elements. Pay attention to the communication between the characters and notice if the myth deals with the ideas of "right" and "wrong."
Legend	Legends may have some truth to them, but they also include made-up material (the truth has been stretched, or exaggerated).	Chart the story elements.
Folktale	Plot is of first importance. Often the lesson to be learned is that good wins over evil. Folktales are different from fairy tales: folktales deal with ordinary people, but fairy tales deal with imaginary beings with magical powers. A tall tale is one type of folktale.	Pay close attention to the plot and to the lesson learned.

	Features of Genre	Strategies for Success
Fantasy	The story could never really happen. Usually the characters and the setting are made up (imaginary), such as other worlds with wizards and dragons.	Pay special attention to the following 3 story elements: setting, characters, and time.
Science Fiction	The main events might really happen, but they are not likely to happen.	Look for the use of time travel, animals that talk, or imaginary beings from other planets.
Adventure Stories	Action-packed tales are filled with suspense and daring characters. Characters, especially the main character, face larger-than-life situations; they need to take risks to solve a problem.	Pay attention to the exciting action and events that make up the plot. Look for brave heroes and mean characters (villains). Note the risks taken for a successful solution to the problem.

POETRY

	Features of Genre	Strategies for Success
Poetry	Usually, poems are made up of few words, but there is much meaning packed in the words. Poetry shows the beauty of language: words are often used in a musical way. Poetry shows the power of language: word pictures are often used in a powerful way to describe the mood and the author's experiences and feelings. Poems do not have to rhyme, but often have a rhythm.	Reread the poem: think about the feelings, thoughts, and experiences the poet is trying to describe. Note the use of figures of speech such as personification, similes, and metaphors.

APPENDIX 3—CHARACTER TRAITS: ADJECTIVES FOR PEOPLE

adventurous

brave
bright

calm
careless
cheerful
clever
confused
cooperative
courageous
cowardly
creative
cruel
curious

daring
determined
disagreeable

energetic

fearful
forgetful
forgiving
friendly
fun-loving
funny

generous
gentle
gloomy
greedy

handsome
hard-working
helpful
honest
humorous

imaginative
intelligent

jolly
joyful

kind

lazy
loud
loveable
loyal

messy
mischievous

nagging
neat

obedient
organized

patient
patriotic
playful
pleasant
pleasing
polite
poor
popular
pretty
proud

quarrelsome
quiet

relaxed
respectful
responsible
rich
rude

selfish
sensitive
short
shy
smart
sneaky
stingy
strong
stubborn
studious
successful

talkative
tall
thoughtful
timid
trusting

unfriendly
unkind
unselfish

wise

APPENDIX 4—FREQUENTLY FOUND WORDS

a
about
after
again
all
always
an
and
any
are
around
as
ask
at
ate
away

be
because
been
before
best
better
big
black
blue
both
bring
brown
but
by

call
came
can
carry

clean
cold
come
could
cut

did
does
done
don't
draw
drink

eight
every

fall
far
fast
find
first
five
fly
for
found
four
from
full
funny

gave
get
give
go
goes
going
good
got

green
grow

had
has
have
he
help
her
here
him
his
hold
hot
how
hurt

I
if
in
into
is
it
its

jump
just

keep
kind

laugh
let
light
like
little
live
long
look

made
make
many
may
me
much
must
my
myself

never
new
no
not
now

of
off
old
on
once
one
only
open
or
our
out
own

play
pick
please
pretty
pull
put

ran
read
red
ride
right
round
run

said
saw
say
see
she
sing
sit
six
sleep
small
so
some
soon
start
stop

take
tell
thank
that
the
their
them
then
there
these
they
think
this
those
three
to

today
together
too
try
two

under
up
upon
us
use

very

walk
want
warm
was
wash
we
well
went
were
what
when
where
which
white
who
why
will
wish
with
work
would
write

yellow
yes
you
your

APPENDIX 5—SAMPLE LISTENING/WRITING RUBRIC

Quality	Excellent	Good
Meaning: The extent to which the answer shows understanding and interpretation of the task	- fulfill all or most of the requirements of tasks -address the theme or key elements of text -show an insightful interpretation of text -make connections beyond text	-fulfill some requirements of the tasks -address many key elements of the text -show literal interpretation -make some connections
Development: The extent to which ideas are elaborated, using specific and relevant details and examples	-develop ideas fully with thorough elaboration -make effective use of relevant and accurate examples from the text	-may be brief, with little elaboration, development sufficient to answer question -use relevant and accurate examples to support ideas -may include minor inaccuracies
Organization: The extent to which the response shows direction, shape, and coherence	-establish and maintain a clear focus -shows a logical, coherent sequence of ideas through the use of appropriate transitions	- is generally focused but may include some irrelevant details -show logical sequence of ideas

Developing	Beginning
-fulfill some requirements of the task -address basic elements of text, make some weak connections -show some understanding of text	-fulfill few requirements of the task -miss basic elements of text -show evidence that the student understood only parts of the text -make few if any connections
-may begin to answer the questions, but are not fully developed -give some examples and details	-may include a few accurate details
- may attempt to establish a focus -show a clear attempt at organization - may include some irrelevant details	-may focus on minor details or lack focus -show little or no organization

Quality	Excellent	Good
Language Use: The extent to which the answer shows an awareness of audience and purpose through effective use of words, sentence structure, and sentence variety	-is fluent and easy to read, with vivid language -style is sophisticated, using challenging vocabulary	-writing is fluent and easy to read, with vivid language -using some sentence variety and challenging vocabulary
Conventions: The extent to which the answer shows conventional spelling, punctuation, paragraphing, capitalization, grammar, and usage	The writing shows control of the conventions.	There are few, if any, errors and none that interfere with comprehension. Grammar, capitalization, punctuation, and paragraphing are correct. Misspellings are minor or repetitive.

Developing	Beginning
-is mostly readable, with some sense of engagement -primarily uses simple sentences	-is often repetitive, with little sense of voice -uses minimal vocabulary
The writing shows partial control of the conventions. There are errors that may interfere somewhat with readability but do not interfere with comprehension.	The writing shows minimal control of the conventions. There may be many errors that interfere with readability and comprehension.

APPENDIX 6—COMMONLY MISSPELLED AND CONFUSED WORDS

accept = to receive or to agree with

> I accept your apology.

except = other than

> Everyone except Sam went swimming.

all ready = completely ready

> We're all ready to go camping.

already = tells when

> I have already finished my homework.

all right = correct

> **all right is always two words**

> Her answers were all right.

a lot = many

> **a lot is always two words**

> I have a lot of baseball cards.

Note: Try not to use the word "a lot" in your writing;
Use synonyms such as "several" and "many."

> I have several baseball cards.

> I have many baseball cards.

all together = people and things in one place at one time

> Our class must stay all together on this field trip.

altogether = completely

> I am altogether tired.

does = performs (a duty, job, or task)

> She always does a splendid job.

dose = amount of medicine

> She needs a dose of cough medicine.

hear = what you do with your ears

> Can you hear me?

here = a nearby place

> Please put the keys here.

hole = an opening through something

> I have a hole in my shirt.

whole = complete or entire

> Please do not eat the whole bag of popcorn.

hour = time

> We will eat dinner in one hour.

our = belonging to us

> Our house has high ceilings.

it's = a contraction for it is

> It's a beautiful day.

its = belonging to it

> The adorable puppy wagged its tail.

knew = the past tense of the verb know

> Jerry knew the answer.

new = the opposite of old

> Ellen has a new baseball bat.

loose = free, unfastened

> My tooth feels loose.

lose = to be unable to find something

> Did you lose your backpack?

meat = food

> Carnivores, not herbivores, eat meat.

meet = to come upon

> It is a pleasure to meet you.

passed = to move beyond

> I passed an apple tree on my way to school.

past = a time gone by

> In historical fiction, the setting is a time and place of the past.

peace = freedom from fighting and war

> Martin Luther King, Jr., dreamed of world peace.

piece = a part of something

> I would enjoy a piece of pepperoni pizza.

principal = person in charge of a school *or* the most important part

> A principal is like the mother or father of a school. A principal is our *pal*.

> My principal (main) complaint is that children cannot roller-blade in Seagull Park.

principle = idea

> The Statue of Liberty is founded on the principle of freedom.

quiet = making very little noise

> During a fire drill, our class is as quiet as an ant in the library.

quit = to stop

> Please quit leaving your toys on the floor.

quite = completely

> She is quite a talented singer.

than = shows a comparison

> Pamela enjoys playing the flute more than anyone in her family.

then = tells when

> Then she ran around the track five times.

their = belonging to them

> Their favorite sport is soccer.

there = points out a location (place)

> The soccer ball is over there.

they're = contraction for they are

> They're playing soccer now.

threw = tossed

> Molly threw the baseball like a major league pitcher.

through = in one side and out the other

> The refrigerator could not fit through the door.

to = in the direction of (toward)

> I went to the store to buy a skateboard.

too = also or too much (very)

> Jack bought a skateboard too.

> The red skateboard is too expensive.

two = the number 2

> Theresa purchased two skateboards.

weather = what it's doing outside

> The weather is delightful.

whether = a choice

> Whether or not I will go depends upon the weather.

who's = contraction for who is

> Who's knocking at the door?

whose = belonging to whom

> Whose lunch box is this?

wood = what trees are made of

> I needed wood to build a doghouse.

would = part of the verb will

> If I had candy, I would share it with you.

you're = contraction for you are

> You're a math wizard.

your = belonging to you

> Your bedroom looks like a toy store.

APPENDIX 7—SYNONYMS FOR OVERUSED WORDS

Instead of using	Try this word	Or this	Now you try
said	exclaimed	screamed	
	muttered	whispered	
good	wonderful	splendid	
bad	terrible	awful	
great	fantastic	excellent	
nice	pleasant	agreeable	
happy	delighted	pleased	
sad	heavyhearted	blue	
like	enjoy	appreciate	
hate	dislike	despise	
big	huge	enormous	
small	petite	tiny	
fast	rapidly	swift	
slow	gradual	unhurried	
fun	amusing	entertaining	
walk	march	stroll	
quiet	hushed	still	
loud	noisy	booming	
scary	creepy	frightening	
look	stare	glance	
tall	towering	lofty	
very	extremely	truly	
kid	youngster	child	
funny	comical	amusing	

APPENDIX 8—ADJECTIVES

Adjectives are describing words that tell what kind, how many, or which one. They make your writing more colorful and give readers a clearer picture of what you're describing.

amazing	lazy	rainy
	long	rare
beautiful		red
black	magnificent	round
blue	many	
bright	mean	sad
	mighty	scary
clever	mushy	short
		silly
dull		splendid
	nasty	stingy
fabulous	new	strange
friendly	nutritious	striped
funny		
	odd	tall
gigantic	orange	tender
gorgeous	ordinary	tough
green	outstanding	tricky
grumpy		
	precious	ugly
handsome	pretty	
horrible	purple	vast
huge		
humorous	quaint	wonderful
	quick	
jolly	quickest	
	quiet	
kind		

APPENDIX 9—"PEOPLE" WORDS YOU SHOULD BE ABLE TO READ AND SPELL

actor
actress
Americans
artist
astronaut
athlete
aunt
author

baby
baby-sitter
baker
banker
boss
bride
brother
builder
bus driver

caretaker
carpenter
character
chauffeur
chef
child
children
citizen
classmate
clown
coach
conductor
cousin
crossing guard

dancer
dentist
director
doctor

editor
electrician
engineer

family
farmer
father
firefighter
friend

gardener
grandchild
grandparent
groom
guard
guide

hairdresser
hero
heroine
husband

infant
illustrator
inventor

judge

king

lawyer
leader
librarian
lifeguard

mail carrier
manager
mechanic
mother

neighbor
nephew
niece
nurse

operator
owner

painter
parent
person
people
photographer
plumber
poet
police officer
politician
president
prince
princess

queen

relative
reporter

salesperson
scientist
seamstress
secretary
senator
singer
sister
student

tailor
teacher
tutor

uncle

waiter
waitress
wife

APPENDIX 10—"GREAT OUTDOOR" WORDS YOU SHOULD BE ABLE TO READ AND SPELL

airplane
American flag
animals
ant
automobile

backpacking
barbecue
baseball
basketball hoop
bay
beach
bee
bicycle
birdbath
blanket
boots
branch
breeze
bridge
bus
butterfly

campsite
canoeing
carnival
caterpillar
chipmunk
clothesline
clouds
compass
cool breeze
curb

daisy
deck
deer
doghouse
driveway

environment

farm stand
field
fire hydrant
flower
football
forest
fresh air

garden hose
gardening
gloves
grass

hiking
hill
hopscotch
horse
hot dog stand

ice-cream truck
ice skating
icicles
insects

jogging
jumping rope

kite

lake
lampposts
lawn mower
leaves
lemonade
lemonade stand
lily
lounge chair

map
mail box
mittens
moonlight
mosquito
mountains

nature
neighborhood

ocean
outdoor concert
outdoor truck

pail
parade
park bench
path
patio
pebbles
picket fence
pinecone
planet
plant
playground
pollen

pond
pool

rabbit
raccoon
rain
rake
recreation
river
road
rocks
rose
running

sailboat
sandbox
scuba diving
seaweed
scarf
scooter
shells
shovel
sidewalk
skateboard

skiing
sky
sledding
snow
soccer
sports
sprinkler
squirrel
stadium
star
stream
street
street lights
summer
summer camp
sun
sunglasses
suntan
surroundings
swan
swimming

telephone pole
temperature

tennis
tent
trail
train
tree
tree house
truck
tulip
twigs

umbrella

valley

walking
wild berries
wildlife
wind
wind chimes
woods
worm

yard sale

APPENDIX 11—SAMPLE WRITING RUBRIC

Quality	3 points
Meaning: The extent to which the answer shows understanding and interpretation of the task	-fulfill the requirements of task -demonstrate insight and make connections
Development: The extent to which ideas are elaborated, using specific and relevant details and examples	-develop ideas fully with elaboration -use relevant and accurate examples to support ideas
Organization: The extent to which the answer exhibits direction, shape, and coherence	-establish and maintain clear focus -show logical sequence of ideas
Language Use: The extent to which the answer shows an awareness of audience and purpose through effective use of words, sentence structure, and sentence variety	-writing is fluent and easy to read, with vivid language -using varied sentence structure and challenging vocabulary
Conventions: The extent to which the answer shows conventional spelling, punctuation, paragraphing, capitalization, grammar, and usage	The writing demonstrates control of the conventions of written English. There are few, if any, errors and none that interfere with comprehension. Grammar, capitalization, punctuation, and paragraphing are correct. Misspellings are minor or repetitive; they occur primarily when a student takes risks with sophisticated vocabulary.

0 = The responses are completely irrelevant or incoherent

2 points	1 point
-fulfill some requirements of the task -make some connections	-fulfill few requirements of the task -make few connections
-may be brief, with little elaboration -provide some examples and details	-may contain a few examples or details
-are generally focused, may contain irrelevant details -show a clear attempt at organization	-may focus on minor details or lack focus -show little or no organization
-are readable, with some sense of engagement -primarily uses simple sentences	-are often repetitive, with little sense of voice -uses minimal vocabulary
The writing demonstrates partial control of the conventions of written English. It contains errors that may interfere somewhat with readability but do not interfere with comprehension.	The writing demonstrates minimal control of the conventions. There may be many errors that interfere with readability and comprehension.

APPENDIX 12—TRANSITION WORDS

Transition words help organize your writing. They are the words that connect thoughts and ideas. The chart below gives three examples for each purpose.

Purpose	Example	Example	Example
To add or show sequence	first	next	last
To show likeness: show how things are alike	also	in the same way	similarly
To contrast: show differences	however	yet	but
To show cause and effect	because	as a result	due to
To give examples	for example	such as	for instance
To show time	now	soon	later
To show place or direction	nearby	far	above
To summarize or conclude	therefore	thus	so

APPENDIX 13—PUNCTUATION TIPS

Ending a Sentence

Period   I think it is a splendid idea.

Question mark   Do you like the idea?

Exclamation mark   I love the idea!

Commas

In dates   February 2, 2004

In addresses   222 Main Street, Hometown, New York

Items in a series   Plants need water, light, and soil to live.

With introductory information   Yes, that is a fabulous idea.

Quotation Marks

Direct quotations—Ms. Hoops said, "Let's continue to work."

Capitalization

Proper Nouns—Proper nouns name a specific person, place, thing, or event

Example: Robert visited the White House on Tuesday, January first. After leaving Washington, D.C., he went to see the Empire State Building in New York City.

First word in sentences and quotations

Titles of works (books, articles, poems, stories)

APPENDIX 14—FIGURATIVE LANGUAGE: SIMILE, METAPHOR, HYPERBOLE, AND PERSONIFICATION

Simile: A simile compares two unlike things using the words "like" or "as." Writers use similes to paint a strong, clear picture in the reader's mind.

Literal Language	Figurative Language: Simile
Joey is tall.	Joey is as tall as the Empire State Building on stilts.
The audience watched me perform on stage.	When I was performing on stage, the audience paid such close attention to me that I felt like an insect being observed under a magnifying glass.
Dayna is pretty.	Dayna is as beautiful as a sunset.

Metaphor: A metaphor compares two unlike things without using the words "like" or "as." It often uses some form of the verb "to be" (is, are, was, were) to compare and link the unlike things. Like similes, metaphors make it easier and more enjoyable for readers to form pictures in their minds.

Literal Language	Figurative Language: Metaphor
Mrs. Lapinski dances gracefully.	Mrs. Lapinski is a ballerina.
Jean's hair feels soft.	Jean's hair is silk.
Transition words and phrases connect ideas.	Transition words and phrases are bridges that connect ideas.

Hyperbole: A hyperbole is an exaggeration. It stretches the truth to create a special effect for the reader.

Literal Language	Figurative Language: Hyperbole
Uncle Victor has a lot of energy.	Uncle Victor is so full of energy that he can recharge a dead battery just by touching it.
Rocco swims many laps in his pool.	Rocco swims so many laps in his pool that the chlorine tablets get seasick from all the motion.
Ms. Oliverio's students pay close attention to their reading material.	Ms. Oliverio's students can get so "lost in a book" that even the police and FBI can't find them.
Elinore's house is very clean.	Elinore's home is so clean that the one tiny speck of dust living there is lonely.

Personification: Personification gives human qualities to nonhuman things.

Literal Language	Figurative Language: Personification
The ice-cream cone fell on the floor.	The ice-cream cone cried vanilla tears when it fell on the floor.
Bruce's muscles are in good shape.	Bruce's muscles sing and dance to celebrate their fine health.

APPENDIX 15—ON-LINE RESOURCES

Graphic Organizers

http://www.graphic.org/goindex.html

Language Arts Site

http://www.english-zone.com/

Spelling and Usage

http://itc.sulross.edu/raustin/spelling.html

Aesop Fables

www.AesopFables.com

Many fables to hear online

New York State Education Department—Assessment Information

http://www.emsc.nysed.gov/ciai/ela.html

Go to the English Language Arts page for sample tests.

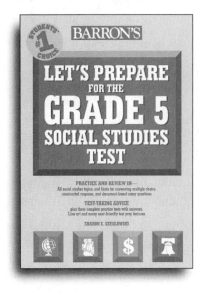

NOTES